£17 50

The Treatment of Homosexuals with Mental Health Disorders

The Treatment
of Homosexuals
with Mental Health
Disorders

Edited by
Michael W. Ross, PhD

The Treatment of Homosexuals with Mental Health Disorders, edited by Michael W. Ross, was simultaneously issued by The Haworth Press, Inc., under the title *Psychopathology and Psychotherapy in Homosexuality*, a special issue of *Journal of Homosexuality*, Volume 15, Numbers 1/2 1988, John P. De Cecco, journal editor.

Harrington Park Press
New York • London

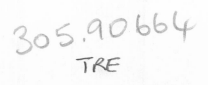

ISBN 0-918393-47-7

Published by

Harrington Park Press, Inc., 12 West 32 Street, New York, New York 10001
EUROSPAN/Harrington, 3 Henrietta Street, London WC2E 8LU England

Harrington Park Press, Inc., is a subsidiary of The Haworth Press, Inc., 12 West 32 Street, New York, New York 10001.

The Treatment of Homosexuals with Mental Health Disorders was originally published as *Journal of Homosexuality*, Volume 15, Numbers 1/2 1988.

Cover design by Marshall Andrews.

LIBRARY OF CONGRESS
Library of Congress Cataloging-in-Publication Data

Psychopathology and psychotherapy in homosexuality.
　　The Treatment of homosexuals with mental health disorders / edited by Michael Ross.
　　　p. cm.
　　Reprint. Originally published: Psychopathology and psychotherapy in homosexuality. New York : Haworth Press, c1988.
　　Includes bibliographies.
　　ISBN 0-918393-47-7
　　1. Homosexuals—Mental health. 2. Psychotherapy. I. Ross, Michael W., 1952-　　. II. Title.
　　[DNLM: 1. Homosexuality. 2. Psychopathology. 3. Psychotherapy. WM 615 P9744]
RC558.P786　　1988
616.89—dc19
DNLM/DLC
for Library of Congress
87-30826
CIP

CONTENTS

ABOUT THE EDITOR

Michael W. Ross, PhD, is the Coordinator of the AIDS Program for the South Australian Health Commission, Adelaide, Australia, and Clinical Senior Lecturer in Psychiatry and Community Medicine, Flinders University Medical School, South Australia. He has published extensively in the areas of homosexuality, venereology, and gender dysphorias.

The Treatment
of Homosexuals with
Mental Health Disorders

Preface

James A. Paulsen, MD

Stanford University
Palo Alto Medical Foundation

Although homosexual behavior emerged as an integral part of human development, it has been widely observed by scientists in numerous non-human species, particularly in primates. From the vantage point of science, homosexuality appears to be an intrinsic part of the natural order. But the kingdom of Nature differs markedly from the kingdom of Humankind!

Since the middle ages, for those Western institutions that have wielded great power, particularly government and church, homosexuality has been, to say the least, problematic. These institutions have forged attitudes and proscriptions regarding homosexuality that, during the most persecutory periods, have been reminiscent of the Nazis killing Jews.

Such inquisitorial treatment of homosexuality was not the case in the ancient world. Then it was perceived by the reigning oligarchies as neither nuisance nor threat. In ancient Egypt, Greece and Rome, homosexuality was both tolerated and condoned as was unabashed polytheism. In fact, it would appear that the polytheism of the ancient world, which dispersed power among several gods, as well as its oligarchies, in which power was broadly shared, left sexual expression, including homosexuality, largely unrestricted.

With the advent of monotheism, history shows that the world was divided between the "we" of the believers, who wielded the power to impose their convictions, and the "they" of the powerless infi-

Dr. Paulsen is Lecturer Emeritus and retired Clinical Associate Professor in Psychiatry and Behavioral Sciences at Stanford University School of Medicine. From 1978 to 1983, he chaired the Task Force and Committee on Gay, Lesbian, and Bisexual Issues of the American Psychiatric Association. He was a partner and former Head of the Department of Psychiatry and Clinical Psychology of the Palo Alto Medical Foundation. Correspondence should be addressed to 720 Gough Street, #53, San Francisco, CA 94102.

dels. Goodness and righteousness became the exclusive property of the believers, while evil and wrongdoing were the sole domain of the non-believers.

This was even true in ancient Egypt which had a brief affair with monotheism in the 18th Dynasty (c. 1375 B.C.). The Pharaoh, Ikhnaton, assumed absolute power and forced monotheism upon the people. All the polytheistic gods and their priesthoods were ruthlessly banished or destroyed, and replaced by Aton. The Pharaoh proclaimed Aton, symbolized and worshipped as the sun, the only true God and declared himself the son of God. After the pharaoh seized the priests' power and, not insignificantly, their wealth, he abandoned Thebes, the revered capital, and built Akhetaton, far to the North, to symbolize the new religious and political order. Egypt was thereby divided into the "We" of the true believers and the "They" of the outlawed polytheists. This brief and bloody excursion into monotheism in the ancient world lasted 17 years, about 5 years longer than the Third Reich. The forsaken Egyptian priests and their gods, with majesty and military might, ultimately reclaimed their religion, power, and, of course, their wealth, returning their civilization to the polytheistic path.

Western history shows that intolerance of homosexuality has accompanied both the rise of monotheism in its Judaic and Christian forms and the increasing concentration of power in the hands of one mighty ruler who was above the law, subject only to the vagaries of heredity disease and assassination. In the 16th century, Henry VIII, for example, brilliantly epitomized the pyramid of religious and political power and the intolerance of homosexuality when he wrenched England from the Roman Catholic papacy. It was during his reign that the first English law against homosexual behavior was enacted, the Buggery Act of 1533. During the 19th and 20th centuries, England evolved from an island nation to a world empire, forever espousing "We-ness" and establishing its notoriety for the persecution of homosexuals.

Empires that followed, Prussia and Germany, the United States, and Tsarist and Soviet Russia, aped the British Empire in their treatment of homosexuality. The culmination of persecutory "We-ness" was reached in Nazi Germany when an estimated 250,000 homosexuals, along with Jews, gypsies, political dissenters, and the mentally ill, were put to death in what was intended as the final solution of the problem of "They-ness."

A lesson can be learned from this history of persecution: The more political and moral power are concentrated in the hands of the few, the "We," the greater the probability that there will be fear, hatred, resentment, intolerance, and ultimately, persecution of the "They." We now call the latter *minorities*, who as victims of oppression, we are slowly learning, can develop an acrid distaste for government, religion, and the social order. Since World War II these minorities have risen against their oppressors. During that war Jewish groups resisted and fought the Nazis. In the sixties blacks in the United States formed a collective front against racism. Galvanized by the Stonewall riot of 1969, when a group of gay men resisted the periodic queer-bashing of the New York City police, the long-smoldering gay community demanded tolerance from both the government and from a relatively new power group within the medical profession, American psychiatry.

The processes and functions of medicine generally reflect and are fused with the society in which it exists. Thus law and social mores influence the medical hierarchy, particularly psychiatry, which deals more with the mind than the body. Prior to the 19th century, people deemed mentally ill were handed over primarily to social and religious institutions. Subsequently a medical specialty evolved, called neurology, which dealt with diseases of the brain and peripheral nervous system. Toward the end of the 19th century lively attention was devoted to "nervous conditions," those partly characterized by a partial or total absence of physical disease. Taking over the treatment of mental conditions, psychiatry gradually emerged as a medical subspeciality of neurology even though it has always been as much art and teaching as medical treatment.

To the extent that psychiatry considers itself the caretaker of the mental health of American citizens, it shoulders an awesome and, at times, agonizing responsibility. In the past two decades a notable portion of psychiatry's agony derives from its position on homosexuality as a psychopathology. *Pathology*, in this context, can be defined in two ways: (1) the science or study of the origin, nature, and course of diseases (for example, AIDS, the most horrifying pandemic since the spread of influenza during the period of World War 1); and (2) any deviation from a healthy, normal, or efficient condition. Since homosexuality has been viewed as pathological on the basis of one or the other definition or on both, as a psychopathology, it has been the source of much confusion regarding psychiatric practice and research.

But not all is confusion. In 1957, Professor Evelyn Hooker published the first study of "normal" homosexuals, men who had never been treated for mental illness in hospitals, prisons, or private consulting rooms. When the psychological adjustment of this group was compared with that of heterosexual controls, no significant differences were found. Sociologists and anthropologists, in their research on homosexuality, followed Hooker with similar findings. All this influenced the American Psychiatric Association, which, at the same time, was being pressured from without by gay activists and from within by its open-minded membership. Astounding enough in a homophobic world, the American Psychiatric Association in 1973 declared that homosexuality was *not* a disease or psychopathology. Furthermore, it defended the civil rights of gay people by deploring all forms of discrimination against them, an action that recalls President Lincoln's emancipation of the blacks almost a century earlier.

The question remains: What is to be done with homosexuality? Answers to this are still avidly sought by researchers, including geneticists, psychologists, psychiatrists and others who diligently seek the *causes* of homosexuality, *ad infinitum* and, not rarely, *ad infantum*. Presupposing that homosexuality is an *entity*, like the human body, these researchers are chronically enmeshed in almost eloquent but kaleidoscopic confusion. As understandable as this confusion may be, it is hardly justifiable, when it is recalled that homosexuality is not an *entity* but *behavior*. As *behavior* it derives its meaning and value from the personal, cultural, and historical context in which it occurs. It is certainly more complicated than left-handedness, but surely less complex than those murky pre-conscious portions of the brain crucial to the survival of our ancestors 50,000 years ago, but which are now a potent contributor to world paranoia and the possibility of war in the nuclear age.

Amidst all this research on homosexuality we ought to remember that a homosexual is not a *thing*. *Homosexual* should be used as an adjective, requiring a noun, which *is* a thing. Thus we can speak of homosexual fantasy or lust, a homosexual couple or neighborhood, or a homosexual act. One who rapes is not called a *rape*, but a rapist; those who oppress racial minorities are not called a *race*, but racists. Accordingly, if we need a noun, an individual who engages in homosexual acts should be called a *homosexualist*. Unfortunately the powers that have elevated the adjective *homosexual* to the status of a noun still prevail as the pejorative "faggot" or "queer," words painfully reminiscent of "kike" and "nigger."

In 1972, a psychologist, George Weinberg, coined *homophobia* to denote the irrational fear and dread of homosexuals and homosexuality. However, with regard to its Latin roots, homophobia literally means fear of humankind. In this latter sense the ceaselessly bellicose stance of the world's nations represents one form of homophobia in action. The other form is the veritable state of war on homosexuality primarily by Western governmental and religious institutions. Most of the 5 billion inhabitants of this planet are oppressed by homophobia in one or both forms. Because this has always been so does not necessarily mean that it must or will continue. Indeed, future survival of the human species depends on change. Regarding homosexuality, the articles in this volume explore and elucidate what these changes are and how they can be realized. Read them, and be changed.

Ego-Dystonic Heterosexuality: A Case Study

Michael W. Ross, PhD

Flinders University Medical School

SUMMARY. This study reports a case of a heterosexual male who was not psychotic and expressed a wish for a homosexual orientation. The psychodynamics of this patient are discussed, and the classification of ego-dystonic states discussed. It is concluded that DSM-III diagnoses should reflect underlying psychological disorders rather than sexual orientation.

The disorder of Ego-Dystonic Homosexuality (302.00) in the American Psychiatric Association's Diagnostic and Statistical Manual of Mental Disorders (APA, 1980) emphasises both the patient's negative appraisal of his or her homosexual arousal and a positive desire for heterosexual relationships. Clearly, the patient's evaluation of the merits of either lifestyle cannot be considered to be independent of their development experiences and socialization in a culture that values heterosexuality and highlights its advantages, such as bearing children, and that designates homosexuality as less socially acceptable. Thus, the "ego-dystonic" dimension arises, at least in part, as a consequence of society's attitudes toward, and assumptions about, homosexuality. It is not accompanied by a corresponding disorder of ego-dystonic heterosexuality because it has been suggested that the only cases of ego-dystonic heterosexuality occur in schizophrenics who attempt to deny all sexuality (Bayer, 1981). The definition of ego-dystonic homosexuality thus rests on the assumption that it is ego-dystonic because it is unacceptable.

Dr. Ross is Coordinator, AIDS Program, South Australian Health Commission, Adelaide, Australia, and Clinical Senior Lecturer in Psychiatry and Community Medicine, Flinders University Medical School, Adelaide. Requests for reprints may be directed to Dr. Ross, c/o AIDS Program, South Australian Health Commission, P.O. Box 65, Rundle Mall, Adelaide, SA 5000, Australia.

However, with rapid changes in society's attitudes toward sexual orientation and reports that a substantial proportion of the population in some major cities are homosexual, this assumption may not stand close scrutiny.

If cases of ego-dystonic heterosexuality do appear, the alternatives would appear to be either inclusion of a new category for this disorder or deletion of the category of ego-dystonic homosexuality. A case of ego-dystonic heterosexuality is reported below.

CASE HISTORY

Mr. A. is a 24-year-old white single male college student. He presented to the Gender Clinic of a university teaching hospital seeking removal of the hair on his arms, trunk, and chin, and advice on the effects of exogenous estrogens on hirsutism. He indicated that he would not want gender reassignment even if this were offered. However, he did indicate he would be happier for reasons involving both anxiety reduction and social comfort if he were homosexual.

On examination, he presented as a tall and appropriately dressed individual, but was initially reticent to provide detailed information. Upon mental status examination, his affect was initially found to be nervous, but he was eager to interact and developed good rapport. Conversation was normal in form and content. Intelligence was assessed as above average, and he had some insight into his situation: There was no evidence of impaired cognition. Psychological testing on the MMPI revealed only an elevation on the *Mf* scale, suggestive of atypical perception of social sex-roles.

There was no history of cross-gendered behavior in childhood or adolescence, and no cross-dressing apart from two or three occasions during play with peers as a child. Nor was there any history of homosexual behavior or of homoerotic attraction, dreams, or masturbatory fantasies. However, a history of occasional heterosexual intercourse from age 18 on was elicited. Within the past year he had felt some anxiety over intimate contact with female peers. There was no past psychiatric history or relevant medical history, nor a history of alcohol or drug abuse.

The family background was unusual. Mr. A. had been adopted shortly after birth into a family with one other child, a daughter. Six months prior to his presentation he had managed to trace his biological family and met a 15-year-old biological sister, also adopted, whom he felt bore a strong physical resemblance to him. Objectively, this was also apparent from photographs. Their mother had put up for adoption four other full-siblings, and two half-siblings from an earlier liaison (all males). She was still living with the father of the patient, and Mr. A. had met them 3 months prior to presentation. Mr. A. had been most distressed to find that he and six other full-and half-siblings had been put up for adoption because his mother had simply "not wanted to be bothered" with children, and he had argued with her on this point, and expressed his feelings of rejection. Mr. A. also began to dislike his biological sister, whom he had fallen in love with. The reason he gave for his increasing distaste was intellectual incompatibility: He claimed that she was only interested in boys, smoking, and getting drunk.

In the course of exploratory psychotherapy following his first visit, it became apparent that Mr. A. harbored considerable anger toward his biological mother and jealousy toward his biological sister. In the case of his mother, this was because of her rejection of him as evidenced by adopting him out, and in the case of his sister because of his jealousy toward her many boyfriends. His attempt to feminize himself through depilation had been activated by his need to identify with his sister prior to his realization that they had little in common apart from a strong similarity in appearance. While Mr. A. expressed a great degree of anger at his female biological relatives, he also indicated a preexisting distaste of stereotyped sex-role behavior in women and a strong dislike of women who expected him to take a conventional overbearing and controlling male role. He far preferred to interact with numerous friends who were homosexual, who socialized without being limited by sex-roles, and who found him attractive.

Mr. A. did not fulfill diagnostic criteria for any specific DSM-III axis I diagnosis except 302.89, "Psychological disorder not elsewhere classified." On axis II he did not satisfy criteria for personality disorder, although some lack of self-esteem was evidenced.

Following 15 sessions of psychotherapy, Mr. A. was able to express and understand his strong hostility toward his mother and jealousy of his sister, at one stage threatening to kill them, and not only gave up his wish for depilation, but also grew a beard and moustache and took up body building. His wish to become homosexual, however, remained. He indicated that if the "right man" came along he might become sufficiently aroused to respond sexually, but realized that this was unlikely, and therefore continued to respond socially to homosexual men and to fantasize about sexual encounters with women who were intelligent and assertive.

DISCUSSION

This case demonstrated the presence of ego-dystonic heterosexuality in a non-schizophrenic individual in whom apparent dislike of female gender-typed characteristics was independent of the desire to become homosexual. Of particular interest was the fact that the desire to become homosexual was based on the perceived positive aspects of that lifestyle, i.e., social comfort with homosexual men and their acceptance of non-stereotypical sex-role behavior as opposed to a distaste for the previously socially sanctioned conventional sex-role in which women are seen as weak individuals with dependent personalities. In the present case there was also a negative attitude toward women arising from the patient's experiences with his biological family; the psychodynamic parallels between the preexisting dislike of conventional sex-roles and the precipitating anger at his biological mother and sister were striking.

The question has previously been raised as to why, in the case of ego-dystonic homosexuality, the sexual orientation has been singled out from other cases of distress (Bayer, 1981). Marmor (1977) has argued that if an individual is distressed by his or her sexual orientation, the disorder should be characterized by the underlying psychological disorder; for example, anxiety reaction in the present case. This argument is supported by Serber and Keith (1974), who report that homosexual men who requested help to change their sexual orientation were content to remain homosexual after receiving social skills training which enabled them to initiate social and sexual contacts. Thus, the source of their ego-dystonic homosexuality was their inability to make same-sex contacts, rather than distress about their sexual orientation. This is supported by a reported case of heterosexual panic in a homosexual male in which the psychodynamics, rather than sexual orientation, were of central importance (Goldberg, 1984).

The presence of at least one case in which the disorder comprises a wish to change from heterosexual to homosexual does suggest that nosological criteria based on the cause of distress, rather than the nature of the presenting phenomenology, are inappropriate. Indeed, the whole philosophy of DSM-III is to base diagnoses on observable phenomenology, not upon presumptions regarding underlying etrology. Rather than introducing a category of Ego-Dystonic Heterosexuality or even Ego-Dystonic/Socio-Dystonic behavior, the latter nomenclature bringing psychiatry back into the role of arbiter of social mores, it may be more appropriate to recognize the progressive changes in attitudes toward sexual orientation and delete the category of Ego-Dystonic Homosexuality, as has occurred subsequent to this report being accepted for publication.

REFERENCES

American Psychiatric Association (1980). *Diagnostic and statistical manual of mental disorders* (3rd Ed.) Washington, DC: Author.

Bayer, R. (1981). *Homosexuality and American psychiatry: The politics of diagnosis*. New York: Basic Books.

Goldberg, R. L. (1984). Heterosexual panic. *American Journal of Psychoanalysis, 44,* 209-211.

Serber, M. & Keith, C. G. (1974). The Atascadero project: Model of a sexual retraining program for incarcerated homosexual pedophiles. *Journal of Homosexuality, 1,* 87-97.

Homosexuality and Neurosis:
Considerations for Psychotherapy

Robert P. Cabaj, MD

Harvard University

SUMMARY. Though there is no correlation between mental illness and homosexuality, there are unique concerns that play a role in symptomatology and psychotherapy around neurotic and characterological issues in gay patients. Homophobia, both in the therapist and in the patient, external and internalized, is the significant "hidden" factor. Lack of training around transference and countertransference issues with gay patients and lack of teaching about homosexuality in training programs contribute to the difficulties encountered in psychotherapy with gay people. There are some problems and concerns specific to being homosexual that may bring patients to therapy: "coming-out," deciding on sexual orientation, desire to change orientation, and a unique "AIDS neurosis." The therapist needs to have an objective knowledge of the gay community and be willing to examine personal beliefs and reactions to work effectively with gay patients.

The attempt to link mental illness and homosexuality continues to have a fascination for many in the mental health field. These efforts continue, despite ample research showing no difference in the emotional adjustment and amount of mental illness in homosexuals as compared to matched heterosexuals (Reiss, 1980).

Efforts also continue, now often in the guise of biomedical research, to show an "abnormal" hormonal balance or other measurable signs to indicate deviations from a norm and find potentially "treatable" factors in developing homosexuality. Reports still flourish on "curing" homosexuals through various means. Though

Dr. Cabaj is an instructor in Psychiatry at the Harvard University Medical School, a Clinical Associate in Psychiatry at Massachusetts General Hospital in Boston, and is President of the Association of Gay and Lesbian Psychiatrists. He is also in private practice in Boston. Correspondence may be addressed to the author, 93 Ivy Street, Brookline, MA 02146.

this research clearly sees homosexuality as an illness or disease needing to be treated, the current psychiatric literature is often more subtle in its homophobia and biases in assuming homosexuals are "sicker," if not ill, just by being homosexual.

There is no evidence of any correlation between any mental illness and homosexuality or any increase of mental illness in homosexuals. There does seem, however, to be a higher rate of alcoholism and possible substance abuse in both gay men and lesbians — up to 30% in the homosexual populations studies verses 10% in the general population (Ziebold & Mongeon, 1982).

There are many factors that affect the treatment of homosexuals when they come for psychotherapy, and some concerns that are unique to being homosexual that often play a role in therapy. Community mental health programs provide a valuable model in working with homosexuals by demonstrating that some neurotic symptoms and concerns can be better understood with clear and objective knowledge about homosexuality, gay literature, and the gay community. Therapists wishing to work with gay patients must be willing to gain such knowledge in order to accept and empathize with them.

From the initial meeting and evaluation through the actual therapy, the major factor that plays a role in psychotherapy with gay men and women, no matter what the presenting complaints may be, no matter what the orientation of the therapist may be, is homophobia. Homophobia affects transference, countertransference, and symptomatology because most, if not all, people have been brought up in homophobic societies. Very few training programs for therapists offer gay or gay-positive models or address treatment issues unique to the gay population.

REASONS FOR PSYCHOTHERAPY

Very few gay men or lesbians come to therapy for a change in orientation; most come to therapy for the usual reasons — depression, anxiety, loneliness, phobias, difficulty establishing relationships, having troubles in a current relationship, and so on. A few come to understand their sexual orientation better or to seek help in "coming-out" that is, accepting their gay identity and letting others know about it. With the advent of Acquired Immune Deficiency Syndrome (AIDS) and the devastating effects it is having on the gay community, many gay men are seeking therapy around changes in their lifestyle resulting from their attempts to reduce their risk of exposure to the viral agent suspected of causing AIDS, which appears to be transmitted through sexual contact or exposure to contaminated blood; some have developed extreme fear of contagion or even a unique "AIDS neurosis," often with some conversion symptoms of AIDS itself (Forstein, 1984). In addition, many gay men and women and their families need support around the loss of loved ones, and some need help in coping with the disease itself, either in themselves or in a lover or a family member.

In looking more specifically at homosexuality and the treatment of neurotic conditions or symptoms, it is important to recall that the American Psychiatric Association, after a long and bitter battle in the early 1970s, no longer considers homosexuality an illness as such, but had established a recently eliminated diagnosis in its diagnostic manual called "Ego-Dystonic Homosexuality" (American Psychiatric Association, 1980). This category covered gay people who were dissatisfied with being homosexual. Though few in number, these people continue to be the joy of traditional analysts, people who use religious means for "conversion," and many heterosexual sex therapists. Yet when treating people who claim dissatisfaction with being homosexual, therapists must make objective evaluations, rather than just assume that the person has decided to be "normal" and needs encouragement. There may be many reasons for dissatisfaction with being gay, but usually there is something else going on in the patient's life that explains the discontent. Many patients fear the psychotherapeutic community and feel that in order to be treated—or even listened to—they have to present themselves as wishing to change.

Many neurotic patients present with a sweeping desire to change everything; sensitive and nondirective exploration of the issues will bring to light the real issues—the loss of a lover, impotency, difficulties at work, family troubles, and so on. Inward-directed homophobia, as evidenced by self-hatred and low self-esteem, may be the main operative dynamic and is often the dynamic manipulated, rather than treated, by those clinicians who are convinced that homosexuality is bad and must be cured or at least subdued, without regard to the patients' fantasies or desires.

Some patients present with what could be called "reactive heterosexuality." Such confused behavior may arise during a period of loss or change, and may be symptomatic of a regression to basic bisexual feelings, projection of sexual feelings to the opposite sex, or a fear of AIDS, resulting in an attempt to "flee" into heterosexuality.

All of the above presentations may be part of a patient's dissatisfaction with a homosexual orientation, but such may also occur in a patient who is comfortable with being gay. If the patient is truly dissatisfied, once the evaluation is completed, he must be clearly advised of the difficulties involved in attempting to change one's sexual orientation and the unlikelihood that any such attempt would be successful. Better use of therapy would be to help the patient accept his orientation and explore his fears of and resistance to being homosexual. If the patient insists, a referral to a sensitive therapist willing to work on changing orientation may be in order, but only if such a therapist is objective, not biased against homosexuality, and can help the patient accept homosexuality if change is not possible.

HOMOSEXUALITY AND THERAPY
FOR NEUROTIC DISORDERS

The major difference in working with gay men or lesbians, as opposed to heterosexuals, around other neurotic and characterological issues may be the feelings the therapist and the patient hold about homosexuality. Homophobia is a force operative in both parties, no matter how accepting both may be about being gay and about gay lifestyles. Many gay and heterosexual therapists are accepting and relatively free of prejudice on the surface, but few have ever fully explored their countertransference feelings and thus may be operating with subtle homophobia around certain issues, issues arising from myths such as: (a) All gays are basically unable to establish deep relationships; (b) older gays are lonely and sad; (c) given a choice, gays would elect to be heterosexual; and, (d) gays can not have lives as fulfilling as their heterosexual counterparts. It goes almost without saying: A therapist who believes homosexuality is an illness and not an accepted variation of sexuality should not treat gay or lesbian patients.

Psychotherapy around depressive symptoms triggered by losses will be very difficult if the lost object is a loved one of the same sex and the patient feels inhibited about homosexuality. The therapist must be able neutrally to ascertain sexual orientation and let the patient know that homosexual choices and desires can be talked about openly. Some patients have been known to set up a facade of heterosexuality, making up opposite-sex names for loved ones, and so on — an extension of the defensive position they take in response to a generally homophobic society.

Social phobias around interacting in gay environments will be difficult to discuss and treat if the therapist is unfamiliar with the aspects of the lifestyle discussed, and even more difficult if the therapist projects his or her own values ("Who wants to go to a smoke-filled bar anyway," or "It is not safe to go to the baths"). Antidepressant or antianxiety medications are helpful for many gay people with extreme phobic anxiety. Anxiety disorders may be more difficult to treat, given the increased situational anxiety many gay people feel in their everyday environments. The anxiety around dealing with accepting homosexuality also may be extreme enough to require medication.

When relevant to therapy, discussions about sexual behavior may be even more difficult for the homosexual patient due to the natural embarrassment of talking about sex, coupled with the homophobia described. If the patient's sexual behavior includes sadomasochistic (S & M) variations, this may be particularly uncomfortable for both the patient and therapist to discuss. Many men feel they are supposed to more "manly" and aggressive sexually, and feel that it is wrong to enjoy being in a more passive or receptive role. Women are at times confused by the desire to have children, with the concomitant belief that heterosexual interaction is needed for such, when in fact artificial insemination may be a true alternative.

The patient may believe the therapist is biased just by being associated with the "establishment," even if the therapist is openly gay. Self-doubt and internalized homophobia will emerge in all ongoing therapy with gay people because of the general cultural homophobia and lack of positive gay role models. The therapist must find a way successfully to show empathy and understanding, without seeming to be condescending or insincere.

HOMOPHOBIA, TRANSFERENCE, AND COUNTERTRANSFERENCE

In looking more closely at the role of homophobia in transference and countertransference, it is important to recognize that homophobia refers not just to an unwarranted fear of homosexuals (the literal meaning) but to hatred, loathing, or fear of homosexual desires as well as homosexuals themselves. Internalized homophobia in the gay patient or the therapist may be apparent as such extremes, but is manifest more often as self-doubt, a belief in inferiority, acceptance of the popular myths, a self-imposed limit on aspirations, or belief that others will be rejecting only on the basis of homosexuality. A "counterphobic" stance may also operate, in which the patient or therapist acts as if orientation has no role, or that it is only the problem of other people who cannot accept homosexuality openly.

A subtle collusion may occur around issues. The patient may say he has no problems with being gay and not be questioned by the therapist, who may feel relieved not to explore this uncomfortable topic. Yet the patient may operate under many myths and limits. The therapist might believe the patient is right in not trying to advance his career or become more involved in public affairs, given the potential homophobic reactions of the others. Both therapist and patient may act as if a gay relationship cannot be as strong or as valid as a heterosexual bond. Therapists may encourage their patients simply to "make the best of it" and learn to operate within certain limits, without challenging them to question whether some of the perceived limits are societal and cultural, or symptomatic of the patient's own narcissistic issues.

Couples or family therapy may not be considered, even if it is the preferred therapy, if it is felt that relationships are transient or that families cannot be unconditionally loving and accepting. Group therapy, especially in clinics or health maintenance organizations, may be suggested too readily. Though recommended in the "best" interest of the patient ("They will be better off with people more like themselves"), this may be a subtle form of homophobic segregation and not take into account what is really best for the patient. It also does not allow gay and heterosexual patients the chance to learn from each other. Sex therapy and work around sexual dysfunction may also be difficult because the process may be confusing, especially in a person without a steady partner, and because of the transference complex. More research needs to be done in how to work with homosexual sexual dysfunction.

The patient will be sensitive to the therapist's reactions to topics, and may be more so than the heterosexual counterpart. He or she may see the heterosexual therapist as reacting too positively to discussions about the opposite sex or the gay therapist dismissing the discussion of the same. In the heterosexual therapist, discomfort around discussion of sexual behavior may be evident and a lack of knowledge about the gay community and gay behavior may become irritating to the patient and seem a waste of time to explain. There is the possibility, too, that a heterosexual patient may object to an openly homosexual therapist, feeling the therapist is inadequate in some way because of his or her sexual orientation.

The therapist must always remember that there is no uniform gay lifestyle. Many gay people believe that once they "come out," they will have to act certain ways or adopt certain styles. The stereotypic effeminate gay male and masculine lesbian images are hopefully now being laid to rest. Within the gay community, men and women behave in a wide range of styles, and the therapist and patient must be open to understanding and accepting whatever style is comfortable for the patient. This is especially true around sexual practices and in forming relationships. Men may be promiscuous (even in the age of AIDS), asexual, or in open or closed relationships (allowing or not allowing sexual contact with others). Women have the same options, and are not always in relationships, or not promiscuous, as is often believed.

Gay people rarely assume fixed roles in sexual interactions and often need basic education about gay sexual behavior because it is not usually taught—either at home, in the streets, or in school. There are small subcultures such as the leather or S & M group that may have specific sexual and social patterns. Gay men and women may be parents, married, or in bisexual relationships, all of which may make for unique issues in therapy. The question of leaving a spouse and family is increasingly common as more people, through public awareness, learn to identify their homosexual yearnings.

Countertransference issues are woven throughout the above discussion. More directly, positive feelings for one's patient may be confusing and frightening for the heterosexual therapist, especially if they are sexual in nature. For the gay (as well as heterosexual) therapist, without a comfortable supervisory or collegial setting to discuss such issues, sexual feelings for the patient may become intense and lead to premature termination if they cannot be addressed in the therapy. Such feelings are primarily part of the transference-countertransference reaction, unless they were there from the beginning (in which case the therapist should probably not have ventured into therapy with that particular client, if such an option was available).

To be too positive and accepting may blind the therapist to pathology and lead one to miss dynamic issues or, at the least, slow down the therapeutic process and prevent open discussion on difficult issues. Negative feelings may arise, as in any therapy, but the therapist who is homophobic may not look beyond his own homophobia for the cause of such negative feelings. A gay-positive therapist may become angry at the patient who seems to refuse to change, to accept his or her gayness openly, who "acts out" sexually with heterosexuality partners, or who cannot limit promiscuous behavior in the face of high-risk health concerns. The patient may be aware of the therapist's beliefs, or believes he or she knows them, and be too embarrassed or ashamed to talk about certain topics. Obvious signs of resistance will become evident and must be addressed directly as soon as the therapist is aware of it.

Insight-oriented psychotherapy, including psychoanalysis, of true neurotic disorders with homosexuals has received little attention and almost no psychoanalytic theoretical study. The Oedipal issues for and developmental stages of homosexuals may well be different than traditionally expected; this alone may explain transference and countertransference problems. More research clearly needs to be done in examining Freudian, Jungian, and Ericksonian psychology in gay people.

PROBLEMS AND ISSUES SPECIFIC
TO HOMOSEXUALITY

To varying degrees, unique issues and problems may be the reasons for therapy with gay men and women and will affect therapeutic success. These include the "coming out" process, alcoholism, sexual compulsive behavior, and concerns around AIDS.

"Coming out," accepting a gay identity, is a complex process, and one on which research has begun only in recent years. Some patients come to therapy to help with this process, to explore fears and misgivings, examine stereotypes and myths, and obtain support in the process of acknowledging a homosexual orientation not only to themselves, but also to friends, work colleagues, or family. The process of accepting a sexual orientation that is neither promoted nor modeled in society is often difficult and life-long, and is an issue in most therapies with gay men and lesbians, no matter what the issues of treatment are. In treating most depressive or anxiety-related problems, the issues of coming out play a role and are a prime area from which hidden homophobia can emerge during the therapeutic process. The steps involved, followed often in overlapping patterns or with back and forth patterns, are: self-recognition, disclosure to others, socializing with other gay people, positive self-identification, and integration and acceptance (McWhirter & Mattison, 1984).

Patients seeking help for a variety of these coming-out issues may be anywhere in the continuum. The therapist needs to know, not just assume, where the patient is in that process, and must be careful not to impose his or her bias as to how the patient should go about coming out, such as recommending being quiet at work or not letting family know. Such advice may support poor self-esteem in the patient and limit the chances for patient and therapist to explore relevant issues fully. The process may seem settled, but then challenged again with job changes, significant family gatherings, or having a lover who has established a somewhat differing lifestyle.

Many patients question why they are gay, an issue which may come up in any therapy, but obviously in one focused on sorting out and accepting one's sexual orientation, as well as issues relating to parents and upbringing—these are a part of every therapy looking at neurotic problems. Therapists who, with good intentions, attempt to diminish their patients' guilt, self-doubt, and anger too quickly by giving accurate information of what is known about how homosexuality comes to be, before the patients can explain and explore the concerns around the issue, may miss the chance to help their patients examine some of their feelings around the parenting they received and their interactions in childhood situations.

It will be a relief for some patients to learn that there is no evidence that parental upbringing plays a role in sexual orientation development, but such information may serve to cut short the anger being expressed toward their parents in the therapy, anger that may really be tied to other parent-child issues. The probable role of genetics and biological and biochemical factors in utero may serve to confuse some patients and obscure the target of anger if the patient resents his or her orientation. This anger, often not understandable to the patient or the therapist, may intensify transference reactions because the patient may see the therapist (one of the targets) as being too accepting and objective, and as avoiding or dismissing the patient's feelings. The common wish to blame someone or something for a perceived problem, whether it be sexual orientation or failed relationships, may help obscure the poor self-esteem of the patient, which is only intensified by internal homophobia.

As mentioned earlier, the rate of alcoholism appears to be higher in the homosexual population—male and female, rural and city

(Lohrenz, Connelly, Coyne, & Spare, 1978)—without regard to cultural background or nationality. The illness of alcoholism must always be considered in evaluating a gay patient, especially since alcoholism causes depression, anxiety, phobias, and social isolation—common complaints for seeking psychotherapy. Gay AA and gay Al-Anon groups are especially helpful once the patient and therapist recognize and accept the diagnosis of alcoholism. Recovery is often hampered by the lack in many gay communities of social outlets that are not alcohol-related, leaving some recovering gay alcoholics without a solid social network.

Many gay men find themselves locked into sexual promiscuity and may wish to change for health reasons, or in order to establish an intimate relationship. Such obsessive-compulsive behavior can be treated by traditional means, but group therapy seems to be particularly useful. Following the addiction model and using such supports as the increasingly popular Sex Anonymous type groups may be the only way to help break the cycle. Often, major depressive issues emerge as the patient successfully abandons the old patterns and begins to deal with the painful aspects of intimacy.

Finally, AIDS has created a major set of psychological problems, along with the medical ones. Besides the obvious need for sensitive care and support of AIDS patients and their loved ones, the "worried well" and patients with AIDS-Related Complex (ARC) may need specific care for hysterical conversion symptoms, depressive reactions with possible suicidal feelings, debilitating social phobias, and extreme anxiety that may interfere with normal functioning. After insuring that the medical needs of patients are well taken care of and fully evaluated, therapists may conclude that psychotherapy and psychopharmacology are also necessary.

SUMMARY

Though there is no higher incidence of neurotic or other mental health problems in the homosexual population as compared with the heterosexual population, therapy for neurotic issues will be greatly affected by the sexual orientation of the patient and the therapist. In addition, the higher rate of the disease of alcoholism among homosexuals must always be considered. Homophobia will inevitably play a role, but the willingness of the patients to be aware of transference issues, and of therapists to seek to understand countertransference issues, should prevent homophobia from being an obstacle and, in fact, allow it to be part of the learning and growing experience of psychotherapy. And finally, knowledge of the gay community and awareness of gay issues such as "coming out" are absolutely necessary for therapists working with gay men and women.

REFERENCES

American Psychiatric Association. (1980). *Diagnostic and statistical manual of mental disorders* (3rd ed.). Washington, DC: American Psychiatric Press.

Forstein, M. (1984). AIDS anxiety in the "worried well." In S. E. Nichols & D. G. Ostrow (Eds), *Psychiatric implications of Acquired Immune Deficiency Syndrome* (pp. 49-60). Washington, DC: American Psychiatric Press.

Lohrenz, L. J., Connelly, J. C., Coyne, L. & Spare, K. (1978). Problems in several midwestern homosexual communities. *Journal of Studies on Alcoholism, 39,* 1956-1963.

McWhirter, D. P. & Mattison, A. M. (1984). *The male couple: How relationships develop.* Englewood Cliffs, NJ: Prentice-Hall.

Reiss, B. F. (1980). *Psychological tests in homosexuality.* In J. Marmor (Ed.), *Homosexual Behavior.* New York: Basic Books.

Ziebold, T. O. & Mongeon, J. E. (Eds.). (1982). Alcoholism and homosexuality [Special issue]. *Journal of Homosexuality, 7*(4).

Alcoholism and Non-Acceptance of Gay Self: The Critical Link

Robert J. Kus, RN, PhD

The University of Iowa

SUMMARY. As part of a larger research project designed to generate grounded theory on the nature of gay sobriety, this study was designed to explore the etiology of alcoholism among gay American men and how etiology is related to gay bars or non-acceptance of gay self or both. In-depth interviews were conducted in Seattle, Iowa City, Chicago, and Oklahoma City with 20 gay recovering alcoholic men, each of whom had at least one year of sobriety. It was found that: (a) Gay bars were totally unrelated to the etiology in any of the informants, yet most thought that this gay bar ethnotheory could explain why there was a high incidence of alcoholism in the gay community; (b) none of the men saw being gay as a positive thing before sobriety, yet many didn't realize their non-acceptance until after sobriety was chosen; (c) accepting being gay as a positive aspect of self occurred only after sobriety was chosen and lived; and (d) not accepting being gay as a positive thing may therefore explain the etiology and thus the high incidence of alcoholism among gay American men.

Alcoholism in the gay (same-sex oriented male) and lesbian (same-sex oriented female) adult American communities has long been recognized to be pandemic.[1] Fifield (1975), for example, found that 31.4% of gays and lesbians in Los Angeles could be considered alcoholic or at least heavy drinkers. Lohrenz, Connelly, Coyne, and Spare (1978), by administering the Michigan Alcohol-

Dr. Kus, a nurse-sociologist specializing in gay studies, is an assistant professor in the College of Nursing, The University of Iowa. Thanks go to Elizabeth M. Burns, PhD, for her helpful comments and suggestions. This article is based on a paper presented at the conference, "Nursing Research—Hawaii '85," Honolulu, June 1985. Correspondence may be addressed to the author, 110 Hackberry Street, North Liberty, IA 52317.

ism Screening Test (MAST) to a gay sample, found that 29% of these men could be categorized as alcoholic. Saghir and Robins (1973) also found high incidence of "excessive drinking behavior" or "alcohol dependency" among both gays and lesbians at some point in their lives. Specifically, they found 35% of the lesbians fit this pattern compared to only 5% of heterosexual women, and 30% of gays compared to 20% of heterosexual men.

How are etiology and the high incidence of alcoholism in gays to be explained? In this article, which is part of a larger study on gay sobriety, this question is addressed.

EXPLANATIONS OF THE ETIOLOGY/INCIDENCE OF ALCOHOLISM IN GAYS

Three types of explanations for the etiology and incidence of alcoholism in gays have been reported: (1) gay bar ethnotheory; (2) multi-factor theories; and (3) gay non-acceptance theory.

(1) *Gay bar ethnotheory*. To account for the common observation that gays have a higher incidence of alcoholism than heterosexual men, gays have developed a particular ethnotheory, or folk explanation. According to this ethnotheory, the etiology and incidence of alcoholism in gays can be explained by the fact that gay bars are often the only, or main, place where gays can meet other gays. Thus, somehow one can "catch" alcoholism in such settings by being surrounded by what the Gay Council on Drinking Behavior (1982) calls "the fraternity syndrome" or the acceptance of excessive drinking. For a detailed discussion of the gay bar ethnotheory refer to Silverstein and White's *The Joy of Gay Sex* (1977, pp. 46-48). According to these authors, the gay man's search for sex partners and companionship in gay bars leads him to drinking, and, before he knows it, he's drinking more and more and communicating less and less, and thus alcoholism is developed.

(2) *Multi-factor theories*. These theories hold that, indeed, gay bars probably account for the etiology and incidence of alcoholism; however, the explanation is expanded to include stress factors which gay men experience in a homophobic society. These theories (e.g., Nardi, 1982; Ziebold, 1978; Moses & Hawkins, 1982; and the Gay Council on Drinking Behavior, 1982), hold that internalized homophobia (self-hatred, shame, and so on), the external oppression of[2] a homophobic society, and hiding one's identity (being "closeted") are as important as gay bars in understanding the etiol-

ogy and incidence of alcoholism in gays. Strangely enough, the gay bar ethnotheory is held even in the absence of evidence that gay bars lead to alcoholism. For example, in the introduction to a book of first-hand accounts of recovering gay and lesbian alcoholics, *The Way Back: The Stories of Gay and Lesbian Alcoholics* (Gay Council on Drinking Behavior, 1982), this theory was discussed in detail. However, in not one of the stories included in the book was there any evidence of gay bars having any role in the development of alcoholism in the authors.

(3) *Gay non-acceptance theory*. This theory, put forth in the writings of Kus (1980, 1985a), holds that gay bars in no way account for either the etiology of alcoholism in the gay man nor the high incidence of alcoholism in the gay community. Rather, the etiology and incidence of alcoholism in gays can only be explained by the dynamics observed in the coming out process, specifically, in the stages of the process preceding Acceptance, the stage wherein the gay person accepts gayness as a positive aspect of self. This theory recognizes the social oppression discussed by the multi-factor theorists, yet holds that it is the internalized homophobia prior to having reached the stage of Acceptance in the coming out process which is the root of alcoholism in gay men. The gay who sees being gay as a positive thing, regardless of his living in a homophobic society, will not develop alcoholism because of gay factors. According to this coming out model, each stage is characterized by a typical health picture. In Stage I, Identification, the gay man recognizes his gay identity. Thus, his lifelong feelings of "differentness" are now explained. In this stage, the health picture is often one of internalized homophobia (guilt, low self-esteem, shame, depression symptoms, and so on), as well as behaviors emerging from this internal stress, such as alcohol abuse leading to alcoholism. Stage II, Cognitive Changes, sees the gay, who still sees being gay as a negative state of being, trying to rid self of this homophobia by learning about the gay world, usually while passing as straight. In addition to having the same negative health picture as in Stage I, the gay passing as straight also is wasting a tremendous amount of energy in his effort to pass as straight and is very fearful of discovery. Stage III, Acceptance, sees the gay man accepting his gay identity as a positive aspect of self and, therefore, becoming freed from the negative health elements characteristic of the first two stages of the process. He not only is free from guilt, low self-esteem, shame, and so forth, but he should have a lessened need or dependency on alcohol, even

though alcoholism, a life-long disease, remains present. Kus (1980, 1985a) assumed that acceptance will lead the gay alcoholic to sobriety. The fourth stage of the coming out process, Action, is characterized by behavior based on acceptance of gayness as a positive thing. Thus, an openly gay man who does not accept his sexual orientation as a positive thing has not reached the stage of Action as he hasn't reached the most critical (from a mental and therefore physical health point of view) stage of the process, Acceptance. In the Action stage, typical behaviors include self-disclosure, participation in gay political activity, changing friendship circles to include more gays, and the like. In the Action stage, the health picture is positive except for the possibility of rejection arising from self-disclosure, and the workaholism commonly observed in high-achievers, a characteristic of many gay American boys and men.

PURPOSE

The purpose of this section of a larger study on gay sobriety was to uncover the etiology of alcoholism in gay American men and, thus, explain the high incidence of alcoholism in the gay community. The three common theories of gay alcoholism etiology/incidence, gay bar ethnotheory, multi-factor theories, and gay non-acceptance theory were tested to see if any of them could explain gay alcoholic etiology and incidence. The hypotheses which emerged and which were explored in this section of the study were: (a) the etiology and thus the incidence of alcoholism in gay American men are unrelated to gay bars; (b) the etiology and incidence of alcoholism in gay American men are related to non-acceptance of gayness as a positive aspect of self; and (c) acceptance of gayness as a positive aspect of self leads to gay alcoholic sobriety.

METHODS

To generate grounded theory of gay sobriety, ethnographic procedures were used. The study was conducted in Seattle, Chicago, Iowa City, and Oklahoma City. The core of the study was formed from in-depth interviews obtained through theoretical sampling (Glaser & Strauss, 1967) with 20 gay recovering alcoholic men, each of whom had achieved at least 1 year of sobriety. Each man signed a consent form which indicated his voluntary participation in the project and the fact that his true name would not be used in order to protect his anonymity. Seventeen of the interviews were conducted using the observer-as-participant role, as I knew these persons only within the research role, and three were conducted using the participant-as-observer role, as I knew and interacted with these men outside the research role (Gold, 1969). No difference was found in the type or depth of information given by informants known to me from those not known at the time of the interview. Formal interviews were conducted only once with each informant.

Each participant was first given a paper-and-pencil questionnaire designed by the researcher to provide demographic information and an alcohol history. This questionnaire was read to each informant, and responses were recorded by the researcher. After completion of the questionnaire, each man was audio-taped formally. This interview explored how the informant had come to choose sobriety, how he maintained sobriety, and how sobriety had affected significant aspects of his life.

The taped interviews were structured, yet allowed the informant to discuss relevant material emerging during the interview. The taped interviews were analyzed in groups of four or five from which major concepts or categories emerged. Subsequent interview questions were designed to focus on specific categories and their indices, or characteristics, until the categories were saturated, i.e., until no new information was forthcoming.

To test the specific hypotheses which emerged early on in the study, the following specific questions were asked.

1. To test Hypothesis #1, which holds that the etiology and thus the incidence of alcoholism in gays are unrelated to gay bars, questions were asked about when the person began drinking alcohol regularly, when drinking became a problem for him, and when his alcoholic drinking began in relation to frequenting gay bars. Data analysis revealed that an additional question was needed, i.e., when did the person begin drinking alcoholically, a question different than when he recognized problems with alcohol. "Drinking alcoholically" refers to the type of drinking characterized by rapid consumption of alcohol for the purpose of getting drunk.

2. To test Hypothesis #2, that alcoholism has its roots in not accepting one's gay identity as a positive thing, I asked each informant questions such as if he accepted being gay as a positive aspect of self now, if he did while drinking, and so on.

3. To test Hypothesis #3, I asked each informant questions ex-

ploring how accepting being gay as a positive thing was related to his sobriety, and which came first, sobriety or acceptance.

FINDINGS AND DISCUSSION

Sample Characteristics

All informants were English-speaking men born and raised in the United States, except for one who was born in New York but raised in Poland and Germany. Informants hailed from 12 states: Illinois, Indiana, Iowa, Michigan, Nebraska, New Jersey, New Mexico, New York, Oklahoma, Tennessee, Texas, and Washington. There were 19 caucasians and one who identified himself as Hispanic. Age of the informants ranged from 26 to 55, with the average age being 37.9 years, and income ranged from $0-40,000, with the mean salary being $19,000. Educationally, one man had completed only 4th grade and held a G.E.D., four had some college, 11 held at least one bachelors' degree, and 4 held at least one masters' degree. Religions represented were Roman Catholic (3), Protestant (10), Deist (1), and Buddhist (1); 5 claimed no religious identification. Political identifications listed were Democrat (7), Republican (3), Independent (3), none (5), Libertarian (1) and "moderate left" (1). Ten of the men were coupled in gay relationships and 10 were single. Occupationally, 17 out of 20 were employed; of those unemployed, one was a college student, one was retired, and one found employment shortly after the interview was conducted. In terms of occupation, two salespersons, two waiters, an arts administrator, a public service clerk, a museum curator, a playwright, an architect, a street vendor, a teacher, a word processor, a licenced practical nurse, a controller, a drafter/illustrator, an accountant, and a machinist.

Alcoholic sobriety ranged from 1 year to 10 years, 3 months, with the mean sobriety length being 3 years, 4 months. All of the informants had attended Alcoholics Anonymous (A.A.) at one time, and 17 out of 20 were still attending A.A. meetings at the time of the interview. Of those who still were attending, one went only to gay meetings, one went only to non-gay meetings, and 15 went to both gay and non-gay meetings. While drinking, all but two informants reported using other mind-altering drugs such as hallucinogenics (2), pot (marijuana) (17), uppers (9), downers (10), and cocaine (2). One reported he had used "poppers" (amyl nitrate).

Others may have used poppers yet did not report it as they didn't define it as a mind-altering drug. Interestingly enough, many of these drugs were legally prescribed, including one man's prescription for 120 mg of Valium per day. At the time of the interview, four continued using pot on occasion, but avoided other mind-altering drugs.

The Myth of the Gay Bar in Etiology and Incidence

All of the informants in the study began drinking alcohol abusively before attending gay bars for the first time. Therefore, hypothesis #1 is supported: The etiology and thus the incidence of alcoholism in gay American men is unrelated to gay bars. Gay bar ethnotheory was rejected as an explanation for etiology/incidence of gay alcoholism, as were the multi-factor theories as they include in their explanation, gay bar ethnotheory.

In addition to finding support for the hypothesis, other interesting related data emerged. For example, all informants were cognizant of the high incidence of alcoholism in the gay community. When asked if "25-33%" sounded about right, informants said it sounded about right or too low, but none thought it too high an estimate. When questioned about why they thought such a high incidence occurred, virtually all explained it by discussing gay bars as the only place for gays to meet other gays. So, while recognizing that gay bars had nothing to do with the etiology of alcoholism in themselves, they believed that was why other gay men became alcoholic. Thus, most of the men saw their own etiology as unique. Personal experience did nothing to hamper their holding of the gay bar ethnotheory.

Finally, an entirely unexpected finding was revealed from the initial demographic/alcohol history form questions. The responses from the questions about when the informant began drinking alcohol regularly, and when trouble developed, led me to ask a third question not on the form; specifically, "When did you begin drinking alcohol abusively?" While the average age for beginning regular alcohol use was 18.55 years, noting trouble with alcohol wasn't recognized by many informants until years later, the mean age for recognizing "trouble" being 23. However, when I asked when they began drinking alcohol abusively, 18 out of 20, or 90%, reported that they drank abusively "with my very first drink." The remaining two informants admitted that perhaps they drank abusively from their very first drink, but they were unsure or could not remember.

In summary, the following was found: (1) The etiology and thus the incidence of alcoholism in gay American men is unrelated to gay bars (Hypothesis #1); (b) all informants were cognizant of the high alcoholism rate in the gay community, and all thought that 25-33% was either a low estimate or just about right; (c) even though gay bars had no role in their becoming alcoholic, virtually all men thought that gay bars were responsible for the etiology of other gay men's alcoholism and thus for the high incidence of alcoholism in the gay community; and (d) most, if not all, informants reported drinking alcohol abusively from their very first drink.

Non-Acceptance and Etiology/Incidence: The Critical Link

In exploring the relationship between alcoholism and non-acceptance of being gay as a positive aspect of self, it was found that 100% of the informants admitted non-acceptance of gayness while drinking. This finding, combined with findings to be discussed later, led to the acceptance of Hypothesis #2, which holds that not accepting one's gay self as positive is the prime etiological factor in alcoholism in gay American men.

For some, the relationship between non-acceptance and alcoholism was clearly seen once sobriety was chosen, as shown in the following two accounts.

> The day I was able to admit my alcoholism was the day I was able to admit to that gay part of me, and they came together hand in hand. I kind of honestly think that the reason my previous attempts with trying to recover from alcoholism failed had something to do with my inability to accept not only the fact that I was an alcoholic but that I was also gay. I could not be honest about that at all. I couldn't tell anybody about that. I really let it smolder inside for a long time.

And,

> I used alcohol as an anesthesia around unresolved conflicts. I just denied and refused to deal with a whole lot of [issues], not the least of which was my sexuality. And I would drink to make the pain go away. I was just so torn and in turmoil that

alcohol was the only thing that would make that go away. Plus, when I drank, I reached a certain point that I allowed myself to act out my homosexuality which I didn't do in sober states. So I would drink to a certain level and then get in the car and go to the baths, or the bars, or wherever.

Others, however, reported that they "thought" they had accepted being gay as a positive aspect of self before sobriety, but they learned differently once sobriety was chosen. This is clear in the following two accounts.

I began working on my 4th step [taking A.A. moral inventory] in June of 1982, and I had been 5 months sober at that time. Somewhere in the course of my 4th step, I believe I accepted the fact that, hey, it's okay for me to be this way. I had for years been saying, "I am a child of God and God doesn't make junk," but that was a defense mechanism rather than a true belief. Somewhere in the 4th step, I actually believed it.

And, from one of the two men who still didn't accept being gay as a positive thing:

When I was 16 and realized I was gay I really thought I had the world by the balls. And I began to be a militant, and I began to tell everyone that I was gay. But at the same time, I don't think I ever accepted it. And I don't know why.

Related data supported this hypothesis also. One, informants reported that they virtually always needed to drink before having sex with other men to buffer guilt feelings. Further, many men reported initial difficulty enjoying sex in sobriety; only as they came to accept being gay as a positive aspect of self did sexual enjoyment increase to—or exceed—pre-sobriety levels (Kus, 1985b). And two, while some of the men reported offering prayers of thanksgiving to the Higher Power for being gay after sobriety was chosen, all said that while drinking they didn't see being gay as anything to be thankful for, to say the least. In fact, a great deal of anger was often shown while drinking toward the Higher Power for having created them gay (Kus, 1985c).

In summary, the following was found: (a) Not accepting being gay as a positive self-attribute was observed in drinking gay alcoholics and can most probably explain the etiology; (b) because not accepting being gay as a positive aspect of self is the most likely factor explaining the etiology of alcoholism in gay American men, logically that would most likely account for the high incidence of alcoholism in the adult gay community; (c) some recognized their non-acceptance of their gay self while they were still drinking; (d) some gays recognized their non-acceptance of their gay self while drinking only after sobriety was chosen; and (e) the practice of virtually always having to drink before sex to buffer guilt in the drinking alcoholic leads one to conclude that they hadn't accepted being gay as a positive aspect of self.

Sobriety and Accepting Being Gay as a Positive Aspect of Self

One hundred percent of the informants admitted not accepting being gay as a positive thing before sobriety was chosen. In sobriety, 18 out of 20, or 90%, reported accepting gayness in a positive way. All 18 of the accepting men agreed that sobriety came first, as seen in this account:

> I didn't really come to terms with being gay until after I stopped drinking. I came out when I was 17 or 18 in the respect that I would sleep with men all the time and had lovers here and there. But I just never accepted it. I mean I was ashamed of it in that respect. And going through treatment and working on being sober for a while, that began to change. I didn't feel good about being gay all the time I was drinking and still didn't, until after I achieved sobriety. I started work on accepting it through telling other people and talking about it. The sobriety came first.

Therefore, Hypothesis #3, which states that accepting one's gay self as positive would lead to sobriety, was rejected. Thus, Kus (1980) was correct in tying the positive acceptance of gay self to sobriety, but wrong in the direction of which came first. Of the two persons who still didn't accept being gay in a positive way, both admitted they were working on it and hoping at minimum to achieve a "neutral," if not "accepting," state. One of those two men, it's interesting to note, had just moved to a city having a gay A.A. group and, therefore, had not had the benefit of gay A.A. to discuss notions such as acceptance of gayness and its link with alcoholism.

In addition to rejecting Hypothesis #3 on the basis of its faulty direction, four factors that the accepting men found helpful in their acceptance process were revealed. (a) Extending the "powerlessness" over alcohol concept to cover being powerless over one's gay orientation was seen as helpful in accepting self.

> I wanted it [gay self-acceptance], and I've done a lot of things to work on it. I see my accepting my homosexuality or gayness as being, again, part of an acceptance of things over which I am powerless. And I never was able to have that insight until I got sober.

(b) Many informants reported that self-acceptance was facilitated by doing the A.A. 4th step, making a "moral inventory," which includes things such as listing one's resentments and anger. Because the non-accepting gay is usually resentful and angry about being gay, acknowledging these resentments and angry feelings and working on reducing them has been found facilitative of acceptance. This was reported in an earlier account.

(c) Recognizing that non-acceptance of gay self in a positive way will make sobriety quite difficult to maintain over time and will make serenity, or peacefulness, impossible, leads many to work on acceptance, as seen in this account:

> It wasn't until I sobered up that it became real clear to me that I had to make peace with that [gay] issue in order to stay sober. And if I didn't stay sober, I was just going to die real soon. So it was a forced decision to accept being gay. It was a real life and death matter at that point. And being gay had been absolutely denied up to that point.

(d) Positive gay acceptance is related to meeting other gay people. Thus, gay A.A. meetings and gay groups of all types may be helpful. However, because the gay doesn't achieve true self-acceptance of being gay until after sobriety is chosen—and lived for awhile—initial contact with gay A.A. groups may be uncomfortable. An example of this is the account of a young man in alcoholic treatment who was advised to attend gay A.A. groups where he might be able to be more open to sharing his gay concerns:

And then finally as the group got to know me better, they said, "If you don't want to talk about those things here, why don't you go somewhere where you can talk about it, gay A.A." So that's when I did start going to gay A.A. And I HATED it! Oh, I did. I hated gay A.A. but I made myself go. I told myself that it would be good for me to go and that it was just like all these other things that I had experienced — the change and being frightened and it being painful and it being difficult. And yet, something inside me told me that it would be good for me, and my group and the people that I knew and trusted told me that it would be good for me. And so it was like taking medicine that doesn't taste good. I said, well, I'm going to commit to keep on going whether I like it or not. And now I really like it. But it took me awhile to get there.

In time, gay A.A. meetings effectively help the homophobic gay man achieve acceptance. In the following account, a young man describes how his negative stereotypes about gays changed when he went to gay A.A. meetings and to an event where he could see large numbers of gays:

[I saw] some people who didn't fit that negative gay stereotype in my mind. People that preferred to not go to bars and people who preferred not to have sex and people who preferred just to sit around and talk and do funny things — go to the zoo or to a play or something and just be friends and do things. I began to see things in those people that I liked and wanted . . . I think the thing that helped me a lot was realizing just how many gay people there are. And the big event that came up was going to the march on Washington in 1979 and seeing a couple hundred-thousand gay people there. I was about 4 months into sobriety, and I saw all those people and all the activities and all the different organizations. Then it was at that point that I can consciously remember saying that I was happy to be gay. That's probably lucky in some ways.

In summary, sobriety is necessary for acceptance of gayness to occur on any meaningful level. Further, ways in which accepting men achieved acceptance in sobriety include: (a) expanding the "powerlessness" concept of A.A. to include their sexual orientation, (b) doing the moral inventory in the 4th step, (c) recognizing that sobriety will be difficult to maintain without seeing being gay as a positive thing, and (d) attending gay A.A. meetings and meeting many gays.

IMPLICATIONS

The findings of this research have implications for recovering alcoholic gay men, for the gay community at large, clinicians, gay A.A. members, and researchers.

For the Gay Community

For the gay community, the striving for alcohol-free alternatives to the gay bars will unlikely lower the incidence of alcoholism in the gay community. However, it will provide a place for non-drinkers and recovering alcoholics to meet other gays and, therefore, enhance the possibility of recovering gay alcoholics to maintain sobriety.

Because alcoholism is linked to non-acceptance of gayness, the community should continue striving to (a) reduce homophobia in society at large and thus reduce social oppression toward gays, and (b) increase gays' self-esteem in all ways possible. The gay community should also be a strong, visible presence for alcohol treatment centers and be ready to counsel and assist treatment staffs whenever possible. Finally, the community should strongly encourage gay A.A. groups to be formed, not just co-sexual gay-lesbian groups. Men need pure gay groups as much as women need lesbian groups.

For Clinicians

Clinicians working with gay alcoholics in treatment are advised first and foremost to assist the client work toward sobriety, rather than trying to assist the client achieve the Acceptance stage of the coming out process. Clinicians in treatment centers should also keep in mind that the gay client is often working on two very serious issues, being gay and being alcoholic. Therefore, extra support is needed. The client should be encouraged, not forced, to attend gay A.A. groups or to talk with gay therapists or men from A.A. groups. On treatment units, information relative to gay A.A. meetings should be posted in conspicuous places, and positive gay literature should be included with other literature on these units. Clinicians should be aware that the life experience of gays is quite different from lesbians. Therefore, not only should this study not be applied to lesbians, but the clinician should avoid thinking that a lesbian therapist is the same as a gay therapist. Finally, if the clinician finds herself or himself homophobic toward gay men, she or he should refer the client to another therapist while working to correct one's homophobia.

For Gay A.A.

Three implications from this study should be helpful to the new gay client. One, consider working on a 4th Step model specific to gay men, as this step has been helpful to other gay men accept being gay as a positive aspect of self. Two, discuss acceptance of gay self along with acceptance of powerlessness over alcohol. Many gay men need to hear that. Finally, urban gay A.A. groups should be encouraged to provide a "loner" network for rural gays who don't have the benefit of gay A.A. This can be accomplished through letters, phone calls, visits, and the like.

For Researchers

One, the specific dynamics by which gays progress from being negative to being positive about their orientation should be explored further. Two, gay ethnotheories upon which much policy is built should be further explored. As this study showed, misinformation about gay bars is prevalent. Three, the nature of A.A.'s Step 4 should be explored in greater depth to determine how it works for gay men. Four, findings gleaned from gay studies apply only to gays. It is questionable whether researchers in lesbian studies would uncover identical findings of lesbians.

SUMMARY

Through ethnographic procedures, three hypotheses were tested, findings analyzed, and implications of the study presented. The major findings were as follows: (a) The etiology and thus the incidence of alcoholism in gay American men are unrelated to gay bars; thus, Hypothesis #1 was accepted; (b) all informants were cognizant of the high alcoholism rate in the gay community, and all thought that 25-33% was either a low estimate or just about right; (c) even though gay bars had no role in their becoming alcoholic, virtually all of the men thought that gay bars were responsible for the high incidence of alcoholism in the gay community; (d) most, if not all, informants reported drinking alcohol abusively from the very first drink; (e) not accepting being gay as a positive aspect of self can explain the probable etiology of alcoholism in gay American men, and thus explain the incidence of alcoholism in the gay community; therefore, Hypothesis #2 was accepted; (f) some gays recognized their non-acceptance while drinking, yet others, who "thought" they had accepted being gay, discovered after achieving sobriety that indeed they had not; (g) sobriety leads to positive acceptance of being gay, not vice versa; thus, Hypothesis #3, that acceptance would lead to sobriety, was rejected; and (h) men who chose sobriety found four factors especially helpful in gaining a positive acceptance of being gay: (1) extending the concept of "powerlessness" over alcohol to include being powerless over one's sexual orientation; (2) doing the A.A.'s 4th Step or "moral inventory"; (3) recognizing that not accepting one's sexual orientation as a positive aspect of self will make sobriety very difficult to maintain over time and will make serenity virtually impossible to experience; and (4) meeting and relating to as many other gay men as possible, both in gay A.A. meetings and outside of A.A.

NOTES

1. Clinicians, in order to establish and maintain trust in their clients, should always choose their words carefully. In the United States, the term "homosexual" to refer to persons with a same-sex sexual orientation is considered by many as "quaint" at best and offensive at most. As a black gay man once told me, "Homosexual: colored or Negro — gay: black." In other words, persons using the word "homosexual" are out of touch with current vocabulary and, it would seem, therefore out of touch with gay and lesbian issues. Likewise, many persons have told me they would be much more likely to disclose their sexual orientation to someone who used the words "gay" and "lesbian" than to one who used the word "homosexual"; "persons who use the word 'homosexual' I think might be homophobic." In the United States, the word "gay" referring to men with same-sex sexual orientation is most often preferred to the word "homosexual." The word "lesbian" referring to women with same-sex sexual orientation is usually preferred to the word "homosexual" also. Although there are still some lesbian Americans calling themselves "gay," this is becoming passé. Gay men's oppression, culture, and society are vastly different from lesbians' oppression, culture, and society. Therefore, in this article, "gay" refers only to same-sex oriented men and "lesbian" refers only to same-sex oriented women. Clinicians are strongly advised to learn the words gays and lesbians in their country prefer to avoid offending these clients.

REFERENCES

Fifield, L. (1975). *On my way to nowhere: Alienated, isolated, drunk*. Los Angeles: Gay Community Services Center & Department of Health Services.

Gay Council on Drinking Behavior. (1982). *The way back: The stories of gay and lesbian alcoholics*. Washington, DC: Whitman-Walker Clinic.

Glaser, B. G. & Strauss, A. (1967). *The discovery of grounded theory: Strategies for qualitative research*. Chicago: Aldine.

Gold, R. (1969). Roles in sociological field observations. In G. J. McCall & J. L. Simmons (Eds.), *Issues in participant observation* (pp. 30-39). Reading, MA: Addison-Wesley.

Kus, R. J. (1980). *Gay freedom: An ethnography of coming out*. Unpublished doctoral dissertation. University of Montana, Missoula.

Kus, R. J. (1985a). Stages of coming out: An ethnographic approach. *Western Journal of Nursing Research, 7,* 177-198.

Kus, R. J. (1985b, November). *Sex & sobriety: The gay experience*. Paper presented at the National Symposium of Nursing Research Conference, San Francisco.

Kus, R. J. (1985c, September). Gays and their higher power: An ethnography of gay sobriety. Paper presented at the National Association of Lesbian and Gay Alcoholism Professionals Convention, Chicago.

Lohrenz, L., Donnelly, J., Coyne, L. & Spare, K. (1978). Alcohol problems in several midwestern homosexual communities. *Journal of Studies on Alcohol, 39,* 1959-1963.

Moses, A. E. & Hawkins, R. O., Jr. (1982). *Counseling lesbian women and gay men: A life-issues approach*. St. Louis: C. V. Mosby.

Nardi, P. M. (1982). Alcoholism and homosexuality: A theoretical perspective. *Journal of Homosexuality, 7*(4), 9-25.

Saghir, M. & Robins, E. (1973). *Male and female homosexuality*. Baltimore: Williams & Wilkins.

Silverstein, C. & White, E. (1977). *The joy of gay sex*. New York: Crown.

Ziebold, T. (1978). *Alcoholism in the gay community*. Washington, DC: Whitman-Walker Clinic & Blade Communications.

APPENDIX 1

Gay-Lesbian Oriented Alcoholism Literature

— NALGAP Bibliography
204 West 20th Street
New York, NY 10011

— Ziebold, T.O. & Mongeon, J.E. (Eds.). (1985). *Gay and Sober: Directions for counseling and therapy*. New York: Harrington Park Press. [Originally published as *Journal of Homosexuality, 7*(4), 1982.]

Gay-Lesbian Alcoholism Organizations

— Local gay, lesbian, or gay/lesbian A.A. groups

— International Advisory Council (for Gays & Lesbians in A.A.)
  P.O. Box 492
  Village Station
  New York, NY 10014

— Lambda Service Group (for gay & lesbian recovering alcoholics)
  606 Barry Street
  Box 231
  Chicago, IL 60657

- National Association of Lesbian & Gay Alcoholism Professionals (NALGAP)
  1208 East State Blvd.
  Fort Wayne, IN 46805

Alcoholism Literature & Information — General

— Alcoholics Anonymous
  Box 459
  Grand Central Station
  New York, NY 10017

— CompCare Publications
  Box 27777
  Minneapolis, MN 55427

— Hazelden Educational Materials
  Box 176
  Center City, MN 55012

Special Issues in the Etiologies and Treatments of Sexual Problems Among Gay Men

Rex Reece, PhD

West Hollywood, California

SUMMARY. Some of the special circumstances and issues involved in both the causes and treatments of sexual problems among gay men are discussed. Reported frequencies of specific dysfunctions are discussed, and desire, arousal, and orgasmic phases are used to describe the special problems gay men have. These categories are also used to explore some of the probable contributing factors and specific treatment issues and suggestions that have been found useful. Since there is some indication that inhibited ejaculation is a somewhat frequent problem among gay men and has been more difficult than some dysfunctions to treat, emphasis has been placed on possible causes and treatments that have been helpful. A category of sexually inexperienced gay men is also discussed.

It seems to be true, as McWhirter and Mattison (1978) have written, that gay men experience a range of sexual dysfunctions similar to other men and most can also be treated successfully. They have also seen in their gay male clinical population (1980) communication problems, lack of insight into their relationship needs, performance pressures, lack of sexual knowledge, sex negative attitudes, incidence of underlying psychopathology, and resistances to sex therapy similar to comparable heterosexual male sex therapy clients. Therefore, the general process of sex therapy with gay men is not unlike sex therapy with anyone, and is described well in other places. The comments in this article are limited to the aspects of frequencies, etiologies, and treatments of sexual dysfunctions, and

Dr. Reece is a psychologist in private practice in Los Angeles. Correspondence may be addressed to the author, 9229 Sunset Boulevard, Suite 608, West Hollywood, CA 90069.

some other problems that are special in sex therapy with gay men. The extensive literature on sex therapy with heterosexuals will not be reviewed nor will accepted principles and practices of sex therapy in general be described.

REPORTED FREQUENCIES
OF DIFFERENT DYSFUNCTIONS

In the few published reports on sexual dysfunctions among gay men, there is little uniformity in the wording of survey questions or in the definitions of terms in reports of clinical experience. Therefore, the actual frequency and types of such problems in this population are as of yet only suggested. Bell and Weinberg (1978) reported from their survey of the San Francisco Bay Area gay male population that 27% of their respondents experienced somewhat or very much of a problem with "coming" too fast, 21% had difficulty in getting or keeping an erection, and 14% complained of lack of orgasm. Published reports on clinical populations reveal a somewhat different ratio of problems presented. Masters and Johnson (1979) reported on 59 cases of impotence (5 primary, 49 secondary, and 3 situational), and 2 cases of premature ejaculation. Although they were not presented with any cases of ejaculatory incompetence during their 10-year study, they acknowledged the likelihood that such problems must exist among gay men. Some reports on clinical experience have used Kaplan's (1974) tri-phasic model of desire, arousal, and orgasm to classify dysfunctions. Paff (1985) interviewed 10 Southern California psychotherapists and asked them to estimate, based on their memories, the frequencies of dysfunctions in each category they had found among their gay male sex therapy clients. These therapists recalled that approximately 25% had presented with desire disorders, 50% with arousal disorders, and 25% with orgasmic disorders. Out of 50 dysfunctions in 31 clients in group sex therapy, Reece (1981/1982) found that only 5% presented with problems of desire, while 50% reported erectile dysfunctions and 40% orgasmic problems. This difference in desire phase disorders can be partially accounted for by the fact that Paff included in his 25% those men who presented with a lack of interest in, discomfort with, or aversion to anal sex, while such clients were not included in Reece's groups; Reece's were designed primarily for treatment of erectile and orgasmic dysfunctions. McWhirter and Mattison (1978) found 9% of their 22 couples presenting with desire disorders, 45% with arousal problems, and 59% with orgasmic dysfunctions.

While secondary erectile dysfunctions seem to be the most frequently reported disorder among gay men, there are some indications that inhibited ejaculation may be more frequent among gay men than in heterosexual male populations and may be presented more frequently as a problem than rapid ejaculation. If so, that is just the reverse of the frequencies of the two aspects of orgasmic phase disorders commonly reported in non-gay male populations. This trend is not supported by Bell and Weinberg's (1978) survey, however. Twenty-seven percent of their respondents reported somewhat or very much of a problem with "coming" too fast and 14% with lack of orgasm. While McWhirter and Mattison's (1978) report on 22 couples, wherein 36% presented with premature ejaculation, and 22% with retarded ejaculation, supported Bell and Weinberg's results, these same authors have written (1980) that premature ejaculation seems to be seen less frequently in gays than in heterosexuals, and that among their caseload in general, delayed or retarded ejaculation is the most commonly presented orgasmic phase dysfunction. Based on his interviews with psychotherapists, Paff (1985) wrote that rapid ejaculation is reported with far less frequency among gay men than among heterosexual men and that retarded ejaculation is a far more significant problem for gay men. Green and Miller (1985) also had the impression that retarded ejaculation may be more common among homosexual men than heterosexual men, and Reece (1981/1982) found that of the 40% of orgasmic disorders in his treatment groups, only 10% were problems with rapid orgasm while 30% were problems with inhibited orgasmic response.

DESCRIPTIONS AND ETIOLOGY

Desire Phase

When doing sex therapy with gay men, the definition of desire phase disorders needs to include not only the situations and problems that are discussed by Kaplan (1977, 1979) and others, but also expanded to include problems with certain sexual acts more common among gay men. As Paff (1985) indicated, the most frequent desire issues are with anal sex, but a lack of interest in fellating a partner because of an aversion to semen or odors and difficulty overcoming a gag response are sometimes expressed problems. McWhirter and Mattison (1980) have mentioned that mutual masturbation is occasionally a problem as well.

Morin (1981) has written extensively on anal sex. His study and group treatment of 143 subjects indicated that perhaps the primary cause of what he called anal spasm (discomfort with being penetrated) was lack of experience. Organic etiologies may be related to a history of medical problems in the rectal area, such as hemorrhoids, warts, fistulas, fissures, or traumatic sexual experiences. Attitudinal contributors to anal spasm include associations with "dirtiness" or attributions of "femininity" to one's being penetrated. Paff (1985) mentioned that some of the therapists he interviewed found that some clients felt that anal sex was too intimate. It is likely that aversions to semen or experiencing the gag response while attempting to fellate a partner can come from associations of "dirtiness" with the genital area. However, like anal spasms, the gag response seems most often to be overcome with experience. To the degree these problems with oral sex exist, they can be serious inhibitors to satisfying sex between men, since oral sex seems to be the most common sexual act experienced by gay men (Bell & Weinberg, 1978; Jay & Young, 1977). Anecdotal reports of discomfort with mutual masturbation reveal difficulty in teaching one's partner to stimulate one's genitals in a way that is as exciting and pleasurable as one can do oneself, either because of self-consciousness about asking or having an uncooperative partner.

Reece (in press) has expanded the discussion of desire phase issues from the perspective of low desire as a problem of an individual or one partner to desire discrepancies in gay men based on Kaplan's (1979, 1983) multi-causal, multi-level model for desire disorders. Following Zilbergeld and Ellison's (1980) argument, he emphasized that most desire discrepancies are based in couple dynamics which may be confounded by lack of information about sex and each other, and range from poor communication through the unconscious repetition of unresolved childhood conflicts on the part of one or both partners.

In recent years some gay men have been withdrawing from sex completely, except perhaps for self-stimulation. This includes not only some gay men with AIDS or ARC, but some of those who test positive for HIV antibodies, or even otherwise physically healthy men who are particularly anxious about AIDS. Many of these men seem unable to make the transition to safer sex practices. Often they have been very active sexually with multiple partners and are now struggling with guilt about past sexual practices and internalized negative feelings about homosexuality. They are not likely to seek sex therapy for desire problems because they are not interested in overcoming their sexual withdrawal, but may come to therapy or be in psychotherapy for other reasons, often because of fears of succumbing to AIDS and terror that some rather common or minor physical problem is a symptom of AIDS.

Arousal Phase

The most frequent manifestation of dysfunction in this phase of sexual response is the loss of erection during attempts to penetrate one's partner anally. Many clients speak of responding with erections during initial kissing, caressing, or petting, but as disrobing is completed, or other conditions allow for, and the partner's communications indicate a desire to be anally penetrated, arousal sufficient for entry diminishes. For others, physical arousal is interrupted earlier in this sequence or is completely absent in the presence of an available partner. Some men complain of a lack or loss of erectile response with oral or manual stimulation. Occasionally the response failure extends beyond partner interaction to private self-stimulation, but, although there are reported cases of primary arousal disorders, this seems rare (Masters & Johnson, 1979).

The causes of such problems for any one gay man or male couple may be varied and not unlike those for their heterosexual counterparts. However, there are a few special considerations in working with gay men with such concerns. Some cases of erectile dysfunction in gay men seem to develop as a result of the fear of not being able to reach an orgasm with a partner. When one takes the history of the dysfunction, it is not uncommon to find that concern over not being able to reach an orgasm developed earlier than the erectile dysfunction. Such a client will also often recognize that, for example, loss of erection just after penetration began because of worry about not reaching an orgasm during that specific activity.

Many gay men move in a social, sexual milieu where sexual arousal is expected immediately or soon after meeting someone. If response is not rapidly forthcoming, rejection is very likely. In private clubs, baths, public restrooms, parks, bookstores, liaisons in automobiles, back rooms of bars, and other places where sex with strangers has been available, a gay man is often required, when a desirable partner comes along, to indicate desire and desirability by displaying an erect penis, or at least becoming obviously aroused with minimal stimulation—often under conditions that are anxiety-producing. Unless the gay man becomes aroused easily, the prospective partner may soon move on to other available partners. Some men have developed their anxiety about erectile response from such settings and carry that fear of failure into their repeated sexual experiences with the same partner, and sometimes the lack of response generalizes.

As suggested from these comments, some men have difficulty responding easily with strangers. And for some of those the etiology is not just in performance anxiety, but is likely associated with a more personal objection to sex under these circumstances. Perhaps, in spite of placing themselves in these situations, they have learned too well to associate sex with love or they may be seeking to satisfy other emotional needs through physical intimacy and are unable to dismiss completely those inner attitudes and needs and simply perform erotically.

The other side of the coin seems to be the case for certain other gay men. These are the men who respond satisfactorily with relative strangers, but who are not responsive during repeated sexual experiences with the same partner, especially as affection, closeness, and intimacy develop. Incidentally, this lack of response with an ongoing partner may not be limited to the arousal phase of the sexual response cycle, it may also be expressed with either rapid or inhibited ejaculation, and certainly expressed in the desire phase.

Two more aspects of anal sex that can contribute to erectile failure are worth mentioning. Worrying about hurting one's partner upon initial penetration is sometimes discussed as a problem. Because it is common, even for those experienced in anal receptivity, to have a few seconds of discomfort until muscle relaxation can occur, concern over a partner's suffering may contribute to sufficient diminution of excitement to prevent penetration. Second, due to concern about AIDS and the commitment many men have made to safer sexual practices, the use of condoms is now generally accepted as advisable for use during anal sex. However, many gay men lack experience using them, and having to interrupt foreplay in order to put the condoms on causes many men to lose their erections before they can penetrate their partners.

Orgasmic Phase

There seems to be little that is special about rapid ejaculation in gay men, either in its manifestation, etiology, or treatment, except that the frequency may be less than among heterosexual men. However, inhibited ejaculation may be more frequently a problem in this population. The most common manifestation of this complaint seems to be difficulty in reaching an orgasm except through self-stimulation, never or infrequently with some type of stimulation from one's partner. As with erectile dysfunctions, difficulty ejaculating is sometimes limited to one specific type of stimulation, such as with anal or oral stimulation. In many years of treating sexual problems in gay men, this author has encountered only one case of primary orgasmic dysfunction.

There is no evidence to indicate that most of the intrapersonal, interpersonal, or cultural contributors to inhibited ejaculation for men do not apply to gay men. However, there are a few considerations that are perhaps special to understanding and treating this dysfunction in gay men. For some men both etiology and treatment are suggested by some specific behaviors associated with this problem. A large number of gay men presenting with inhibited ejaculation describe their masturbatory patterns in remarkably similar ways. Self-stimulation, especially during the later part of the plateau phase, usually includes *very* rapid stroking of the penis, applied with great pressure and often accompanied by tensed abdominal and leg muscles. Not only is the body rigid, but the position — usually reclining on the back — seldom varies. Many men also have a specific fantasy that accompanies these activities and aids in their efforts to achieve an orgasm. A small but not insignificant number of men say they reach orgasm in masturbation by lying on their stomach and thrusting against the bed clothes, a pillow, or some other fabric or object beneath them. Closer questioning often reveals that the primary area of sensitivity is the frenulum and just the right amount of friction between that area of the penis and the material below allows excitement to build to orgasm. Such rigid patterns are difficult to duplicate with a partner, and when orgasm is dependent on these specific conditions, climaxing is not likely to occur with a partner.

There is another aspect of sex between men which may contribute more to inhibited ejaculation than to rapid ejaculation. Most men seem to accept that stimulation from receptive anal intercourse alone is unlikely to result in an orgasm. There may be some disappointment on the part of either or both partners if the penetrating partner's orgasm abbreviates the pleasure of prolonged anal sex, but that event does not typically interfere with the two of them changing to another activity that allows the recently anally receptive partner to experience an orgasm during that sexual encounter. The receptive partner may become the penetrating partner, or they may get involved in some combination of oral or manual stimulation that builds to orgasm. In other words, generally between men, one partner's orgasm does not render the other's unlikely. With many accepted ways to reach an orgasm, the penetrating partner may not feel the pressure that heterosexual men sometimes feel to last long enough during intercourse for their partner to climax. Without such performance pressure, the frequency of rapid ejaculation is likely to be lower.

There are probably many factors that contribute to inhibited ejaculation between men, and some of the following can contribute to the performance pressure often involved, which in turn can inhibit orgasm. Generally, men masturbate at an earlier age than women, and do so more frequently. Because masturbation usually leads to orgasm, men are more likely to expect orgasm to be a part of sex. In writing of the fantasy model of sex, Zilbergeld (1978) mentioned that women are not necessarily expected to reach orgasm during each sexual encounter, but men are. Two men together are even more likely to be orgasm-oriented. In sexual encounters with relative strangers, many men are understandably primarily interested in the release of sexual tension through an orgasm and not so much in the possibility for intimacy or prolonged sensual pleasure. Gay erotic films often slow the speed of the action at the time of orgasm, reflecting the importance of this aspect of sex for gay men. These expectations and attitudes can sometimes create enough performance anxiety to contribute to ejaculatory difficulties.

Sexual Inexperience

Although neither a phase disorder nor a specific dysfunction, lack of sexual experience with men is another type of sexual problem that is not common, but is presented frequently enough by gay men to merit some discussion. Gay men with this problem are most often in their thirties or early forties, and their history, if presenting with little or no sexual experience, most commonly reveals men whose sexual interest in women has been slight or nonexistent and whose attitudes and fears about homosexuality have kept them from becoming involved with men. They are likely to have been painfully shy and isolated as children and exhibit some aspects of social phobia or exhibit avoidant or schizoid personalities as adults. Exceptions to such a history or adult characteristics include the client who may have been a priest or follower of some other religious discipline that proscribes sexual activity and who has decided to express his homosexual sexual desires. These clients are usually very frightened about getting sexually involved and often ask basic questions about sex; they usually have little idea how and where to meet people, how dating happens, or have any of the basic social skills most people learn as teenagers. One such client's statement, "I'm approaching middle age, yet when it comes to sex, I feel as awkward as a young teenager," illustrates the fear and embarrassment experienced by some of these men.

The other subtype of client, less frequently seen, is likely to be or have been married and yet is motivated to become involved with men. His presenting complaint is also usually sexual and social. Although he may have felt sexually secure in heterosexual relationships, when faced with an unfamiliar social milieu in the context of which he intends to finally act on proscribed, yet intense feelings, he is prone to feel very anxious.

Other Contributing Factors to Sexual Problems for Gay Men

Although some special factors do contribute to problems within each particular phase of the sexual response cycle for gay men, there are some issues special to gay men that bear mentioning because they can have an effect on problems within any phase. These points have implications both for etiology and treatment.

Performance anxiety seem generally accepted by most sex therapists as a factor in the etiology of various dysfunctions. Of course, it is not unusual for heterosexual men to feel they must prove their masculinity through sex, but for gay men there is often an added burden resulting from two related factors. In their investigation, Bell, Weinberg, and Hammersmith (1981) found in significant numbers of gay men's histories abundant examples of gender nonconformity. Yet typically, these "sissy" boys grew up to be attracted to, as most gay men are, "masculine" men. Therefore, in order to be attractive to such partners, the assumption is that one has to be especially "masculine." Some of these men fear their "feminine" side is just below the surface and that it will be exposed as they become more sexually and emotionally intimate with another man. This anxiety can contribute a particular character to the performance anxiety that is otherwise common in different sexual problems.

Malyon (1981/1982) traced how developmental experiences typical of gay men contribute to internalized negative attitudes about homosexuality. To the degree that such values continue to exist, consciously or unconsciously, they can be expressed through various sexual dysfunctions. Some men have difficulty becoming vulnerable and intimate with other men, perhaps partly because of the cultural norms that men should be strong, active winners. These attitudes can make it difficult for some gay men to seek the tenderness and affection, to ask for specific stimulation or sexual activities, or to allow the closeness to develop with another man that may be necessary for their sexual response to flow naturally.

Fifield (1975) reported on the relatively high incidence of alcohol abuse among Los Angeles gay men and lesbians. Although the specific degree of abuse is uncertain, most gay people and professionals working with gay populations would probably agree that alcoholism and drug use and abuse is common. Therefore, more attention to these possible organic bases for various sexual problems in this population is warranted.

TREATMENT

General Issues

McWhirter and Mattison (1978, 1980) mentioned certain characteristics of gay men in their clinical work that may have some impact on the sex therapy process. They found, as did Blumstein and Schwartz (1983), that gay men are much more likely to have had sex outside of a primary relationship. Their impression was that gay men are less rigid in their sexual attitudes and roles and are less likely to use sex as a weapon. They found gay men not only less likely to blame the partner for the dysfunction, but actually more likely to empathize with him.

There are further considerations when doing sex therapy with male couples. Gay male love relationships are more at risk than most heterosexual marriages. Again, McWhirter and Mattison (1978, 1980) mentioned the lack of cultural and institutional support for such pairings. Popular ideas that gay relationships do not last contribute to a self-fulfilling prophecy and, because extra-relationship sex has been so common and acceptable, many couples have the attitude that if sexual problems arise, the practical solution is to seek outside partners rather than work within the relationship. This may contribute to less tolerance of the stresses involved in and commitment necessary for sex therapy.

There is considerable opportunity to work with single men in sex therapy; this presents a special problem, particularly when a cooperative, ongoing partner seems necessary for therapeutic success. Reece (1981/1982) did group treatment for men without partners, and had appropriate clients who were in individual treatment work with surrogate partners. Everaerd et al. (1982) had four gay men in a male-only treatment group of 21 men.

McWhirter and Mattison (1978, 1980) emphasized that the single most important factor in treating male homosexual sexual dysfunction is a total absence of homophobia in the therapist. They also emphasized the frequent necessity of consciousness-raising to counter internalized negative attitudes about homosexuality, no matter what the sexual dysfunction or problem being treated is. If the client has internalized negative attitudes about gay sexuality and homosexuality, a strong, clear positive role model can be very beneficial.

Desire Phase

Treatment of the desire problems in gay men that parallel those found in heterosexual men have been covered in other research. Morin (1981) essentially treated anal spasms with much information and permission-giving and the use of progressive insertion exercises, similar to the technique used in the treatment of vaginismus. Reece's (in press) multi-causal, -level, -treatment approach to desire discrepancies is too lengthy and detailed to be summarized here. Treating aversions to oral sex in gay men is not substantially different from the same treatment process for heterosexual women. Permission-giving and learning new communication processes are usually sufficient to overcome resistances to mutual masturbation. And withdrawal from sex because of fears related to AIDS can probably best be approached as an anxiety disorder rather than a sexual problem.

Arousal Phase

As with most sexual dysfunctions in gay men, the treatment of arousal phase disorders is essentially comparable to the treatment of similar problems in heterosexual populations. It is helpful to keep the special context in mind, however.

As mentioned above, there seems to be a relatively high incidence of orgasmic dysfunctions, particularly problems with inhibited ejaculation, in the history of gay men with erectile disorders. When the development of the orgasmic dysfunction predates the beginning of arousal problems, then the relationship must be determined and both dysfunctions treated. This does not mean that the inhibited ejaculation needs to be treated first; they can be treated concurrently. As a matter of fact, prohibiting orgasm during sensate focus or pleasuring exercises is usually necessary to regain and maintain erectile function in these cases.

Zilbergeld (1978) emphasized the importance of a man's having his conditions met before he can expect to respond sexually, a principle many gay men have tried to deny. For some, spending enough time to become comfortable with a potential partner before expecting erectile response is a necessary condition. At one time, that might mean a few minutes of talking or physical affection in an otherwise "impersonal" situation; at another, a series of social experiences together may be necessary. Sometimes, just the understanding that erectile response cannot necessarily be expected without certain conditions being met will allow one to relax and therefore make response more likely. Generally, for those men who have difficulty responding in repeated sexual opportunities with the same partner, some individual therapy directed toward issues of intimacy or internalized homophobia is necessary.

Some direction to experiment and play with condoms during masturbation experiences or encounters with a trusted partner can be helpful in overcoming the fear of losing one's erection for those inexperienced with condom use. If a client understands that loss of excitement is natural when an interruption of the cycle occurs — such as taking time to slip on a condom — and that excitement naturally returns when one refocuses on pleasurable sex play, the anxiety that blocks erection can often be relieved. A sexual couple tends sometimes not to pause to apply a condom until they are both ready for anal intercourse. Learning to put on the condom during the initial stages of sexual interaction can be helpful.

A little education about the anatomy and physiology of the anal sphincter and some reassurances from one's receptive partner that the initial discomfort eases quickly is likely to reassure most men who lose erections for fear of hurting their partner upon penetration.

Orgasmic Phase

McWhirter and Mattison (1978) found rapid ejaculation the easiest dysfunction to treat and Masters and Johnson (1979) hinted that it may be easier to treat in gay men than in heterosexual men.

However, McWhirter and Mattison (1978) also found inhibited ejaculation the most difficult to treat. Their impression was that there is more psychopathology found in men with this dysfunction, and sometimes the deeper disturbances cannot be bypassed to treat only the sexual dysfunction. It is also the current author's impression that the treatment of inhibited ejaculation in gay men takes longer and success is somewhat less likely than treatment of the other dysfunctions. Often issues such as internalized homophobia and fears of dependency and intimacy interfere and must be addressed. Highly anxious or obsessive-compulsive personality styles seem to be involved for many of these men.

Successive approximation, a process of gradually moving the desired response (orgasm) toward the desirable stimulation (direct interaction with a partner) with progression dependent on success at each step, is a commonly used behavioral approach for treatment of delayed ejaculation. This author has not found it to be very successful unless used in combination with other processes due to the necessary repetitive and tedious steps. A combination of concurrent processes seems most successful, the specifics depending on the individual case. If the client exhibits some variation of the masturbatory style mentioned above, several processes can be helpful. General body self-pleasuring that is gentle and slow with lots of concentration on physical sensations, then later including genitals, can be suggested. The client must learn to masturbate, with orgasm prohibited, with a similar slow, gentle, attention-focused rhythm. Detailed discussions with the therapist about the bodily sensations, especially in the pelvic or genital area, can help focus the client on feelings and distract him from a goal orientation. On other occasions, the client can be encouraged to develop a clear fantasy of reaching orgasm under the desired conditions and stimulation, then while masturbating according to his usual pattern and to his familiar fantasy, replace this with the new fantasy at the point of ejaculatory inevitability. A variation is simply and consciously to relax, instead of continuing the tension at that point. With repeated experiences, the fantasy or the relaxation or both can be pushed further back into the plateau stage.

Other processes that help vary rigid orgasmic patterns include changing positions just before orgasm or exaggerating the physical movement and vocalizations that may naturally occur as orgasm approaches and occurs. Some men are so expressively inhibited that some practice in physically "letting go" seems to help release the orgasmic response. Repeating some of these experiences in the presence of a partner before gradually getting the partner more directly involved is a step that is usually helpful. Learning then to respond to physical and mental stimulation that is possible with a partner seems a necessary next step.

Inexperienced Gay Men

Work on social skills is often necessary for sexually inexperienced gay men. Participation in an all-gay male therapy group can be useful, as can becoming involved in gay community events, groups, or organizations. Often this is not easy for such clients, but progress can be made with time and patience. Because social interaction can be so difficult for some, fears of rejection and failure abound in relationship to sex. Sometimes a trusted friend of the client is suitable for progressive sexual exercises and experiences, but when appropriate and available, surrogate partners can be particularly useful.

REFERENCES

Bell, A. P., & Weinberg, M. S. (1978). *Homosexualities: A study of diversity among men and women*. New York: Simon & Schuster.

Bell, A. P., Weinberg, M. S. & Hammersmith, S. K. (1981). *Sexual preference: Its development in men and women*. Bloomington, IN: Indiana University Press.

Blumstein, P., & Schwartz, P. (1983). *American couples: Money, work, sex*. New York: William Morrow.

Everaerd, W., Dekker, J., Dronkers, J., Rhee, K. van der, Staffeleu, J. & Wiselius, G. (1982). Treatment of homosexual and heterosexual sexual dysfunction in male-only groups of mixed sexual orientation. *Archives of Sexual Behavior*, *11*, 1-10.

Fifield, L. (1975). *On my way to nowhere: Alienated, isolated, drunk*. Los Angeles: Gay Community Services Center and Department of Health Services.

Green, J. & Miller, D. (1985). Male homosexuality and sexual problems. *British Journal of Hospital Medicine*, *33*, 353-355.

Jay, K. & Young, A. (1977). *The gay report: Lesbians and gay men speak out about sexual experiences and lifestyles*. New York: Summit Books.

Kaplan, H. S. (1974). *The new sex therapy*. New York: Brunner/Mazel.

Kaplan, H. S. (1977). Hypoactive sexual desire. *Journal of Sex & Marital Therapy*, *3*, 3-9.

Kaplan, H. S. (1979). *Disorders of sexual desire*. New York: Brunner/Mazel.

Kaplan, H. S. (1983). *The evaluation of sexual disorders*. New York: Brunner/Mazel.

Malyon, A. K. (1981/1982). Psychotherapeutic implications of internalized homophobia in gay men. *Journal of Homosexuality*, *7*(2/3), 59-69.

Masters, W. H. & Johnson, V. E. (1979). *Homosexuality in perspective*. Boston: Little, Brown.

McWhirter, D. P. & Mattison, A. M. (1978). The treatment of sexual dysfunction in gay male couples. *Journal of Sex and Marital Therapy*, *4*, 213-218.

McWhirter, D. P. & Mattison, A. M. (1980). Treatment of sexual dysfunction in homosexual male couples. In S. R. Leiblum & L. A. Pervin (Eds.), *Principles and practice of sex therapy* (pp. 321-345). New York: Guilford.

Morin, J. (1981). *Anal pleasure & health*. Burlingame, CA: Down There Press.

Paff, B. A. (1985). Sexual dysfunction in gay men requesting treatment. *Journal of Sex and Marital Therapy*, *11*, 3-18.

Reece, R. (1987). Causes and treatments of sexual desire discrepancies in male couples. *Journal of Homosexuality*, *14*(1/2), 157-172.

Reece, R. (1981/1982). Group treatment of sexual dysfunction in gay men. *Journal of Homosexuality*, *7*(2/3), 113-129.

Zilbergeld, B. (1978). *Male sexuality: A guide to sexual fulfillment*. Boston: Little, Brown.

Zilbergeld, B. & Ellison, C. R. (1980). Desire discrepancies and arousal problems in sex therapy. In S. R. Leiblum & L. A. Pervin (Eds.), *Principles and practice of sex therapy* (pp. 65-101). New York: Guilford.

Psychopathology, Homosexuality, and Homophobia

Jaime Smith, MD

University of British Columbia

Before 1973 the official nosology of the American Psychiatric Association specified homosexual adjustment as psychopathological (American Psychiatric Association, 1968). The International Classification of Diseases of the World Health Organization continues to do so (World Health Association, 1977). Although the current Diagnostic and Statistical Manual of Mental Disorders of the A.P.A. (American Psychiatric Association, 1980) explicitly states, ". . . homosexuality itself is not considered a mental disorder," this official view is not unanimous and a significant number of psychiatrists in North America and elsewhere remain convinced of the inherent psychopathology of homosexuality.

The relationship may be represented by a Venn diagram in which the large rectangle encloses the set of all individuals, the larger circle the set of all those who exhibit psychopathology, and the smaller inner circle the set of all those who are homosexually adjusted. Thus in Diagram 1, homosexuality implies psychopathology, and one is led to invoke the medical model of disease, with etiology, treatment, "cure," and so forth with which researchers are familiar.

On the other hand, taking the DSM-III view that not all instances of homosexual adjustment are necessarily psychopathological, a different Venn diagram results: in Diagram 2 the rectangle again represents all individuals, but now the two circles intersect, so that some homosexual individuals may be considered psychopathological and others not.

Dr. Smith is Clinical Assistant Professor of Psychiatry at the University of British Columbia and the Director of the Psychiatric Short Stay Unit at St. Paul's Hospital in Vancouver. Correspondence may be addressed to the author, St. Paul's Hospital (C2A), 1081 Burrard Street, Vancouver, BC V6Z 1Y6, Canada.

This is a much more interesting situation both theoretically and clinically, for it allows us to entertain the question of when and under what circumstances are homosexually adjusted individuals psychopathological. Further, if the homosexuality is related to the psychopathology, what can be done to facilitate a shift from a pathological adjustment?

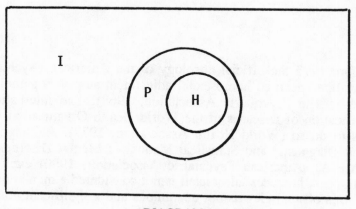

DIAGRAM 1
I = Set of all individuals
P = Set of all psychopathological individuals
H = Set of homosexually adjusted individuals

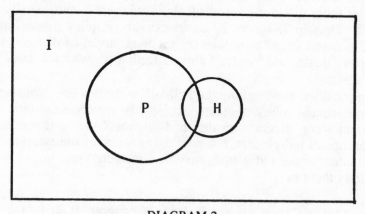

DIAGRAM 2
I = Set of all individuals
P = Set of all psychopathological individuals
H = Set of homosexually adjusted individuals

In the discussion which follows, I will use "psychopathology" to mean presence of an axis 1 or axis 2 psychiatric diagnosis in the sense of DSM-III. By "homosexual" I mean those same-sex thoughts, feelings, or behavior present in an individual with more than incidental occurrence, i.e., Kinsey numbers 5 or 6 (Kinsey, Pomeroy and Martin, 1948). As seen in Diagram 2, there are clearly individuals with homosexual adjustment who do not exhibit psychopathology in the above sense; similarly, there are persons whose mental status is consistent with the presence of psychopathology but who do not display homosexual adjustment. Of special interest here is the intersection of the two sets, those individuals who are both homosexually adjusted and who display psychopathology.

An understanding of the intrapsychic and psychosocial factors contributing to psychopathology in homosexually oriented persons requires a clear appreciation of the role of homophobia. Irrational prejudice against homosexuality has been a feature of Judeo-Christian culture for millenia, waning and waxing in intensity from amused but derogatory tolerance to outright genocide. Negative attitudes are internalized early in life, prior to the self-discovery of sexual orientation in most persons; in homosexually adjusted individuals this internalized homophobia becomes self-directed and plays a major role in the development of dysphoric states which must be worked through to attain stable adjustment.

In addition to internalized homophobia, homosexual persons are subjected to the effects of social stigmatization, including overt disapproval of lifestyles, lack of protection against discrimination in housing, employment, and association, and in many jurisdictions, criminal sanctions against the expression of love and affection. It is therefore not surprising that those individuals with immature or maladaptive coping styles become psychologically wounded by the constant application of this stigmatizing process. What *is* notable is the resiliency of the human spirit in the face of such adversity and the strength of character attained by so many of the survivors.

A particularly insidious effect of homophobia arises from the involvement of homophobic therapists in the treatment of homosexual persons. One may see direct or indirect support of psychological defenses working against self-acceptance, or even the promotion of an ego-dystonic state where none existed before. Such efforts are clearly antitherapeutic in that they inhibit the formation of a mature psychosexual identity in the context of minority sexual orientation.

The remainder of this article will consist of an examination of the diagnostic categories of DSM-III with respect to what can be said about homosexuality and psychopathology in each of these areas, and how internal and external manifestations of homophobia contribute to the clinical pictures.

DISORDERS USUALLY FIRST EVIDENT IN INFANCY, CHILDHOOD, OR ADOLESCENCE

Mental Retardation is usually diagnosed at an early stage and of course persists lifelong. Sexual needs are experienced by the mentally handicapped as much as by the remainder of the population, and that includes those with homosexual adjustment. If the retardation is mild or borderline, the individual may attain a reasonable adjustment in adulthood, though naiveté may render the young adult or teenager susceptible to exploitation. For those with a more profound handicap, the attitude of caregivers is important; the desire for sexual release may be interpreted as "acting-out" rather than the expression of a legitimate need, and this is more of an issue when the adjustment is homosexual because of the pervasive homophobia in our culture. On the other hand, caregivers who themselves are homosexual may be in a precarious position and vulnerable to accusations of "condonement" of homosexuality if they encourage or facilitate sexual expression between their clients.

Bell, Weinberg & Hammersmith (1981) have described atypical gender role behavior as a marker for possible later adult homosexual adjustment in children. This lack of same-sex peer socialization is an extremely common finding in retrospective histories taken from adults with homosexual adjustment. "I knew I was somehow different from other boys (or girls)" is a familiar phrase to those who have explored life histories with this population. There is thus a clear psychodynamic mechanism to account for avoidant or over-anxious disorders of childhood in that subset of the prepubertal population destined to evolve into homosexually adjusted adults. Clinicians working with these children must bear in mind that this is not an uncommon situation, but on the contrary, one of the more likely explanations for this type of childhood psychopathology.

Adolescence is particularly risky for the evolving homosexually adjusted child, for this is when awareness of sexual orientation usually occurs, and the cultural homophobia already has been internalized. Various reactive states may ensue: "normal" reactive depression, denial, and reaction formation leading to aggressive conduct disorders directed against obvious homosexuals, and the ego-dystonic state (Smith, 1980). Identity disorder may be the presenting picture, arising from conflicts not only over sexual identity, but also over religious and moral values, group and family loyalty, and exacerbated by the lack of social support systems. It is imperative that psychiatrists and other mental health workers understand the ubiquity of homosexual adjustment and the potential for adolescent psychopathology arising out of these conflicts. We are discussing 10% of the population, not some unusual and rare variation such as transsexualism.

On my consulting room wall there hangs an engraving of a yellow-billed cuckoo, whose developmental history is a metaphor for the growth and development of the homosexually adjusted individual: born and raised in a family perceived as inexplicably different from the self as a child, it is only with maturing and "spreading one's wings" that one discovers one is not alone after all in one's identity, and a sense of community and belonging becomes possible in a way fundamentally different from the family of origin. This developmental process is not without perils and it is reasonable to suggest that childhood mental disorders in some instances may arise from these circumstances.

It should be noted also that many of the developmental tasks of adolescence, such as peer socialization, sexual exploration, and experiments with intimacy and tentative love attachments, which occur in the second decade for the most part in the heterosexual majority, are developmentally delayed in the homosexual minority. Thus, some homosexually adjusted persons may in the third decade of life display some of the turbulence and emotionality of the teenaged heterosexual. The developmental delay is understandable in the context of social homophobia preventing the individual from undertaking his or her normal developmental tasks; the manifestations of the working-through of these tasks should not be confused with personality disorders.

ORGANIC MENTAL DISORDERS

It is difficult to imagine any difference in psychopathology between the homosexually oriented and the heterosexually oriented in the group of organic mental disorders. Although there is an increased amount of alcohol-related brain syndromes because of a greater amount of alcoholism among the former (Saghir & Robins, 1973), the syndromes themselves are the same in both populations. Similarly, the brain syndromes resulting from acquired immune deficiency syndrome (AIDS) related neoplasms and infections are seen mainly among the homosexually oriented, since they constitute the majority of AIDS patients at the present time. One would not expect that the pathology itself would differ with the sexual orientation of the patient.

The identification of an anatomical or biochemical factor in the central nervous system of individuals which is related to their sexual orientation remains elusive. I have noted sinistrality among 18 of 100 successive clients at a venereal disease screening clinic for homosexually adjusted males. With a general population prevalence of 7% sinistrality, this result is attributable to chance in less than 1 time in 1,000. Evidently there is something going on here of interest, but just what it is remains to be elucidated.

SUBSTANCE USE DISORDERS

It has been already noted that there is an increased prevalence of alcoholism in the homosexual population. That this should be so is not surprising for a number of reasons. First, the normal developmental process in the context of sexual minority status is anxiety-provoking. Second, alcoholic beverages are socially sanctioned and freely available anxiolytic drugs which are self-administered. And finally, the usual social setting in which potential partners are initially encountered is often the bar. Given all this potential, it is surprising that there is not a greater amount of alcohol abuse in the homosexually adjusted population.

Specialized counseling services are becoming available for the homosexual alcoholic, and the Alcoholics Anonymous organization has groups in all major centres specifically for these persons (Ziebold & Mongeon, 1982). Clinicians working with this population should be aware of the developmental dynamics and their contributions to the etiology of the disorder, including self-directed homophobia. These issues must be addressed in therapy if a favorable outcome is to be achieved and maintained.

PSYCHOTIC DISORDERS

Delusional material observed in patients with schizophrenia and other psychotic illnesses may involve sexual orientation. Usually the other signs of the psychotic disorder alert the clinician to the situation.

> Ms. B., a 35-year-old registered nurse, requested counseling to facilitate her lesbian adjustment. At the first appointment she demonstrated pressured speech, flight of ideas, and described a decreased need for sleep and the sense of having boundless energy. Following a brief admission with the diagnosis of bipolar affective disorder, manic phase, and initiation of lithium carbonate treatment, she reverted to her usual state, and expressed relief at the correct diagnosis and treatment plan. After 5 years she remained on lithium prophylaxis, had not relapsed, enjoyed an active sex life with male partners, and had no further interest at the time in pursuing same-sex experiences.

A concern is that patients such as Ms. B. will receive counseling by well-intentioned but untrained community advisors, and be encouraged in a direction contrary to the non-psychotic self. The exact reverse also occurs when the emotionally disturbed, perhaps psychotic, homosexually adjusted person seeks "Christian counseling" to facilitate heterosexual adjustment. In either case, a mental status examination should be conducted by a competent examiner before undertaking any form of treatment.

The case of paranoid disorders (or delusional disorders) is of special historic interest. There has been a traditional psychoanalytic linkage between homosexuality and paranoia since Freud's discussion of the Schreber case (Freud, 1911/1958). This connection, however, is spurious, as epidemiological studies disclose no overrepresentation of paranoid disorders among the homosexually adjusted. The great influence of psychoanalytic thinking, particularly in North American psychiatry, has led nevertheless to an unwarranted association in the minds of many clinicians, particulary those who trained some decades ago when the psychoanalytic influence was at its zenith. As there is no substantiating evidence for this association, to maintain now that it exists is suggestive of rationalization based upon homophobia.

What initially may appear to be paranoid thinking in the homosexually adjusted person may, on exploration, turn out to be anticipated rejection subsequent to disclosure of homosexuality. This is often reality-based and not delusional at all, for many homosexual persons have lost employment, housing, peer esteem, and family support as a consequence of disclosure. A psychotic illness should never be diagnosed on the basis of this type of situation; instead, a diagnosis of psychosis must arise from the consideration of other aspects of mental status.

AFFECTIVE DISORDERS

One would not expect to find any difference in the prevalence between homosexual and heterosexual populations of "endogenous" affective disorders such as bipolar disorder or major depression. On the other hand, chronic low-grade depression or dysthymic disorder may arise out of incomplete developmental stages in homosexually adjusted persons, such as the conflict between behavior and values in the nondisclosed or "closeted" homosexual person. Therapy facilitating normal development, disclosure when appropriate, and peer socialization may successfully treat this type of individual. The sense of belonging to a community and the formation of a network of support among friends and family members will protect against decompensation at times of stress. A decrease in social isolation, if present, must be a goal in psychotherapy and may be best attained at times in a small group setting, rather than in individual therapy. Failure to achieve this leaves the individual at risk for depression and suicide, particularly in middle and later life.

ANXIETY, SOMATOFORM, DISSOCIATIVE DISORDERS

These categories include much of what was formerly known as the neuroses. Anxiety disorders are particularly common in the population at large. There is no overrepresentation of homosexuals in these categories and treatment should be straightforward and unrelated to sexual orientation.

The clinician should be cautious about attributing a causative role to sexual orientation in the etiology of these disorders. Psychodynamic rationalization of cultural homophobia, such as characterizing homosexual adjustment as secondary to phobic avoidance of the opposite sex, may be considered to be of only historical interest, although no doubt there are still some homophobic clinicians around who would make such interpretations.

PSYCHOSEXUAL DISORDERS

Among the differential diagnosis for Transsexualism in DSM-III is "effeminate homosexuality." Transsexualism is unlikely to be confounded with the latter by the experienced clinician, but the distinction is necessary because from time to time homosexually adjusted persons may make inquiries about sex reassignment surgery, particulary if young and naive. Gender dysphoria clinics require a lengthy trial period of living successfully in the preferred role prior to sex reassignment surgery, and there is ample opportunity to discontinue treatment before irreversible procedures are undertaken.

> Mr. W. presented to his family physician requesting estrogens because he thought he was transsexual. He was appropriately referred for psychiatric assessment and found to be very feminine but without a strong wish to be rid of his genitals. He was counseled to abandon the quest for medical treatment and attended a group for gay men to facilitate adjustment in his natural style. This was successful and subsequently he supported himself as a creative artist, with a flair for sexual ambiguity in his paintings having sublimated the transsexual strivings.

Gender Identity Disorder of Childhood is of interest because cross-gender peer identification in childhood tends to predict atypical (i.e., nonheterosexual) adult outcome, homosexual or transsexual. It should be noted that transsexualism is a rare condition compared to homosexual adjustment, in the ration of around 2,000 to 1. The treatment implication of gender identity disorder of childhood thus leads into the broader issue of prevention of sexual variation in adulthood. Naturally, all parents wish their children to be happy and to resemble themselves, and if it were possible to prevent homosexual adjustment (not to mention transsexualism), most parents would welcome the intervention. On the other hand, this raises ethical issues along the lines of other "Final Solutions" to minority problems. Certainly the world would be more predictable without variants, but it would also be less interesting; insect societies are stable, but stagnant. The issue is academic at present for the ultimate causes of sexual variation are unknown, but research is continuing and the day may come when these questions must be addressed not only scientifically but politically and ethically as well.

Paraphilias exist in both heterosexually and homosexually adjusted males. Although there is no overrepresentation of pedophilia in particular among the homosexual group, cultural homophobia perpetuates the myth that homosexually adjusted persons are somehow likely to engage in pedophilic behavior, and this argument is employed to deny civil liberties and employment opportunities to homosexual persons. This erroneous belief needs to be exposed and refuted whenever it arises. Pedophilia may be a cultural label rather than anything inherently medical or psychiatric; anthropological findings support this view. The Sambia of Papua-New Guinea, for example, require all male children from the age of 8 onwards to participate in homosexual activity with older boys, as part of their cultural tradition (Herdt, 1981).

Not a great deal needs to be said about psychosexual dysfunctions, other than to note that when they occur in same-sex couples the Masters and Johnson type of treatment approach is similar to that with opposite-sex couples.

"Ego-dystonic Homosexuality" is of particular interest in this discussion, for up to this point all psychopathology considered has been more or less incidental to the sexual orientation of the patient. This diagnosis, however, was defined to include *only* the homosexually adjusted. The byzantine history and acrimonious debates within the American Psychiatric Association leading up to the initial DSM-III diagnostic category of Ego-dystonic Homosexuality has been well documented (Spitzer, 1981). The category represented a compromise which was little liked by participants in the debate; it was deleted in the 1987 revision of DMS-III.

Nosological debate notwithstanding, there is no unanimity of opinion either as to what is one to do with the patient who presents with the wish to change his or her sexual orientation. Some such as Marmor (1980) would attempt to go along with the agenda of the patient and offer "conversion" or "reversion" to heterosexual adjustment. In my view this constitutes siding with the defensive structure of the patient, and impedes natural development of conflict-free adjustment as homosexual. These patients do present with psychopathology, but their psychopathology is not their homosexual thoughts, feelings, and behaviors, but rather their internalized and self-directed homophobia which impairs self-acceptance and the establishment of adaptive and sexually fulfilling lifestyles in the context of minority sexual orientation.

My therapeutic approach to this concern is to teach the patient to redefine his or her problem, and eventually to promote an ego-syntonic state through individual and small group psychotherapy (Smith, 1985). At times an impasse is reached and therapy must be discontinued, but it should be remembered that, as with all developmental issues, time and nature are on the side of the maturational processes, and even an unsuccessful conclusion to therapy may plant the seed for future growth in a healthy direction.

A psychiatric colleague of mine, an analyst and professor at a medical school and psychiatric training program, said to me, "Whenever I see a patient in whom homosexuality is ego-syntonic, I try to make it ego-dystonic." This illustrates the danger of homophobic therapists in working with these patients: They are unable to carry out the first rule of the physicians' code of ethics—*primum non nocere*.

FACTITIOUS DISORDERS

One would not expect to find a difference between homosexual and heterosexual populations in this area. On occasion, a heterosexual person may simulate homosexual adjustment (e.g., to avoid military service), or, more commonly, vice-versa (to avoid exposure, harassment, or ridicule), but these are clearly goal-related behaviors, and hence more akin to malingering and not to factitious disorders (in which the goal is involuntary).

DISORDERS OF IMPULSE CONTROL
NOT ELSEWHERE CLASSIFIED

Those homosexually adjusted men who have developed a pattern of seeking anonymous sexual contacts in settings such as public washrooms, and who perceive this behavior as unwanted and seek therapy to gain control over their sexual impulses, could be classified under this section. This behavior is illegal and police entrapment is often employed to provide some measure of social control. The men who participate in this form of sexual activity may or may not regard it as problematic, so whether it should be considered a mental disorder will depend upon the individual case. Often they will come to clinical attention only after they have been apprehended and charged. (This situation must be distinguished from exhibitionism, in which the display of the genitals is the most important aspect of the behavior, but no actual sexual interaction is sought by the exhibitor.)

Heterosexual males are unlikely to present with this condition, not only because of the custom of separate washrooms for the two sexes, but also because of the difference in the sexual response cycle of the human female and the lesser arousal effects of visual stimuli.

ADJUSTMENT DISORDER

It is part of the human condition to be exposed to psychosocial stressors throughout the life cycle. The individual's coping strategies determine the responses to these events, and may be adaptive or maladaptive. Bowlby's (1980) attachment theory characterized most of these stressors as real or symbolic losses. Adjustment to loss and other changes in life circumstances is necessary for survival and growth; failure to do so leads to stagnation, regression, and overt psychopathology.

Both the homosexually and the heterosexually adjusted will experience those life stressors which arise out of developmental stages, conflicts in interpersonal relationships, and the other vicissitudes of life such as illness and death. Many homosexually adjusted persons who have integrated successfully into mature adults have acquired superior coping skills as a consequence of having worked through the burdens of internalized homophobia and social stigmatization. It may be for this reason that there appears to be an overrepresentation of homosexually adjusted persons in the caregiving occupations and professions (rather than a hypothetical genetic linkage with altruistic behavior traits as suggested by sociobiologists). It seems reasonable to suppose that those who have coped well with loss, and who have adapted adequately to the major life stress of acquiring a positive self-image in the face of so much negative input about their own identity, should be in a good position to be helpful to other people.

PSYCHOLOGICAL FACTORS
AFFECTING PHYSICAL CONDITIONS

What immediately comes to mind when considering this diagnostic category of DSM-III is the phenomenon of acquired immune deficiency syndrome, a lethal viral infection which is thought to be sexually transmitted, and when spread in this manner has mainly affected the male homosexual population in the developed countries. Michael Ross (1984) has considered the psychological aspects of sexually transmitted diseases (S.T.D.) infection in a series of recent publications under the concept of psychovenereology, noting that:

[There is] a common underlying psychological process in homosexuals who are most likely to present with large numbers of sexually transmitted diseases, and it is precisely these individuals who appear to be most at risk of contracting AIDS as a S.T.D. . . . psychovenereology has a role in the understanding of the factors which predispose to AIDS infections.

PERSONALITY DISORDERS

Despite an impression to the contrary among many physicians and other health care workers, there is no demonstrated over-representation of the homosexually adjusted in this diagnostic category. The contrary impression arises from three separate sources which, acting together, support this erroneous belief.

First, individuals who seek psychiatric help or who otherwise come to psychiatric attention are by their nature in a state of emotional disturbance. There is a built-in selection bias here: Homosexually adjusted *patients* do demonstrate psychopathology, including character pathology (as would any other *patient*).

Second, the tendency to generalize is a deplorable but common human characteristic, and this is particularly pronounced when the individuals in question are members of a devalued minority group. Unresolved homophobia in the examiner (whether heterosexual or homosexual) will favor this type of generalization, leading in time to a false impression of the distribution of character pathology or personality disorder in the homosexual population at large.

Finally, as noted in the earlier section on developmental disorders, the phenomenon of delayed adolescence may falsely simulate personality disorder in young adulthood among the homosexually adjusted.

V CODES FOR CONDITIONS NOT ATTRIBUTED TO A MENTAL DISORDER THAT ARE A FOCUS OF ATTENTION OR TREATMENT

This final section in DSM-III allows the diagnostician to classify those complaints and concerns which come to clinical attention but which do not merit inclusion among the previously described diagnostic entities. In my own experience, the most common of these involving homosexually adjusted persons have been "Phase of Life Problems" in predominantly younger persons dealing with their own "coming-out" process, and "Marital Problems" in same-sex couples, where the dynamics of interpersonal conflict differ from those in opposite-sex couples.

Other instances of this category which arise on occasion have been "Adolescent Antisocial Behavior" as a consequence of reaction-formation to homosexual feelings which are unacceptable due to internalized and self-directed homophobia, "Parent-Child Problem" as a consequence of forced disclosure of homosexual adjustments in the case of some AIDS patients, and "Occupational Problem" where conflict arises in the work environment as a result of a homosexual employee being stigmatized or harassed by coworkers or management. This list is by no means exhaustive, but is meant to illustrate the many ways in which external and internal homophobia may negatively affect the quality of life for homosexual persons.

CONCLUSION

The DSM-III view that not all instances of homosexual adjustment are necessarily psychopathological has allowed us to review each of the diagnostic categories in turn and to describe some of the special conditions and considerations which apply when the patient is a member of this sexual minority.

The role of homophobia in both the patient and the clinician has been noted; successful treatment interventions with homosexually adjusted patients are facilitated by an awareness of the potential for harm caused by this irrational prejudice. Resident training programs and continuing education courses should be aware of and address this issue, given the ubiquity of homosexually adjusted persons among both the clinical and the non-clinical populations.

REFERENCES

American Psychiatric Association. (1968). *Diagnostic and statistical manual of mental disorders* (2nd ed.). Washington, DC: Author.

American Psychiatric Association. (1980). *Diagnostic and statistical manual of mental disorders*. (3rd ed.). Washington, DC: Author.

Bell, A., Weinberg, M. & Hammersmith, S. (1981). *Sexual preference*. Bloomington, IN: Indiana University Press.

Bowlby, J. (1980). *Loss*. New York: Basic Books.

Freud, S. (1958). Psychoanalytic notes on an autobiographical account of a case of paranoia (dementia paranoides). In J. Strachey (Ed. and Trans.), *The standard edition of the complete psychological works of Sigmund Freud* (Vol. 12). London: Hogarth Press. (Original work published 1911.)

Herdt, G. (1981). *Guardians of the flutes*. New York: McGraw-Hill.

Kinsey, A., Pomeroy, W. & Martin, C. (1948). *Sexual behavior in the human male*. Philadelphia: W. B. Saunders.

Marmor, J. (1980). Clinical aspects of male homosexuality. In J. Marmor (Ed.), *Homosexual behavior* (pp. 267-279). New York: Basic Books.

Ross, M. (1984). Psychovenereology and acquired immune deficiency syndrome. In *Psychiatric implications of acquired immunity deficiency syndrome*. Washington, DC: American Psychiatric Association.

Saghir, M. & Robins, E. (1973). *Male and female homosexuality*. Baltimore: Williams & Wilkins.

Smith, J. (1980). Ego-dystonic homosexuality. *Comprehensive Psychiatry, 21*, 119-127.

Smith, J. (1985). Treatment of ego-dystonic homosexuality: Individual and group psychotherapies. *Journal of the American Academy of Psychoanalysis, 13*, 399-412.

Sptizer, R. (1981). The diagnostic status of homosexuality in DSM-III: A reformulation of the issues. *American Journal of Psychiatry, 138*, 210-215.

World Health Organization. (1977). *Manual of the international statistical classification of diseases, injuries, and causes of death* (9th rev.). Geneva: Author.

Ziebold, T. & Mongeon, J. (Eds.). (1982). Alcoholism and homosexuality [Special issue]. *Journal of Homosexuality, 7*(4).

Theoretical Considerations in Psychotherapy with Gay Men and Lesbians

Terry S. Stein, MD

Michigan State University

SUMMARY. This paper examines certain issues relevant to psychotherapy with gay men and lesbians. The roles of general factors in psychotherapy in relation to homosexuality, including the theoretical orientation of the therapist, the nature of the presenting problem, the mode of therapy, and the personal characteristics of the therapist, are discussed. Special issues of concern to gay men and lesbians, specifically the question of pathology, the amount of information the therapist has about homosexuality, the sexual orientation of the therapist, and the unique problems of gay men and lesbians, are reviewed. Finally, an overview of the role of homophobia in psychotherapy is presented, and the importance of further exploration in this area is discussed.

Psychotherapy with gay men and lesbians involves factors relevant to psychotherapy in general as well as those which are relevant to gay men and lesbians in particular. In this paper, I will offer an overview of these factors and then discuss the role of homophobia in psychotherapy with gay men and lesbians. Any discussion of psychotherapy in relation to homosexuality must also be informed by an awareness of the stormy history of homosexuality and psychotherapy. Only since 1973, when the American Psychiatric Association agreed that homosexuality as such was not a form of mental illness, has it been possible for gay men and lesbians to be in psychotherapy without being officially designated as deviant or mentally ill because of their sexual orientation (Bayer, 1981).

Dr. Stein is Professor and Director of Medical Student Programs in Psychiatry, Department of Psychiatry, College of Osteopathic Medicine and College of Human Medicine, East Fee Hall, Michigan State University, East Lansing, MI 48824. Correspondence may be sent to the author at that address.

During this period, attempts to understand homosexuality have evolved from examination of the origin and practice of homosexual behavior in the individual to the study of the larger issues related to the development of homosexual and bisexual identities. The work of DeCecco (1981; 1984) and DeCecco and Shively (1983/84) has contributed significantly to the definition of this new conceptual territory. In response to this material, the practice of psychotherapy in relation to homosexuality appears to have changed to some extent since the 1973 decision (Gonsiorek, 1981/82; Marmor, 1980; Paul, Weinrich, Gonsiorek & Hotvedt, 1982). However, theoretical models which incorporate an understanding of homosexuality and of the development of homosexual identities as normal variations of human experience have not been well integrated into psychotherapy during the same time period, at the levels of research, training, or clinical application.

GENERAL CONSIDERATIONS

Differences within psychotherapy are based upon the therapeutic rationale of the therapist, the nature of the patient's problem and personality, the therapeutic modality, and the personal characteristics of the individual therapist. The definition of psychotherapy varies considerably between different schools of therapy, and the panorama of possible therapeutic approaches may be confusing to the individual seeking psychotherapy. In this article I will use a rather classical definition of psychotherapy to refer to a process which involves a verbal interaction between two individuals, one of whom has specialized training and certification to assist the other with an emotional or mental disturbance, and both of whom have agreed to some structured arrangement in order to accomplish this task.

Karasu (1977) surveyed the many different kinds of psychotherapy and divided them into three general types based upon their therapeutic rationale: psychoanalytic or psychodynamic, behavioral, and humanistic. Luborsky, Singer and Luborsky (1975) studied the relative effectiveness of different types of psychotherapy as reported in the literature and found a wide range of variables that had been considered to determine effectiveness, with few consistent conclusions about outcomes. Marmor (1979) described newer approaches to psychotherapy and discussed the need to expand conceptualizations of psychotherapy to include approaches to treatment such as meditation, relaxation training, and certain physical therapies. The proliferation in the number and types of psychotherapy has led to the publication of consumer guides to psychotherapy, and recently even to a guide to psychotherapy for gay men and lesbians (Hall, 1985).

The relevance of the theoretical school or therapeutic rationale of the therapist to the conduct of psychotherapy with the gay man or lesbian has been surveyed extensively from the perspective of examining the approaches within particular schools which have been developed to cure homosexuality or eliminate homosexual behavior (Coleman, 1982). However, the examination of the interaction between theoretical orientation as such and sexual orientation, as distinct from a specific therapeutic technique or application associated with a particular school of psychotherapy, has not been undertaken. Thus, for example, Martin (1984) and Coleman (1982) have offered thoughtful critiques of behavioral treatment approaches that are intended to convert homosexuals to heterosexuals, such as that reported by Masters and Johnson (1979), or to extinguish homosexual arousal (Feldman & MacCullouch, 1965), but little consideration of the contribution of the underlying theoretical system which is associated with these approaches has occurred. Hencken (1982), Herron, Kinter, Sollinger, and Trubowitz (1981/82), and Mitchell (1978) have argued that psychoanalysis does have relevance to psychotherapy with gay men and lesbians; and specific behavioral treatment approaches have been effectively utilized with problems associated with homosexual behavior, such as sexual dysfunction (Masters & Johnson, 1979).

There does not appear to be any inherent characteristic of a given theoretical school which in its nature is antithetical to conducting psychotherapy in a helpful manner with gay men and lesbians, once the belief is removed that homosexuality is by definition an expression of pathology. However, the absence within a school of psychotherapy of specific theories about normal development and identity related to gay men and lesbians could be expected over time to diminish the capacity of a therapist who follows that school of psychotherapy to understand fully the experiences of the gay person. This type of limitation on therapeutic understanding clearly would involve most significantly those therapists who utilize developmental and psychodynamic approaches. Given an objective perspective on the relationship between sexual orientation and psychopathology that is consistent with the absence of a diagnosis of homosexuality as a form of mental illness, the lack of theoretical understanding about the role of homosexuality (or sexual orientation in general) in personality development might be expected to be most detrimental in those forms of therapy which examine early childhood and developmental issues and least relevant to effectiveness when the therapeutic focus is on specific behaviors or experiences. Consistent with this view, effective approaches to the treatment of well-defined problems of gay men and lesbians, such as sexual dysfunction (Masters & Johnson, 1979), and of interpersonal issues, such as those presented within couples therapy by gay men (McWhirter & Mattison, 1981/82, 1984) or lesbians (Kaufman, Harrison, & Hyde, 1984; Krestan & Bepbo, 1980; Roth, 1984), have so far been reported more extensively in the literature than have any form of in-depth psychodynamic therapy. Only very recently have reports of the latter type been available (Isay, 1985; Stein & Cohen, 1986).

A second general factor which must be considered is the type of problem with which a person presents. Evaluation of the nature of the concern, and in particular whether it is primarily psychological in origin or also involves significant physical or biological factors, may determine in some cases what type of professional is most appropriate to work with the person. For example, if significant physical or biological factors are contributing to a person's problems, then a psychiatrist or other professional with knowledge about medicine may be most helpful. If specific learning or neuropsychological problems are present, psychologists or other professionals who have specialized training or experience in these areas might be the most appropriate psychotherapist.

For the most part, the problems of the gay man or lesbian which might influence the selection of a particular therapist based upon areas of training, expertise, or specialization would be expected to parallel those of the general population. However, the level of familiarity on the part of the psychotherapist with the specific problems of gay men and lesbians may be an important additional factor to consider for many individuals. The impact of this knowledge on the conduct of psychotherapy is discussed more extensively below.

Another general factor that must be considered in selecting a psychotherapist is the modality of psychotherapy. Modality refers to whether the therapy is short-term or long-term and whether it is conducted with an individual, couple, family, or group. The criteria for choosing a specific therapeutic modality for a given individual and a particular problem are variable and depend to some extent on the availability of skillful and experienced therapists who practice in a given modality.

No particular mode of psychotherapy appears to be any more effective than another in working with gay men and lesbians if the characteristics of this population are viewed by a therapist as consistent with the treatment offered within a given mode. Thus, if a family constellation consisting of a lesbian couple and their children is viewed by a family therapist as fitting into the scope of family therapy, this couple and their children should be able to receive treatment as effectively as any other family group. The apparent paucity of literature reporting on family and couples therapy with gay men and lesbians is undoubtedly a result, at least in part, of the tendency within traditional psychotherapy to view homosexuality and the capacity for intimacy as mutually exclusive characteristics and not a reflection of any real absence of problems in these areas for gay men and lesbians.

The personal characteristics of the therapist, including especially the capacity to establish an empathic relationship with the patient, may constitute the most important factor in determining the ultimate effectiveness of the therapeutic endeavor. In addition to those personal requirements necessary for a therapist to work with any other individual within psychotherapy, the therapist who works with gay men and lesbians also needs to possess a willingness to encounter the special problems associated with a group that is oppressed within society, and to be open to self-examination regarding one's own reactions to homosexuality and gay persons. The implications of internalized homophobia within the therapist for conducting psychotherapy with gay men and lesbians and its role in diminishing the capacity for empathy will be discussed more extensively in later sections of this paper.

SPECIAL ISSUES RELEVANT TO PSYCHOTHERAPY WITH GAY MEN AND LESBIANS

In the preceding section those general factors which must be considered in conducting psychotherapy with any person have been discussed. The remainder of this article will focus on some specific issues relevant to the conduct of psychotherapy with gay men and lesbians. First, I will outline certain theoretical concerns and special problem areas for gay men and lesbians. Then I will discuss the role of homophobia in psychotherapy with gay men and lesbians.

Theory and Practice: The Issue of Pathology

Few areas within psychotherapy present more conceptual complexity and richness than does sexuality. Freud developed much of the foundation for psychoanalysis from his beliefs about infantile sexuality, and later writers have focused extensively on childhood and adult sexuality as a basis for organizing and understanding human behavior, development, and personality. Within this framework, homosexuality has received a great deal of consideration, but it has never resided comfortably in any theoretical niche for a long period of time (Reiss & Safer, 1979).

During most of the middle part of the twentieth century, psychoanalysis and medicine played predominant roles in determining the prominence of a given theoretical position within psychotherapy, and both of these fields represented the belief that homosexuality was a form of mental illness (D'Emilio, 1983). The effect of this theoretical stance was to contribute to the development of a variety of approaches to treating homosexuality within psychotherapy that focused on curing the person of a pathological condition. Extensive research, such as that by Bieber and his colleagues (1962), was also conducted to demonstrate the origin of the disease of homosexuality and to establish the effectiveness of various approaches to its treatment. Unfortunately, the effects of these interventions on persons who were homosexual were frequently extremely negative, serving to reinforce a sense of low self-esteem and rarely affecting any significant change in sexual identity (Martin, 1984).

The monolithic antagonism to homosexuality within psychotherapy has only gradually begun to change in response to research findings. These findings have repeatedly demonstrated the lack of difference between persons who are homosexual and heterosexual on most psychological variables, and that nonclinical groups of homosexual persons demonstrate the same degree of psychological adjustment as nonhomosexual persons (Hooker, 1957). The gay liberation movement and the development of gay political groups which expressed significant social reaction against diagnosing homosexuality as a form of illness also served to point out the negative effects of such a stance on gay men and lesbians (Altman, 1982; Bayer, 1981).

Nevertheless, the strong tradition within psychotherapy of an association between homosexuality and mental illness has not yielded readily to change, even in the face of the overwhelming scientific evidence to the contrary. This resistance to theoretical advancement is reinforced by a strong cultural bias against homosexual behavior and homosexual persons and reflects an underlying individual and institutional homophobia, or fear of and reaction against homosexuality (Weinberg, 1972). The basis for this homophobia has been postulated to lie within both patterns of individual development and societal structures for dealing with difference (Hencken, 1982).

The gay man or lesbian who is in psychotherapy may be at significant risk if they work with a psychotherapist who believes that homosexuality is an expression of abnormality or mental illness. Brown (1976) provided a moving account of his own painful encounter with such a therapist. He described being left with the ". . . overriding message — that I was inherently impaired because of my sexual orientation and that if I would not change it, I was doubly a failure" (p.214). Such an attitude on the part of the therapist would be expected to have a pervasive effect on the conduct of psychotherapy and theoretically to prevent resolution of conflicts because of repeatedly reinforcing the person's own sense of being impaired or defective. If such a view is held either consciously or unconsciously by the therapist, the only fully healthy outcome of therapy is for the client to become someone different from who he or she is.

Even within this belief system, the likelihood of change in sexual orientation is recognized to be extremely small. Thus, the person who is homosexual is required both to accept a sense of being impaired and to struggle with little chance of altering this situation. Obviously, the effect of this therapeutic stance on the patient is extremely negative. Presumably, some persons who are in acute crisis, who seek only support from a therapist, or who are able to sequester off from therapeutic focus those aspects of their personality related to sexuality might not suffer as extensively from such an encounter. But the vast majority of gay men and lesbians who work with a therapist holding such a view are at risk for further psychic injury.

The assumption that homosexuality is a form of mental illness usually involves a corollary assumption about the necessity to change sexual orientation if one is homosexual. This assumption leads to additional considerations regarding the ethical presentation of treatment outcomes by the therapist (Davison, 1982; Krajeski, 1984). Regardless of the beliefs held about the relationship between homosexuality and psychopathology, it is essential for the therapist to represent realistic goals to the person seeking therapy. The issue of change related to sexual orientation is complicated by many factors, including the definition of the outcomes which are believed to represent change. A change in behavior represented by choosing a partner of a different sex with whom to have sexual relations would not seem to be that difficult to achieve, given the belief by many psychotherapists in the underlying bisexuality of the individual. Even on this single dimension of behavioral change, many persons are unable to accomplish any change. More profound changes which represent a true shift in sexual identity appear to be virtually impossible to accomplish, although there are reports of structural changes in patients' lives, such as entering into heterosexual marriages. Whether such outcomes represent a true change in identity or sense of self is difficult to determine and has not been adequately documented in the literature. It is clear, however, that even behavioral changes are rare, and they may occur more frequently outside of psychotherapy, given the few reported instances of change within psychotherapy.

The creation by the American Psychiatric Association of a category of mental illness specifically related to homosexuality, ego-dystonic homosexuality, as part of the official diagnostic nomenclature (American Psychiatric Association, 1980) provided a sanction for those individuals who wished to continue to treat homosexuality or homosexual behavior as a form of mental illness. While the criteria for this diagnosis referred only to the wish to attain a heterosexual arousal pattern and to dissatisfaction with homosexual arousal, it is clear that this label was applied to a large number of persons who were either confused or unclear about the meaning of their homosexual feelings. Hetrick and Martin (1984) examined both the theoretical errors associated with the rationale for this diagnostic category and the practical problems involved in its clinical application. The decision to eliminate this category (American Psychiatric Association, 1987) appeared to reconcile the theoretical inconsistency that was inherent in the diagnosis from the start; namely, the suggestion that homosexuality, in and of itself, was not a form of mental illness, but that it did represent mental illness when a person complained about it.

Knowledge About Homosexuality

The lack of relevant theoretical frameworks for thinking about homosexuality outside of a context of pathology leaves many psychotherapists with a void in understanding with respect to how to treat gay men and lesbians. Each therapist who wishes to work with gay men and lesbians will have to struggle to overcome a lack of formal training and experience in this area. Several topics need to be explored if this deficit is to be overcome, including attitudes about homosexuality and specific sexual acts, awareness of the effects of stigmatization, the relationship between normal development and homosexuality, familiarity with gay lifestyles, knowledge about the patterns and stages of coming out, and the meaning of a homosexual identity.

A lack of knowledge about any of these topics may restrict a therapist's ability to understand or conceptualize about a gay person's experience; and, more importantly, it may limit the therapist's ability to establish an empathic stance toward the gay man or lesbian. Because much of the experience of the gay person has been so thoroughly denied at a theoretical level — or, even worse, distorted to fit into an inaccurate conceptual category — some therapists may find it impossible to be empathic with this population. They are unable even to imagine the gay person's experience, let alone to appreciate the rich contextual meaning of a particular experience for an individual man or woman.

The outcomes of psychotherapy for a gay person may be significantly affected by the failure of a therapist to have any knowledge about homosexuality or homosexual persons outside of a framework of pathology. However, a lack of knowledge or having inaccurate knowledge are deficits that could in theory be corrected by obtaining more or correct information. Some therapists may have no wish to obtain this new information about homosexuality — or even to listen effectively to information that is presented directly by the patient — if their goal is simply to eliminate the homosexuality. Whether this intent is viewed as a form of countertransference, as the result of a simple belief, or as a necessary approach to treatment, it will have a profound effect on the gay person who is in treatment with a therapist who holds it. Therapeutic neutrality is impossible in this situation, and the patient's ability to talk openly about their homosexuality will undoubtedly be severely circumscribed by the therapist's conscious or unconscious need to eradicate, transform, or judge the homosexuality. Mitchell (1978) suggested that it is difficult to obtain any understanding of the dynamic and developmental meanings associated with a person's homosexuality if it is viewed as pathological.

A therapist's willingness to examine and change his or her own attitudes and feelings about homosexuality also seems to be a necessary requirement for working with gay men and lesbians within psychotherapy. It is virtually impossible to imagine anyone — and that includes both therapist and patient — growing up in American society without experiencing some negative feelings about homosexuality. The absence of any ability to acknowledge negative feelings about homosexuality on the part of the therapist may indicate in some cases an unwillingness to examine one's own internalized homophobia. When these reactions are rigidly sealed off from consciousness, the risk is that they may then be acted out unconsciously. Thus, when therapists say too readily that they have no problem with homosexuality, they may simply be unwilling or unable to examine their true reactions and may communicate a similar message to their patients.

The gay person who is seeking psychotherapy may need to ascertain directly the amount of knowledge a therapist has about homosexuality and about gay-identified lifestyles. While a given therapist cannot be expected to know personally about every type of experience a patient discusses within psychotherapy, the patient will need to be informed to some extent about the therapist's familiarity with the issues with which he or she is concerned in order to appreciate the level of communication which is occurring at a given point in time. This is not to say that a patient should have to be in the position either of having to educate or to take care of a therapist over time, but rather that it may be necessary to be informed about the extent to which these functions are required with a particular therapist in order to establish a reasonable amount of communication. For some persons, the assumption that a therapist knows or understands what is being talked about without any form of explanation may itself be an important therapeutic focus, but every patient should be able to be assured of a basic level of understanding on the part of the therapist, such understanding being a precursor to establishing a therapeutic relationship.

If the sexual orientation of a therapist is known by a patient, a higher level of understanding about certain issues may be assumed by some patients if there is a degree of congruence with the patient's own sexual orientation and lifestyle. However, this assumption may be incorrect and does not consider the varieties of life experiences and differences between persons with a particular sexual orientation.

Sexual Orientation of the Therapist

No research findings have been reported that fully explicate the manner in which the sexual orientation of the therapist actually affects the patient. Rochlin (1981/82) discussed some of the possible benefits of a gay or lesbian patient having a therapist who is also homosexual. These benefits include role-modeling and greater familiarity with the gay world. The research methodology which would be necessary to explore this issue in-depth is, however, quite complicated because of the many levels of therapist-patient interaction that remain to be examined. First, of course, the variable of simply having knowledge about the therapist's sexual orientation itself suggests many other dimensions, including how this information is obtained, what it reflects about the therapeutic stance of the therapist, and what other personality and interpersonal characteristics may be associated with this factor.

A second level of interaction which would have to be understood is the meaning of sexual orientation to both the therapist and the patient. Because no other specific personal characteristics can be predicted based upon sexual orientation alone, little can be said about the impact on the patient of knowledge about the therapist's sexual orientation without also examining a large number of other characteristics related to its expression for a given therapist and patient. In addition, the relationship between knowledge about a therapist's sexual orientation to particular content or processes within psychotherapy would need to be understood. For example, did the patient seek out a particular therapist with the knowledge that the therapist was gay, or was this information disclosed by the therapist in response to direct inquiry or to specific material presented by the patient? If this information was disclosed by the therapist, what was the impact of the disclosure on a given patient? What was the intent of the therapist in informing the patient about his or her sexual orientation, and was this intent congruent with the impact it actually had on the patient?

Another important factor in determining the effect of knowledge about a therapist's sexual orientation on a given patient is the attitude the therapist conveys about that sexual orientation. Thus, the degree of comfort and acceptance about sexual orientation which is communicated by the therapist will undoubtedly influence most patients more than the actual knowledge of a particular sexual orientation. In addition, for a gay man or lesbian, the willingness on the part of therapists to disclose his or her sexual orientation within the context of psychotherapy may have unusual significance because of the social proscriptions against sharing this information. An unwillingness to disclose sexual orientation may be perceived by the patient, regardless of the intent of the therapist, as a statement of agreement with societal pressures to keep one's sexual orientation secret when it is homosexual. The therapist must be aware of this special meaning of withholding of information about sexual orientation for the gay man or lesbian, even if the decision not to share this information is the result of a more general therapeutic stance or of a specific rationale for a particular patient. In many instances, especially when the patient has complied with the societal restrictions on disclosure of homosexuality, a therapist's unwillingness to acknowledge a personal sexual orientation may be viewed as a statement that the patient should also continue to keep his or her sexual orientation hidden from others. If such a position is taken by the therapist without any awareness of the possible impact on the patient, the result may be that those aspects of internalized homophobia that are associated with the decision not to disclose sexual orientation may be further removed from the consciousness of the patient.

When the therapist is heterosexual, many of the same issues that occur for the gay therapist related to disclosure and meaning of sexual orientation may still be relevant to working with the gay or lesbian patient. However, in general, if the therapist is not known to be gay and the therapist does not disclose his or her sexual orientation, most persons can be expected to assume that the therapist is heterosexual because of the greater number of heterosexual persons and because of the heterosexual bias (Rich, 1980) in our society. This assumption of heterosexuality obviously may be present on the part of the patient regardless of the actual sexual orientation of the therapist, and in spite of any nonspecific communications by the therapist regarding sexual orientation. The effect of this assumption will be variable for the gay or lesbian patient and may be associated for some persons with a belief that the therapist will be unable to understand certain issues, or that the therapist will in some way look down on the patient in a manner similar to how the larger society, which is predominantly heterosexual, denigrates homosexuality and gay persons.

In this situation, as when the therapist is homosexual, the feelings and beliefs that the therapist communicates about sexual orientation are probably more primary than actual sexual orientation in determining the impact on the patient. The therapist who talks about sexual orientation, either their own or the patient's, in a nondefensive and neutral manner will provide the best setting for patients to present feelings about their own sexuality and to discuss fears about, and experiences with others' reactions to, their sexuality.

The variable of the sex of the therapist may also have an effect on the conduct of psychotherapy in relation to both the sex and the sexual orientation of the patient. Similar to the variable of the therapist's sexual orientation, the sex of the therapist will have conscious and unconscious, as well as actual and symbolic, meaning for the patient. Each of these dimensions may be relevant to therapeutic effectiveness and may need to be discussed within the context of therapy. Examples of the types of interactions related to sex of the therapist that may occur are the different erotic components which can be expected for same and different sex therapist-patient dyads for gay and lesbian patients in contrast to heterosexual patients, and the interplay between the particular gender role attributes associated with the sex of the therapist and of the patient.

Special Problems of Gay Men and Lesbians

A number of special problem areas have been identified for gay men and lesbians that either may lead to psychotherapy or may arise in the course of psychotherapy undertaken for some other reason. Anthony (1981/82) mentioned the following areas for lesbians: (a) establishing and maintaining lover relationships; (b) a greater tendency within the lesbian subculture to meet the therapist outside of therapy; (c) alcoholism; (d) special problems of minority-group, adolescent, disabled, and older lesbians; (e) bereavement; (f) unique issues related to parenting; and (g) problems for a woman in this society associated with not being paired with a man. Gay men share some of these problems, especially those concerned with being in relationships, alcoholism and other substance abuse, issues for subgroups, and parenting. In addition, gay men have special problems with compulsive sexuality, high rates of sexually transmitted disease, and acquired immune-deficiency syndrome (AIDS). Having AIDS, anxiety about exposure to AIDS, and concern about its overall impact are currently among the most important problems for gay men related to their physical and mental health (Holland & Tross, 1985; Nichols, 1985; Nichols & Ostrow, 1984).

Until recently many of these problems have frequently been dealt with through nontraditional approaches to psychotherapy because traditional therapists either have not been informed about how to work with them or have not been able to see past the issue of homosexuality in the gay person's life to appreciate the real nature of the concern with which the gay man or lesbian presents. One result of this failure to respond to the special needs of the gay male and lesbian populations has been the establishment of a number of support and self-help groups, often within independent community centers in large cities where there are high concentrations of gay persons. Some therapists who have traditional training also become specialists in working with gay male or lesbian populations outside of the mainstream professional organizations and settings (see, e.g., Clark, 1977). More recently, the major mental health professional organizations, including both the American Psychiatric Association and the American Psychological Association, have formed separate groups and divisions that are devoted to the study of gay and lesbian issues. Special treatment approaches for gay persons and their problems have not been extensively reported so far, however, in response to the wider recognition of the unique problems of this population of men and women. The lag between recognition of the problems and development of approaches to handle them must be seen in part as a result of the failure within the area of psychotherapy to recognize and accept the need for theoretical study of homosexuality and gay men and lesbians, as well as of the continuing absence of specific training about homosexuality and gay persons in most professional degree programs. To what extent this situation is a reflection of the general anti-homosexual prejudice within American society must also be examined.

THE ROLE OF HOMOPHOBIA

The gay male or lesbian who seeks psychotherapy may have difficulty obtaining help for their emotional problems or mental illness. The tension between the needs of this group of patients and the continued insistence within many schools of psychotherapy and by a large number of psychotherapists that homosexuality is abnormal or pathological places the gay person at risk for iatrogenic damage from the very persons and approaches that are supposed to be available to alleviate their distress. This tension currently exists to some extent across all schools of psychotherapy and within all of the mental health professions. Clearly, some individual psychotherapists persist in the belief that homosexuality is pathological, in a manner which ignores scientific fact (see, e.g., Van den Aardweg, 1984) and suggests some personal rage at homosexuality and gay persons. Given this situation, gay men and lesbians need to adopt an attitude of caution in approaching psychotherapy, and when possible they need to develop skills which will allow them to assess those characteristics of the psychotherapist and the psychotherapy relationship which are relevant to sexual orientation and to working with homosexuality. The role of homophobia within psychotherapy should be of special interest to gay persons.

Malyon (1981/82) described the need for a "gay-affirmative" approach to psychotherapy with gay men in order to work with the consequences of internalized homophobia within the gay male patient. He delineated how this approach to psychodynamic psychotherapy would operate during four separate phases of psychotherapy to help the gay man establish a healthy individual identity and a sense of purpose and place in the world which transcends the limitations imposed by stigmatization. A similar approach to psychotherapy with lesbians would necessarily include a process dealing with the parallel but different manner in which homophobia is incorporated into a woman's identity, as well as with the profound impact of gender socialization as a female. Malyon's model of psychotherapy represents a powerful conceptual tool for understanding how antihomosexual attitudes are incorporated into the individual identity of the gay man and the manner in which these attitudes may be expressed during individual psychotherapy.

In order for Malyon's model to be useful as a framework for a general approach to psychotherapy with gay persons, however, the role played by antihomosexual attitudes in shaping two additional elements in psychotherapy, the psychotherapist and the relationship between the therapist and the patient, need to be examined and explicated more fully. The manner and the extent to which the therapist has incorporated negative societal attitudes about homosexuality in the form of internalized homophobia will shape the nature of the therapist's responses to the material presented by the patient. These responses, in turn, will influence the patient and, to the extent psychotherapy is viewed as an interpersonal crucible within which the patient-therapist dyad re-forms the separate components, can be expected to be internalized in some form by the patient.

The subtle ways in which reactions to homosexuality are woven into male and female identity operate in exactly the same way for the therapist as they do for the patient and, therefore, conscious acceptance (or rejection) of homosexuality represents only one level of the reaction. In some instances unconscious beliefs or feelings may be as prominent as consciously chosen values or attitudes in determining the therapist's reactions to a gay male or lesbian patient. For example, a traditional concept of masculinity includes a defensive rejection of homosexuality. A male therapist who has internalized this concept as a component of his identity, but who also values highly personal freedom and individuality, may communicate contradictory messages to a patient. He may be frightened or repulsed by the homoerotic sexual and affectional behaviors described by a male patient, but he may at the very same time express to the patient an acceptance of these behaviors because of his conscious values. The discordance between the rejection of the homosexuality, which may be communicated nonverbally through signs of discomfort on the part of the therapist, and spoken acceptance of the homosexuality may generate considerable conflict for the patient. The effect of this type of discordance and the complex communication which results from it need to be studied more fully if we are to understand the possible impact of the internalized homophobia of the therapist on the gay patient and, ultimately, understand the interaction between homosexuality and psychotherapy in general.

Certain elements in the relationship between a therapist and patient transcend the individual characteristics of the two persons involved in it and as such may be viewed as separate carriers of societal values and attitudes, including those about sexual orientation. Those elements of the relationship that create structure and provide meaning, both at a general level and in a specific instance, may at times be seen to reflect and reinforce the larger society's views about sexual orientation and its role in the lives of individual men and women. The interaction between these various elements and the attitudes of a particular patient about his or her sexual orientation may be subtle and difficult to determine, but they must be appreciated if the gay male or lesbian's position in relation to psychotherapy is to be understood fully.

An example of a relationship element within psychotherapy is the agreement between therapist and patient to maintain confidentiality. This agreement may have a very different meaning for gay male and lesbian patients than for heterosexual patients. While confidentiality is generally assumed to contribute toward creating a safe environment within which communication can best occur, for a gay person who has felt a life-long need to maintain secrecy about their sexual orientation, confidentiality may also be seen as reinforcing a belief in the shamefulness of being homosexual. Appreciating this very different meaning that some gay persons (similar to incest survivors and others who have been forced to keep secrets) might, as a result of internalized homophobia, associate with the fundamental expectation of confidentiality within psychotherapy is an example of the different type of understanding about certain aspects of the psychotherapy relationship which the therapist who works with gay men and lesbians must be able to achieve.

The purpose of understanding the various ways in which internalized homophobia may be expressed in the specific reactions of the patient or the therapist, and through particular meanings associated with the conduct or structure of psychotherapy, is to understand more fully an individual patient's experience. The origins of the perceptions which arise from internalized homophobia will be seen to lie in both the antihomosexual attitudes of the larger society and in the individual experiences of a given man or woman. Unraveling the layers of personal perceptions and assumptions, both positive and negative, regarding sexual orientation within the setting of psychotherapy should assist any patient, including the person who is heterosexual, to understand sexual identity more completely. If such an understanding is a focus of psychotherapy, as it is for many gay men and lesbians who are in psychotherapy as a result of difficulty in accepting their sexual orientation, this approach should be especially productive in establishing a more integrated sense of sexual identity.

CONCLUSION

A review of theoretical considerations related to psychotherapy with gay men and lesbians necessarily raises more questions than it answers. The evolution of a homosexual identity over the last century in Western society (Altman, 1982; D'Emilio, 1983) is a new phenomenon that has led to the appearance of persons with diverse individual gay and lesbian identities (Paul, 1985). The origin of these identities is only in part a function of individual development and lies also in the convergence of many social and political factors intersecting with human sexuality. Given this situation of flux, it seems that the important task for the psychotherapist working with individual men and women is to learn to understand and value the range of experiences associated with being gay or lesbian in this society, not simply to establish a new set of rigid operational rules with which to approach a larger set of sexual variations.

Many of the issues I have discussed in this paper have been raised previously, but the clinical implications of these issues have not yet been applied extensively within the practice of psychotherapy. The hesitancy to accept these principles cannot be viewed only as a function of lack of familiarity with the ideas or even as a result of valid questions regarding their clinical efficacy. The theoretical constructs underlying psychotherapy have not sufficiently incorporated an understanding of the role of culture in shaping individual sexuality and identity (see, e.g., Foucault, 1978). As a result of this continued narrow focus on the individual within the field of psychotherapy, regardless of the formal theoretical orientation or therapeutic approach of a particular psychotherapist, a large number of persons are unable to be helped with their emotional problems within traditional psychotherapy. The capacity of psychotherapy over time to respond to the special issues for gay men and lesbians related to sexuality, and to appreciate the impact of social forces on their individual identities, may ultimately reflect the ability of psychotherapy to survive in its present form as a social institution that is intended to respond to the needs of a variety of individuals in diverse social groupings.

REFERENCES

Altman, D. (1982). *The homosexualization of America, the Americanization of the homosexual*. New York: St. Martin's Press.
American Psychiatric Association (1980). *Diagnostic and statistical manual of mental disorders (3rd ed.)*. Washington, DC: Author.
American Psychiatric Association (1987). Diagnostic and statistical manual of mental disorders (3rd ed. Revised). Washington, DC: Author.
Anthony, B. D. (1981/82). Lesbian client-lesbian therapist: Opportunities and challenges in working together. *Journal of Homosexuality, 7*,(2/3), 45-57.
Bayer, R. (1981). *Homosexuality and American psychiatry*. New York: Basic Books.
Bieber, I., Dain, H. J., Dince, P. R., Drellich, M. G., Grand, H. G., Gundlach, R. H., Dremer, M. W., Rifkin, A. H., Wilbur, C. B., & Bieber, T. B. (1962). *Homosexuality: A psychoanalytic study*. New York: Basic Books.

Brown, H. (1976). *Familiar faces hidden lives*. New York: Harcourt Brace Jovanovich.

Clark, D. (1977). *Loving someone gay*. Milbrae, CA: Celestial Arts.

Coleman, E. (1982). Changing approaches to the treatment of homosexuality: A review. In W. Paul, J. D. Weinrich, J. C. Gonsiorek & M. E. Hotvedt (Eds.), *Homosexuality: social, psychological, and biological issues* (pp. 81-88). Beverly Hills, CA: Sage Publications.

Davison, G. C. (1982). Politics, ethics, and therapy for homosexuality. In W. Paul, J. D. Weinrich, J. C. Gonsiorek & M. E. Hotvedt (Eds.), *Homosexuality: Social, psychological, and biological issues* (pp. 89-98). Beverly Hills, CA: Sage Publications.

De Cecco, J. P. (1981). Definition and meaning of sexual orientation. *Journal of Homosexuality*, *6*, 51-59.

De Cecco, J. P. & Shively, M. G. (Eds.). (1983/84). Bisexual and homosexual identities: Critical theoretical issues [Special Issue]. *Journal of Homosexuality*, *9*(2/3).

De Cecco, J. P. (Ed.). (1984). Homophobia: An overview [Special issue]. *Journal of Homosexuality*, *10*(1/2).

D'Emilio, J. (1983). *Sexual politics, sexual communities*. Chicago: University of Chicago Press.

Feldman, M. P. & MacCulloch, M. J. (1965). The application of anticipatory avoidance learning to the treatment of homosexuality: I. Theory, technique, and preliminary results. *Behavior research and therapy*, *2*, 165-183.

Foucault, M. (1978). *The history of sexuality: Vol. 1: An introduction*. (R. Hurley, Trans.) New York: Random House.

Gonsiorek, J. G. (Ed.). (1981/82). Homosexuality and Psychotherapy [Special Issue]. *Journal of Homosexuality*, *7*(2/3).

Hall, M. (1985). *The lavender couch*. Boston: Alyson.

Hencken, J. (1982). Homosexuality and psychoanalysis: Toward a mutual understanding. In W. Paul, J. D. Weinrich, J. C. Gonsiorek & M. E. Hotvedt (Eds.), *Homosexuality: Social, psychological, and biological issues* (pp. 121-147). Beverly Hills, CA: Sage Publications.

Herron, W. G., Kinter, T., Sollinger, I. & Trubowitz, J. (1981/82). Psychoanalytic psychotherapy for homosexual clients: New concepts. *Journal of Homosexuality*, *7*(2/3), 177-196.

Hetrick, E. S. & Stein, T. S. (Eds.). (1984). *Innovations in psychotherapy with homosexuals*. Washington, DC: American Psychiatric Press.

Hetrick, E. S. & Martin, A. D. (1984). Ego-dystonic homosexuality: A developmental view. In E. S. Hetrick & T. S. Stein (Eds.), *Innovations in psychotherapy with homosexuals* (pp. 1-21). Washington, DC: American Psychiatric Press.

Holland, J. C. & Tross, S. (1985). The psychosocial and neuro-psychiatric sequelae of the acquired immunodeficiency syndrome and related disorders. *Annals of Internal Medicine*, *103*, 760-764.

Hooker, E. A. (1957). The adjustment of the male overt homosexual. *Journal of Projective Techniques*. *21*, 17-31.

Isay, R. (1985). On the analytic therapy of homosexual men. In A. J. Solnit,

R. S. Eissler & P. B. Neubauer (Eds.), *The psychoanalytic study of the child* (Vol. 40, pp. 235-254). New Haven, CT: Yale University Press.

Karasu, T. B. (1977). Psychotherapies: An overview. *American Journal of Psychiatry, 134,* 851-863.

Kaufman, P. A., Harrison, E. & Hyde, M. L. (1984). Distancing for intimacy in lesbian relationships. *American Journal of Psychiatry, 141,* 530-533.

Krajeski, J. P. (1984). Psychotherapy with gay and lesbian patients. In E. S. Hetrick & T. S. Stein (Eds.), *Innovations in psychotherapy with homosexuals* (pp. 75-88). Washington, DC: American Psychiatric Press.

Krestan, J. & Bepko, C. S. (1980). The problem of fusion in the lesbian relationship. *Family Process, 19,* 277-289.

Luborsky, L., Singer, B. & Luborsky, L. (1975). Comparative studies of psychotherapies. *Archives of General Psychiatry, 32,* 9950-1008.

Marmor, J. (1980). *Homosexual behavior.* New York: Basic Books.

Martin, A. D. (1984). The emperor's new clothes: Modern attempts to change sexual orientation. In E. S. Hetrick & T. S. Stein (Eds.), *Innovations in psychotherapy with homosexuals* (pp. 23-58). Washington, DC: American Psychiatric Press.

Masters, W. H. & Johnson, V. E. (1979). *Homosexuality in perspective.* Boston: Little, Brown.

Malyon, A. (1981/82). Psychotherapeutic implications of internalized homophobia in gay men. *Journal of Homosexuality, 7(2/3),* 59-69.

McWhirter, D. P. & Mattison, A. M. (1984). Psychotherapy for male couples: An application of staging theory. In E. S. Hetrick & T. S. Stein (Eds.), *Innovations in psychotherapy with homosexuals* (pp. 115-313). Washington, DC: American Psychiatric Press.

McWhirter, D. P. & Mattison, A. M. (1981/82). Psychotherapy for gay male couples. *Journal of Homosexuality, 7(2/3),* 79-91.

Mitchell, S. (1978). Psychodynamics, homosexuality, and the question of pathology. *Psychiatry, 41,* 254-263.

Nichols, S. E. (1985). Psychosocial reactions of persons with the acquired immunodeficiency syndrome. *Annals of Internal Medicine, 103,* 765-767.

Nichols, S. E. & Ostrow, D. G. (Eds.). (1984). *Acquired immune deficiency syndrome.* Washington, DC: American Psychiatric Press.

Paul, J. P. (1985). Bisexuality: Reassessing our paradigms of sexuality. *Journal of Homosexuality, 11(1/2),* 21-34.

Paul, W., Weinrich, J. D., Gonsiorek, J. C. Hotvedt, M. E. (1982). *Homosexuality: social, psychological, and biological issues.* Beverly Hills, CA: Sage Publications.

Rich, A. (1980). Compulsory heterosexuality and lesbian existence. *Signs: Journal of Women in Culture and Society, 5,* 631-660.

Reiss, B. F. & Safer, J. M. (1979). Homosexuality in females and males. In E. Gomberg & V. Franks (Eds.), *Gender and disordered behavior: Sex differences in psycho-pathology* (pp. 257-286). New York: Brunner/Mazel.

Rochlin, M. (1981/82). Sexual orientation to the therapist and therapeutic effectiveness with gay clients. *Journal of Homosexuality, 7(2/3),* 21-29.

Roth, S. (1984). Psychotherapy with lesbian couples: The interrelationship of individual issues, female socialization, and the social context. In E. S. Hetrick

& T. S. Stein (Eds.), *Innovations in psychotherapy with homosexuals* (pp. 89-114). Washington, DC: American Psychiatric Press.

Stein, T. & Cohen, C. (Eds.). (1986). *Contemporary perspectives on psychotherapy with lesbians and gay men*. New York: Plenum Press.

Van den Aardweg, G. J. M. (1984). Parents of homosexuals—not guilty? Interpretation of childhood psychological data. *American Journal of Psychotherapy, 38*, 180-189.

Weinberg, G. (1972). *Society and the healthy homosexual*. New York: Anchor Books.

A Pedosexual Pedophile Splitting and Projective Identification

F. van Ree, MD

Bennebrock, The Netherlands

This article is a short summary of the book *The Man Who Killed a Child; A Psychiatric Study,* which was published in Dutch in November 1984.[1] The aim of this book was to demonstrate the possible significance of environmental factors in the genesis of disturbances in both sexual identification and aggression control by use of an in-depth study of a patient suffering from such disturbances. Moreover, it attempts to explain the psychodynamic processes of splitting and projective identification active during the killing of an 8-year-old boy while the patient was in a psychotic state.

The patient (I have called him Bob) suffered during his early years from a Conduct Disorder characterized by negligible social involvement and aggressive behavior (DSM-III code 312.00),[2] though later it became more of a Mixed Personality Disorder (DSM-III code 309.89)[2] with traces of both Antisocial (DSM-III code 301.70)[2] and Borderline (DSM-III code 301.83).[2]

The title of this essay makes a distinction between Pedophilia (DSM-III code 302.83)[2] and Pedosexuality — a distinction not to be found in the DSM classification. One speaks of Pedosexuality if sexual contact takes place without a deeper personal involvement by the perpetrator.[3] Fitch[4] stated that pedosexuals are often the product of inferior environments or broken homes, and invariably also take part in other acts of delinquency. Schorch,[5] too, emphasized the above-mentioned distinction. Bender and Blau[6] observed that pedosexuals invariably display a very strong sense both of morality and of religious standards, and that during pedosexual activity they break through their excessive inhibitions.

Dr. van Ree is a psychotherapist in private practice. Correspondence may be sent to the author, Bennebroekerdreef 20, 2121 CN Bennebroek, The Netherlands.

For splitting and projective identification I refer the reader to Grotstein.[7] Athkar and Byrne[8] argued that splitting is a central defense mechanism in cases of both Borderline and Antisocial Personality Disorders.

Montagu[9] suggested that the regulation of aggression and choice of object are the result of cultural conditioning. Freud, too, stated that to begin with, sexual drive is independent of its object.[10] He described the development of male homosexuality as resulting from a very intense but fleeting fixation on the mother in the earliest years of life. This phase is followed by identification with the mother and the choice of self as sexual object. Moreover, he pointed out that the absence of a strong father in early childhood tends to stimulate such developments.[12]

The author sees fit to assume that homosexual, pedosexual, and heterosexual feelings occur in the lives of all homosexuals, pedophiles, and heterosexuals, and that no strict boundaries exist between these tendencies. Though the patient under discussion was a pedophile, pedosexual behavior also played an important role. The author is quite aware that analysis of a single case history is not enough on which to base a hypothesis on the role of formative factors leading to this condition. In this case, however, a relationship between traumatic events and extreme behavioral characteristics is hard to deny.

BIOGRAPHY

Bob's father was a robust, strict, impressive, hardworking man, his mother a shy, quiet, submissive woman subject to long periods of severe depression combined with melancholia (DSM-III code 296.33)[2] for which she spent some time in psychiatric hospitals. Both father and mother were very strict orthodox Christians.

Bob was born using a forceps delivery. As a small boy he was thin and frail, and as a result was exempt for number of years from gymnastics and sports. However, despite many neuropsychiatric examinations, no evidence of minimal or any other organic brain damage had ever been found. Bob had one sister who was 6 years his senior and very clever. Until nursery school Bob lived almost completely isolated with his sickly mother, playing on and around her bed and being indulged to an extreme. During these first years Bob and his mother enjoyed a genuinely symbiotic relationship.[11]

Father was hardly ever home, his sister regularly away at school.

So during this period Bob rarely had playmates of his own age, and learned nothing of the world outside, let alone how to explore it like others his age.[13] He hardly ever went to nursery school out of fear and recalcitrance, and often quarreled with his sister, who was not only clever but also spiteful. Thus, he began primary school as a shy, anxious little boy and was subsequently teased a lot. At this point his father, in a sudden show of concern, began to expect and demand that his only son be a first-rate scholar and unafraid of his peers. "Learn to stick up for yourself instead of whining!"

Despite being very intelligent (repeatedly confirmed during psychological testing), he was dogged by failure. Four times he was kept from moving up to the next grade, and 3 years running had the same schoolmistress. This teacher despised childishness and lack of achievement, and often humiliated him in front of the class. Bob took revenge on his classmates, especially the cleverest, by stealing such belongings as exercise books, pencils, and sachels and destroying them in his "secret hiding place" by trampling on them, tearing them up, but mostly by burning them. Both at home and at school, he began stealing from purses. The money he stole was used for buying sweets to give to smaller children at school as a way of buying their friendship.

As a result of staying in the same class and because of his fear of those of his own age and older, each year he chose increasingly younger children as playmates. It was now that he needed his mother's support. But she didn't come to school to speak with the teacher and serve as mediator in his conflicts, as other mothers did for their children. During his last year at school, he was increasingly truant. This was around 1942, and because of war-time chaos there was little chance of being caught.

Then, when he was 9 years old, a terrible accident occurred. Bob was late for school as usual, so mother was in a rush to get him ready. In her flurry she fell down a flight of stairs and suffered multiple fractures of the pelvis and one femur, leaving her permanently disabled. After that, she could only hobble a little around the house using crutches and complicated leg-irons. So Bob often had to fetch her things. At such moments she would tell him, "You are my legs, my boy!" He always felt afraid and upset when looking at "those scary irons."

Now and then he played "mummies and daddies" with other children, but didn't understand the grown-up talk of boys at school about "chicks" and "balling." Both his mother and father (but especially his mother) threatened him with damnation and disease if he played "dirty games" either alone or with other children. One day, while Bob was playing in a garden, a 14- year-old boy introduced him to mutual masturbation. From that time on he masturbated frequently, especially when feeling anxious. When he was alone, too, he often used masturbation to pass the time. Yet his practice brought anxiety, and he felt as though God was watching him. Sometimes he played masturbatory games with younger schoolmates or boys on the street.

When Bob was 10 years old, the owner of the house where he lived forced the family to move into a smaller, cheaper dwelling. Bob's father contested this eviction in vain. For weeks he had been boasting to Bob's mother, Bob's sister, and to Bob himself of how he was going to win the case. On top of this he spoke ill to them of the new residents (the owner and his family). The day they were to move Bob didn't want to leave his room. When the owner's two sons burst in he was still there. Remembering his father's wish that he be brave and strong he at last summoned all his courage and, shouting and arms flailing, went for them. To his great horror, his father, after separating them, reacted by, in the presence of those boys and their father, giving him a clip across the ear and demanding that he apologize. "That day I lost my father, whom I respected so much," he was later to write, "He betrayed me." This was a true loss of a strong father in the sense that Freud described.[12] After this calamity, Bob was very upset for weeks. He cried a lot, slept badly, and ate little.

At school not long after that incident, the small son of a highly placed Dutch National Socialist joined his class, and this boy took Bob's side against the others. After school he took Bob home to his family and on free afternoons to a Nazi youth club. There he was fully accepted and allowed to attend sports with the other youngsters. The mother of his friend was caring and affectionate. The father was an impressive, uniformed man who found time to play with the boys. This pair became a second father and mother to Bob and for more than a year provided him with a second home. When Bob's father discovered this acquaintance, he flew into a rage, even thrashing Bob with one of his wife's crutches. From that time on, Bob's behavioral disturbances (stealing, vandalism, and truancy) increased, and he began suffering from panic attacks and headaches.

When Bob was 12 years old his father, aided by the family doctor, had him admitted to a neurological clinic. This was in a way a last ditch attempt to get his son away both from the street and from his Nazi friends. The diagnosis on admission was "headaches and behavioral disturbances." Because of a lack of beds, Bob was placed in a ward with adult males with severe brain damage who suffered attacks and vomited, and others with paralyses and speech disturbances. This was all quite frightening to the young Bob, who was described in the case files as a timid, frightened little boy.

During that year in the hospital three important events took place. First, without any forewarning, Bob suffered a lumbar puncture. He refused to accept his lot, mainly out of fear. This in turn caused him much pain and for 3 days he suffered continually from severe headaches and vomiting. A few days later a laboratory worker and two nurses came to his bed to take a blood sample. Bob acted like a madman and bit one of the nurses in the hand. At the moment that he managed to break free one of the doctors passed by. As this doctor had talked to him a little and played a few children's games with him only the day before, Bob regarded him as a friend and expected support and refuge. He ran toward the doctor's open arms, expecting to be protected. To his bewilderment, however, this doctor pushed him away and slapped his face so hard that he fell on the bed. Then he grabbed Bob and held him down for the blood sample to be taken. "This was my second great betrayal by a man," he confided to his diary. He was greatly shocked by this event, and cried a lot.

Not long after this, the nursing staff and patients all at once broke into shouts of joy and celebration over news that an important National Socialist had been shot by a Jewish woman of the underground. This man turned out to be Bob's second father. In the months that followed Bob was completely beside himself with sorrow and hatred. Finally he was transferred to the children's ward, where he looked for support from a girl a few years his senior wearing a uniform of the Nazi youth club. This girl tried to seduce Bob into playing sexual games, which led to some necking and petting. Bob found this quite exciting and on several occasions had an erection. Some months later when he met her on weekend leave, he made fresh advances but she ridiculed him openly in front of some of her girlfriends. At that time Bob was living at a remand home. A few years later, while working in a factory, he experienced romantic feelings and slight sexual stimulation toward another girl. But she, too, rejected him rather roughly, and since then he had no more such feelings for women.

Hart de Ruyter[13] and others have observed that during postpuberty (from 16 to 18 years), when bisexual orientation ends, the breaking of heterosexual relationships not infrequently leads to homosexual ones. Naturally, other foregoing events play an equally important role in such a choice. In Bob's life, too, we have already remarked on events and situations that influenced his sexual identity.

After a year in the hospital, Bob was transferred to a remand home for boys and young men, far away from the other home. By then he was 12 years old, but looked much younger, while his behavior, too, was very childish. This was why he was placed in a group with youngsters 5 to 8 years old. He played children's games with them and often had masturbatory contact as well. "Dirty talk" about women and girls was absolutely forbidden in this orthodox Christian establishment, as were pamphlets and photographs featuring the opposite sex.

During the last period of Nazi occupation during World War II, part of the hospital building was taken over by the German army. As a result, the older boys and young men were placed with the little ones. They lived and slept together with little supervision. Hunger and cold were the order of the day. Like most others at that time, Bob experienced a lot of war-time deprivations. So he and many other young boys were rewarded with bread and sweets for performing masturbation and fellatio. Meanwhile, his mother had died in a psychiatric clinic where she had been admitted for severe depression. He received the news, weeks after the fact, from the director of the home.

After the armistice, Bob returned to his father's house. By then he was 15 years old. There was no aftercare service of any sort. His father was living in pitiful conditions and suffered from hunger edema. Bob stole here and there and made a little money on the black market. Now and then he was caught, which earned him several spells in an institution. But now, even though still a fragile and quite infantile boy who was given to playing with children's toys, he was put in the company of a rough, criminal element.

While in such an institution, at the age of 18, he experienced his first intense feelings of love for an 8-year-old boy named Billy, who lived with his mother in a house nearby. He filled many pages of his diary with the expression of his love, and though the grammar was bad, the phrases he used were very fine. He fought hard to keep sexuality out of this relationship—and in practice he succeeded. Yet when alone he frequently masturbated, and also played sexual games with other small boys—both of which produced feelings of guilt and anxiety. After some time, the staff of the home prohibited all contact with Billy. In his diary, Bob wrote of him as his little brother; yet on the other hand, he stressed over and over again the desire to be Billy's *mother*. He wrote of his wickedness, his fear of the devil and so on. At this time Bob began consciously grappling with his ideas and feelings about homosexuality and his love of children, especially young boys. It was during this period, too, that he made his first suicide attempt by taking sleeping pills discovered amongst his mother's belongings.

Bob was 20 years old when he was released from one of these institutions on the condition that he find regular employment. So he began work in a factory. However, his colleagues soon heard of his former Nazi associations and his sexual contact with little boys and began calling him "fascist" and "pansy." This hurt him deeply; he began suffering from insomnia and resorted to sleeping pills, even during the day. His work gradually slowed down and he made more and more mistakes, so much so that his employer threatened to dismiss him. This would have meant returning to the correctional institution. One night, in anger and desperation, he set the factory on fire. In this way he hoped to escape discharge.

He kept his responsibility for the fire secret for a year. Then, unable to bear it any longer, he resumed contact with one of his former social workers and begged for psychiatric help. He spoke of his sexual problems and some of his thefts. He also told the truth about the fire. This man then promptly went to the police and told them everything, which resulted in Bob's arrest and several years' imprisonment. "It was the third betrayal," he was to write later.

In prison he found himself among hardened criminals and became acquainted with homosexual prostitution. In the prison workshop he earned only the smallest of salaries. Partly because of this he began serving as a male prostitute for older men. Although he found this abhorrent, he nevertheless enjoyed relieving these "dirty old men" of their money. He himself preferred the company of young boys, and enjoyed getting involved especially if they seemed to be having difficulties at home. He often—too often perhaps—saw them as children in distress who needed his "maternal" protection, help, and affection. At the age of 26 he returned home to his old and lonely father. Sometimes Bob took young boys to his room to play with them and for masturbatory contact, treating them to sweets and toys.

It was in this way that, at the age of 27, he met an 8-year-old boy named Tommy. The boy told him that he was beaten regularly by his father, whom he described as highly aggressive. (One of his older brothers later confirmed these stories.) Then, during a walk in the woods, Bob took Tommy's life. A few weeks after his arrest, his father died. From that day on he always wore his mother's wedding ring.

SPLITTING AND PROJECTIVE IDENTIFICATION

Kohut,[14] Kernberg,[15] and others have called attention to the concept of "splitting." Grotstein,[16] quoting from their work, described it thus:

> Splitting may be defined as the activity by which the ego discerns differences within the self and its objects, or between itself and objects. In the perceptual or cognitive sense, an act of discriminative separation is involved, while in the defensive sense splitting implies an unconscious fantasy by which the ego can split itself off from the perception of an unwanted aspect of itself, or can split an object into two or more objects in order to locate polarized, immiscible qualities separately.[16]

According to Akhtar and Byren:[8]

> Splitting is defined as the separation of mutually contradictory, alternatively conscious self and object representations in order to avoid painful ambivalence and anxiety. In her child observation studies Mahler found splitting common among children whose relationship with their mothers during the first 2 years of life was unsatisfactory. Mahler suggested that the collapse of the toddler's belief in his own omnipotence, coupled with emotional unavailability of the mother, creates hostile dependency on the mother. The resulting intense ambivalence calls for the defense of splitting.[8]

These passages seem to match Bob's experiences very well. And they continued:

According to Kernberg, splitting begins as an inevitable means by which the rudimentary, infantile ego categorizes its pleasurable and unpleasurable experiences of self and objects. Later this same separation of good and bad self and object representations can come to serve a pathological defensive purpose. Contradictory self and object representations are then kept separate to avoid overwhelming and painful ambivalence.

This defensive division of the ego, in which was at first a simple defect in integration is then used actively for other purposes, is in essence the mechanism of splitting.[8]

Positive and negative self and object representations are situated close to each other, denying each other, and being able to change from one extreme to the other, without reciprocal inhibition. Love can change into murder and murder can be replaced again by love. They exist without influencing each other. . . . Positive and negative self and object representations exist together in close proximity while denying each other's existence, and are thus about to switch from one extreme to the other without keeping each other in check. Love can change to murder, while murder can be replaced once more by love. They are able to exist side by side without one influencing the other.[17]

Thus Bob saw his mother as the loving, sweet, and helpless woman who alone cared for him and pampered him during his first years of life ("all good"). Then again, it was she who had let him down completely by leaving him to struggle alone with his problems at school and against his father's aggression. It was she, too, who had spied on him and threatened him with sickness and hellfire for playing sexual games, and who had continually burdened him with feelings of guilt and anxiety by playing on her disability ("all bad"). Nor could Bob have seen his father as a stable and predictable person. On the one hand, he was to Bob a fearless, strapping fellow—an example of devotion and righteousness (all good); and on the other hand, a menacing, aggressive bully who let Bob down without warning and even mishandled him (all bad). His experiences in later years, both with women but especially with men, helped to reinforce these images. The schoolmistress was an aggressive vixen; a woman shot his "second father"; a doctor mistreated him; a therapist betrayed him; and in the end even his "second father" turned out to be a war criminal.

As for himself, Bob saw himself as the only one to attend his loving and helpless mother whom he loved so much (all good), yet also as the cause of her permanent disablement (all bad). Then again he fought for his father during the eviction (all good), yet hated him for the punishment after the fight, for that meted out for his National Socialist activities, and for his "banishment" from home during the war (all bad).

In love with the 8-year-old Billy, he sometimes saw himself as an ideal big brother, but usually he was the child's *pampering mother* (all good), or alternatively the "satanic beast" harboring laviscious feelings for him (all bad). The same splitting phenomena would return in later years in all of Bob's relationships with adults and young boys.

Projective identification has been discussed extensively by Melanie Klein.[18,19] Grotstein[20] described this concept as follows:

> Projective identification is a mental mechanism whereby the self experiences the unconscious [f]antasy of translocating itself or aspects of itself into an object for exploratory or defensive purposes. If projective identification is defensive, the self may believe that through translocation it can rid itself of unwanted, split-off aspects; but it may also have the [f]antasy that it can enter the object so as to (actively) control it, or disappear into it (passively) in order to evade feelings of helplessness. As such it follows the principle of generalization, corresponding to Freud's condensation, which accounts for the unification of objects on the basis of their similarities, contrived or natural.

It thus is the counterpart to the principle of distinction which governs splitting.[20]

If identification means "I am like you," projective identification takes the line "You are like me."

In his diary Bob wrote:

> I often dwell on the fact that Billy can never really be my little brother. When I see him I want to lift him and kiss him. . . . Sometimes I think I have gone mad, for who can have such feelings for a little boy? There is a powerful force pulling me towards him, something that reminds me of my mother. Have I truly taken leave of my senses?

Bob wanted to be for Billy what his own mother should have been for him, and would like to have done for Billy what he himself had missed. So he wanted to lift Billy up and kiss him, as his mother hadn't done. He was both mother and Bob at the same time — thus identifying with his own mother.[21] Later on he was to wear her wedding ring. More recently when someone noticed how Bob carried a baby in his arms, he remarked that Bob did so like a mother, and not as a man would do. On many occasions Bob obviously put himself in the place of his young friends. He often wrote in his diary that he was giving them the support and tenderness he himself had so much missed as a child.

To quote Hoekstra:[22]

> Disturbances in relationships with adults, anxiety, mistrust, and loneliness often make people turn towards children, hoping to realize in their relationship something they feel should have happened to them as a child. The experience of basic security and basic trust missed in the early years of life is sought for most intensely and desperately in intimate physical contact. What is done to the child is partly doing to oneself what should have been done to one when a child. The child is therefore seen not so much as another person, but as an extension of the self.[23]

Wildschut[23] commented:

> Naturally Bob saw himself both as Billy and as himself this, then, is the splitting. But the "dirty old men" to whom he prostituted himself were in fact himself also. This revolted him. In his eyes sex was disgusting and perverted. In these situations it was his bad side at work ("all bad"). Subsequently he was able to be of help to pre-pubertal boys, who were still "all good" this was his other side.[23]

The boys were his all good self, the old men his all bad self.

THE KILLING

One summer day, Bob went for a walk in the forest together with young Tommy. They were in fact trespassing. When Tommy began making noise Bob urged him to be quiet, telling him that they were in a "forbidden forest." The anxious, nervous child started crying loudly. All of a sudden, Bob was gripped by a feeling of agitation terrifying in its intensity. *"Tommy just had to stop crying."* So he snapped at the child. Tommy only cried more loudly and pitifully, whereupon Bob's hand shot out, giving him such a blow across the ear that he fell down. Bob then jumped on the screaming child with his full weight. He pinned Tommy down, pushing his face into the sand, and seized him by the neck. After much kicking and floundering Tommy became still. Then Bob made the terrible discovery that he had killed the child. Panic-stricken, he took to his heels.

The next morning he came back to bury the child. He dug a hole, but in order to squeeze in the entire body he had to fold it double. In doing so some air escaped from Tommy's throat in a loud "burp." Suddenly Bob saw the dead body as an enormous blood-curdling monster that towered over him and seemed to be coming toward him. "It was a monster which both revolted and terrified me." Bob wanted to attack it with his spade. "I believe I did lift the spade then, but even under those circumstances I could do no more than that." He did, however, tighten a cord around Tommy's neck. After covering the body with sand he fled in panic.

Bob's arrest and conviction followed a year later.

SOME PSYCHODYNAMIC ASPECTS OF THE KILLING

In accordance with later judicial reports, Tommy had indeed been an anxious, shy little boy who had had many difficulties with his despotic father, and Bob was certainly aware of this. One of Bob's remarks during the court hearing was: "Who should know the fears and anxieties of a child that has been beaten better than I do?" In other words, Bob recognized in Tommy the fearful little fellow he himself had been. For him this child represented himself as a youngster; this boy whom he had wished to pamper and pet like a mother, something he had longed for during his first years—a definite case of projective identification.

Horwitz[24] noted that projective identification is not only a mechanism of the one projecting, but also an interactional process because of the reaction of the target.

> The mechanism of projection alone is not sufficient to explain the event, since it describes only the process occurring within the projector and does not deal with the effect on the target person. . . . It is both an intrapsychic mechanism and an interpersonal transaction that involves transformation in both the

projector and the external object. . . . The content projected by one person upon or into another begins to influence the behavior of the other person in so far as the target person becomes the repository of the unwanted contents. The identification aspect of the process is one in which the projection emanating from the subject becomes fused with the characteristics of the object; thus the external object begins to take characteristics that have been "put into" him. . . . Segal defined this aspect of projective identification as follows: "Parts of the self and internal objects are split off and projected into the external object which then becomes possessed by, controlled and identified with the project parts."[24]

In such cases splitting impedes any development toward a coherent identity and promotes loss of contact between the patient and external reality. Several diary entries described Bob's reactions to these phenomena during the killing and its sequel the following day:

> I couldn't understand my rage towards Tommy's dead body. It worried and puzzled me for years, and gave me many sleepless nights. In some reports, I read to my dismay that they thought it had been some form of sadism. This upset me terribly. Sadism means the enjoyment of the victim's pain and fear. Fortunately I recognized nothing of all this in myself. Besides, how can you torture someone who is already dead? I had the dreadful feeling that I had wanted to vent my rage on a "human object" that resembled a human being, yet because of rigor mortis and lack of body heat it was, at the same time, a human being no longer. What sort of madness could have possessed me then?[25]

A little later he wrote:

> To me it would have been understandable if my hatred of adults had finally led to an outburst of madness in which I took the law into my own hands. If so I could have attacked a grown-up with a knife or something. . . . But this? What on earth possessed me to do it?[26]

After writing this statement — and indeed 8 years later in prison — he continued worrying about his inexplicable aggression during the killing, and even more so, that toward the child's corpse. One day he wrote in his diary:

How did I discover the truth? It happened quite unexpectedly at a moment when I was not thinking of it at all. I was
busy putting to paper a memory of my second father . . . of
that period of deep sadness. I relived it intensely, as though it
had happened the day before. Not only did I relive all the
sadness but also the anger and insanity of those days. Returning to the blows I had received shortly before this from the
ward doctor, the meaning of it all suddenly dawned upon me.
It was like a flash of lightening through my brain — as if a
flashbulb had exploded before my eyes. . . . All at once I
relived the doctor's slap across the face. . . . That was what
the blow in Tommy's face had been. . . . And then Tommy
had started to cry in utter despair. I had betrayed him and like
a coward had deserted him precisely when he needed me most.
His exclamations of fright and pain and distress pierced me
like a pointed accusation, cutting me like a sharp knife until I
could stand it no longer. . . . My aggression was directed at
his crying and was not intended to be homicidal. While it was
happening I had no idea of my state of mind nor of the force I
was using. With this discovery I suddenly realized that my
violent reactions were directly linked to the grief and conster-
nation generated by the doctor's brutality and all the emotion
of the events of that time. I had associated my feelings of those
days with Tommy's reactions. It was as if I myself had felt his
pain and fear.[27]

Shortly after he wrote:

This discovery consoled me somewhat, but the next morning
my restlessness returned. Where had the rage and aggression
of that second day come from? During the weeks that followed
I felt miserable and had horrible dreams every night. The image of the second day's events kept returning. Again and again
I recalled the sensation that Tommy's corpse had to me become a "thing," a monstrous thing. . . . And I relived that
feeling of wanting to destroy something, of blind rage toward
something. . . . And then all at once I "knew"! When I lifted
the spade and tightened the string, I in fact had one of those
hated men literally by the throat. I was working off my aggression on one of them! When I realized this — again it happened
in a flash — it was as if something inside me snapped.[28]

When asked at other times about the identity of that man, Bob invariably mentioned the doctor, or on occasion the men in the hospital who laughed at the death of his second father. He never mentioned his own father. (Bob was relentless in his denial of any aggression toward him.) As Freud pointed out, tension resulting from a boy's ambivalent feelings toward his father diminishes the moment he shifts his hostile and anxious feelings toward a substitute father.[29]

CONCLUSIONS

In summing up, we can draw the following conclusion. Egodystonic homosexuality, pedosexuality, and criminal behavior require treatment, as does egodystonic pedophilia. As cultural norms rejecting homosexuality and pedophilia increase, so does egodystony. In the case discussed above, the extreme turn of events and the ensuing sexual orientation and aggression regulation disorders could hardly be better matched.

The professional help Bob received as a child failed miserably — admittedly due in part to war-time conditions — and with it the chance of preventing the catastrophic events that followed. Bob's case showed just how soon mutually strengthening derangement processes appear to diminish any hope of therapeutic success. The denunciatory and demoralizing attitude of the parents and those involved on a professional level seemed in this case to have been paramount in encouraging the patient's pedophilia to develop partly into pedosexuality.

As stated in the introduction, no generally applicable hypothesis can be gleaned from a single case. To achieve a better insight into the causes of these characteristics, well-documented studies of case histories are needed. It is the chronic lack of these, however, which must first be remedied.

NOTES

1. F. van Ree: De man die een kind doodde; psychiatrische studie (The Man Who Killed a Child; A Psychiatric Study): Boom, Meppel-Amsterdam, 1984.
2. American Psychiatric Association: Quick Reference to the Diagnostic Criteria from DSM-III: Washington DC; March 1981.
3. E. Brongersma: Over pedofielen en kinderlokkers (On Pedophiles and Child-Enticers): Intermediair, May 2, 1975.

4. J. H. Fitch: A Descriptive Follow-up Study of a Group of Men Convicted of Sexual Offenses Against Children: London Prison Commission, 1961.

5. E. Schrosch: Liberalität reicht nicht: Betrifft: Erziehung 6, 4, 1974.

6. L. Bender, A. Blau: The Reaction of Children to Sexual Relations With Adults: American Journal of Orthopsychiatry, 7, 1937.

7. J. S. Grotstein: Splitting and Projective Identification: Jason Aronson; New York-London, 1981.

8. G. Akthar, J. P. Byrne: The concept of splitting and its clinical relevance: American Journal of Psychiatry, 140; August 1983, pp. 1013-1015.

9. A. Montagu: Aggressie: aangeboren of aangeleerd (original title: The Nature of Human Aggression): A. W. Bruna en Zoon, Utrecht-Antwerp, 1978.

10. S. Freud: Drei Abhandlungen zur Sexualtheorie und verwandte Schriften: Fischer Bücherei; Hamburg, 1961, p. 23.

11. Ibid., 10: p. 21-22.

12. Ibid., 10: p. 23.

13. Ih. Hart de Ruyter: De psychoseksuele ontwikkeling bij zuigeling en peuter (Psychosexual Development in Suckling and Toddler). In: Ih. Hart de Ruyter (Ed). De sexuele ontwikkeling van kind tot volwassene (Sexual Development from Childhood to Maturity I): Stafleu, Leiden, 1976.

14. H. Kohut: The Analysis of the Self: International University Press; New York, 1971.

15. O. Kernberg: Borderline Conditions and Pathological Narcissism: Jason Aronson: New York, 1975.

16. Ibid., 7: p. 3.

17. J. W. Wildschut: Commentaar bij de tekst van "De man die een kind doodde" (Annotation to "The Man Who Killed a Child") (Ibid., 1): p. 26.

18. M. Klein: Notes on some schizoid mechanisms: In M. Klein, et al. (Eds.), Developments in Psychoanalysis; London 1952, p. 292-320.

19. M. Klein: On identification: In M. Klein, et al. (Eds.), New Directions in Psychoanalysis; Basic Books; New York, 1975, p. 309-345.

20. Ibid., 7: p. 123.

21. Ibid., 17: p. 95.

22. R. C. Hoekstra: De ontwikkeling van deviaties en variaties, psychoanalytisch bezien (The Development of Deviations and Variations, Viewed Psychoanalytically): In Ih. Hart de Ruyter, et al. (Eds.). De sexuele ontwikkeling van kind tot volwassene, Deel II, (Sexual Development from Childhood to Maturity, Part II; Stafleu, Leiden. 1976.

23. Ibid., 17: p. 129.

24. L. Horwitz: Projective Identification in Dyads and Groups: International J. Group Psychotherapy, 33(3); July 1983, p. 259-279.

25. Ibid., 1: p. 145-146.

26. Ibid., 1: p. 146.

27. Ibid., 1: p. 146-149.

28. Ibid., 1: p. 149.

29. S. Freud: Totem en taboe: Cultuur en Religie 4 (Culture and Religion 4) Dutch Edition-(Oranje R., Starke J. Transl): Boom, Meppel-Amsterdam: 1984, p. 175.

Homosexuality, Suicide, and Parasuicide in Australia

Neil Buhrich, MD
Carlson Loke, MRC Psych
St. Vincent's Hospital

EPIDEMIOLOGY OF SUICIDE

In Australia the rates for completed suicide among older males have remained fairly constant since early this century, whereas the rates for females, and more recently for the young of both sexes (McClure, 1984), have steadily increased. In addition, there is a steady rise in completed suicide with age for both males and females, and at all ages suicide rates for males are two to three times those for females (Australian Bureau of Statistics, 1983). (Statistics for causes of death in Australia are derived from registrations made with the Registrars of Births, Deaths, and Marriages. Deaths due to suicide are not usually registered until a coroner's inquest has been conducted.)

A number of risk factors for suicide are now well-recognized. Suicide rates fall during periods of war but rise, especially among older males, during times of economic crisis. Suicides are relatively more frequent among the affluent social class, but recently the rates have increased among the less affluent. Up to 90% of those who commit suicide are mentally ill at the time of the suicide; depressive illness can be recognized in 70%, schizophrenia in 3%, and an early organic brain syndrome in 7%. Approximately 15% of alcoholics die by suicide, especially when alcohol has led to adverse social, domestic, and financial repercussions or to a relapse following a period of abstinence (Barraclough, Bunch, Nelson & Sainsbury,

Dr. Buhrich is Senior Staff Specialist and Senior Lecturer and Dr. Loke is Senior Registrar in the Department of Psychiatry, St. Vincent's hospital, Darlinghurst, 2010, Sydney, Australia. Correspondence may be sent to the authors at that address.

1974). More recently, especially among young males, heroin use has become a recognized risk factor in suicide. Suicide is more frequent in those who are divorced or widowed, less so in those who have never married, and less in those who are married (but not separated). Childlessness is another recognized factor in suicide. There is a seasonal variation in suicide, with higher rates in the spring and early summer. Suicide rates also vary for day of the week, being most frequent on Mondays and least frequent on Wednesdays (Australian Bureau of Statistics, 1983).

None of the risk factors listed above are considered to be associated with homosexuality apart from those of being single, being childless, and possibly those related to alcoholism. Single status and childlessness among homosexuals is likely to have less of a negative impact than for heterosexuals. It would therefore seem that the commonly recognized factors for suicide would not place homosexuals at any great risk.

A factor which could lead to an over-estimate of suicide among homosexuals is the tendency for homosexuals who are raised in a rural setting to drift toward an urban community. In Europe urban suicide is reported more frequently than rural suicide. However, this difference may result from different methods of collecting statistics. There are well-documented biases in the collection of data concerning suicide. For example, rates are under-reported in Muslim and Catholic societies where suicide is branded a disgrace. Another factor which may lead to an over-estimate of suicide rates in homosexuals is that the coroner is more likely to categorize death by suicide in someone who is not from his social class or is from an alien social background (Douglas, 1973). A factor which may lead to an under-estimate of suicide among homosexuals is that more homosexuals than heterosexuals live alone, and thus corroborating evidence to substantiate the subject's desire to die by suicide is less likely to be available, leading to an open verdict.

SUICIDE AND HOMOSEXUALITY

Criminal proceedings, blackmail, and threatened exposure concerning homosexuality have been traditionally regarded as factors in homosexual suicide (Allen, 1962). Homosexual behavior is only very rarely reported to the police (Wolfenden et al., 1963), and not infrequently those who threaten the blackmail or exposure are homosexuals themselves (Bell & Weinberg, 1978). Rofe (1983), citing a number of homosexual suicides reported in newspaper articles, considered that threatened exposure is a suicide factor. Rofe emphasized that homosexual suicide is commonly reported by members of the gay community and he reported in some detail the deaths by suicide of several male and female homosexual activists.

It is difficult to interpret such anecdotal reports. Death by suicide of a gay activist is likely to be regarded as being newsworthy. In addition, members of the gay community have a wide network of acquaintances and are therefore more likely to learn that a homosexual acquaintance has committed suicide. It also seems likely that the death of a homosexual in which the cause is uncertain is more likely to be attributed to problems related to homosexuality in the homosexual than would be heterosexuality in the case of a suicide by a heterosexual.

The widely reported homicide-suicide in London in 1967 of Kenneth Halliwell and his lover, Joe Orton, a playwright writing in a macabre humorous style, is not easily forgotten. Less impressionistic studies do not support an increase in dual suicides among homosexuals. Cohen (1961) found that among 58 successful suicide pacts, only one was reported to be a homosexual couple. O'Hara (1963) reported that 3% of 1,281 "forced" and "by agreement" double suicides during 1 year in Japan were homosexual females and 1% homosexual males. The author did not comment on the relatively high female suicide rate, but did emphasize that the attitude of society toward suicide in Japan is far less stigmatizing than that in the West.

Prentice (1974) listed over 2,000 studies in a bibliography concerning suicide. Only two are indexed as related to homosexuality and completed suicide, and both reports were anecdotal. In a bibliography listing over 2,000 studies concerned with homosexuality (Weinberg & Bell, 1972), only five reports were indexed as relating to completed suicide, three were anecdotal, and the other two concerned a total of four single case histories — one which involved an alcoholic, and another a presumably psychotic male who believed himself to be a lesbian.

In summary, systematic literature concerning completed suicides does not support the contention that rates for homosexuals are higher than those for heterosexuals.

TERMINOLOGY AND EPIDEMIOLOGY
OF PARASUICIDE

Statistics concerned with attempted suicide are less reliable than those related to completed suicide. An unknown number of people who attempt suicide do not seek medical attention, and approximately 20% (Stengel, 1964) who are seen by a general practitioner are not referred to a hospital.

The complexity of motivation and variability of outcome in suicidal behavior has been emphasized by many authors and is reflected in the profusion of terminology proposed to categorize such behavior: attempted suicide, pseudocide, suicidal gesture, deliberate self-harm, deliberate self-poisoning, parasuicide.

Stengel (1964) emphasized the different demographic profile in those who completed compared to those who attempted suicide. The latter group were young, predominantly female, frequently came from a deprived background, and led a disorganized social life. Attempted suicide was six to eight times more frequent than completed suicide and the frequency dramatically decreased with age. However, some overlap between the two groups existed; 10% of those who attempted suicide went on to complete suicide, 1% within 1 year (Pallis, Gibbons & Pierce, 1984).

Many subjects who "attempt suicide" are clearly not trying to kill themselves. Typically, the episode occurs on weekend evenings after the subject has consumed alcohol (but not necessarily enough to become intoxicated) and has had an argument with a relative or lover. Two-thirds of such subjects have considered the "attempted suicide" for less than 15 minutes prior to carrying it out (Hetzel, 1971). Frequently the "attempt" is made when somebody is nearby or expected to arrive soon. Thus, there is an element of risk in the behavior.

Not infrequently the subject himself reports to the neighbors and friends that he has made the "attempt," which in the vast majority of situations involves an overdose of drugs. There also may be associated superficial self-inflicted wrist lacerations. A relatively small quantity of drugs may be consumed, but even a very large overdose of, for example, benzodiazepines need not indicate a serious attempt as patients frequently recognize that high doses of such tablets are unlikely to lead to death. On the other hand, the patient may become dangerously physically ill after taking a small quantity of analgesics, which he considers relatively safe. The term suicide gesture has been proposed to categorize the motivation of patients with the typical features described above.

It is frequently not clear, even in the mind of the person who has made the "suicide attempt," what he hoped to achieve or what he expected would be the outcome of his action. Thus the term parasuicide has been proposed to categorize both the suicide attempt and suicide gesture.

The demographic profile of people presenting with a drug-related accidental overdose differ from parasuicide patients in that the former more frequently abuse drugs, come from a deprived background, and show features of antisocial behavior. They also differ in that the motivation for taking the drugs is hedonistic rather than self-destructive. Studies concerned with the rates of "suicidal behavior" among homosexuals should aim to differentiate between suicide attempt, suicide gesture, and accidental overdose.

PARASUICIDE AND MALE HOMOSEXUALITY

Assessment of the rates of parasuicide in homosexuals has been approached in two ways. First, patients presenting for treatment following parasuicide have been asked their sexual orientation; second, homosexuals in the community have been asked whether they have "attempted suicide."

O'Conner (1948) found homosexual "tendencies" in more than 50% of an unspecified number of subjects presenting with suicide and attempted suicide. Spencer (1959) reported 100 male Oxford undergraduates who were referred for psychiatric help, often because they had "complained" to their local medical officer "in whatever guise" about their homosexuality. Forty-one percent of the students were categorized as "persistent" homosexuals in either practice, fantasy, or desire. Two had made a serious attempt, five a suicidal gesture, one was psychotic, one "histrionically" threatened suicide, and one announced that he might harm himself. Nine of the 10 were "persistent" homosexuals. Two episodes followed rejection by a friend. In seven the relationship between homosexuality and parasuicide and threatened suicide was not clear.

Swartzburg, Schwartz, Lieb and Slaby (1972) reported an attempted suicide pact of two homosexual acquaintances, one of whom (R. N.) joined the pact for what seemed to be sado-masochistic reasons rather than a desire to die.

The present authors assessed the sexual orientation of 33 consecutive males who presented to the Casualty Department of St. Vincent's Hospital in Sydney during 1984 following parasuicide by drug overdose. Sexual orientation was categorized depending on the subject's report of sexual interest and activities during the previous 3 months. Non-parasuicide subjects, controlled for sex and age, presenting to the Casualty Department with fractures, lacerations, abdominal and chest pains, and sprains were used as a comparison group. The mean age of both groups was 31 years. Of those presenting with a parasuicide, 20 reported exclusive heterosexuality and 13 reported homosexual interest; of the 13, seven were exclusively or predominantly homosexual, two were bisexual, and four predominantly heterosexual. Twenty-three of the non-parasuicide controls reported exclusive heterosexuality and 10 homosexual interest; of the 10, six were exclusively or predominantly homosexual, and four predominantly heterosexual. The trend for parasuicide subjects to report more homosexuality than control subjects was not significant.

Problems with the Buhrich and Loke study were that, compared to controls, those presenting with parasuicide could be expected to show a more disorganized lifestyle and report more alcohol and drug use, and at least some of these factors may have related to sexual orientation. In addition, the time of day at which subjects presented to the Casualty Department was not recorded. Subjects who are homosexual and who exhibit parasuicidal behavior may be more "nocturnal" than those who present for other reasons and this may have biased the findings to show an association between parasuicide and homosexuality.

The second method of investigating the rates of parasuicide among homosexuals has been to seek the reports of parasuicide from homosexuals in the community.

Roesler and Deisher (1972) interviewed 60 males aged 16 to 22 years who reported homosexual contact to orgasm. Forty were referred by acquaintances, nine were located in gay meeting places, and 11 were referred "after being rejected by the selective service for homosexuality." Over half of the subjects reported heterosexual contact to orgasm and many reported extensive heterosexual interest. One-third regarded themselves as bisexual, and one as heterosexual. The authors did not utilize a comparison group of subjects.

Nineteen of the 60 had made what the subjects themselves considered to be a significant suicide attempt; seven of the 19 reported multiple attempts. The authors did not define what they consider to be a significant suicidal attempt. They drew attention to the distinction made by the subjects between the first (physical) sexual contact with a male and the first (emotional) homosexual experience. The finding that one-third of the subjects had made multiple suicide attempts and half had reported contact with a psychiatrist suggested a high level of psychopathology.

Saghir, Robins, Walbran and Gentry (1970a) compared 89 male homosexuals recruited from homosexual organizations in Chicago and San Francisco to 35 male heterosexuals recruited from a 500-unit apartment block and by word-of-mouth of friends of those from the apartments. Those who were currently married were excluded from the study. Twelve homosexuals and an unrecorded number of heterosexuals who reported hospitalization for psychiatric reasons were also excluded from the study. The authors found that six of the homosexuals reported a suicide attempt, one of whom required brief medical attention. None of the heterosexuals reported such an attempt. The difference between the two groups was not significant.

The rates for parascuicide among the homosexuals in the Saghir et al. (1970a) study may have been higher if the 12 subjects reporting hospitalization for psychiatric reasons had been included in the study. Although the authors termed these episodes suicide attempts, both examples reported were probably gestures; one subject cut his wrist superficially in front of his mother following an argument with her, and the other consumed a total of nine sleeping tablets.

Buhrich (1977) using Australian subjects, compared 34 male volunteer transvestites, 29 male homosexuals seeking treatment concerning their homosexuality, and 20 male-to-female transsexuals seeking sex conversion. A "suicide attempt" for which medical attention was sought or required was reported by 9%, 14% and 24% of the subjects, respectively. In general, homosexuals who seek treatment for homosexuality show more psychopathology than those who do not, and a relatively high rate of parasuicide among such subjects might be expected.

In a large study Bell and Weinberg (1978) recruited homosexuals in the San Francisco Bay area through public advertising, gay bars, gay bathhouses, homosexual organizations, and personal contacts. Six-hundred eighty-six male homosexuals were interviewed concerning their suicidal thoughts and behavior and of these over half regarded themselves as exclusively homosexual in both feelings and behavior. The homosexuals were compared to heterosexuals from the San Francisco general population. Both groups were categorized by sex and race. The authors found that 18% of the white and 20% of the black homosexuals in the study reported an attempted suicide compared to 3% of the white and 2% of the black heterosexual subjects. The first attempt generally occurred in the late teens or early adulthood.

Impressive as the Bell and Weinberg (1978) study is, it was not established whether the reported suicide attempt was in fact a gesture or an accidental overdose, or whether it even took place. The authors' finding that over one-quarter of the subjects had "never imagined" a suicide attempt seems unlikely, and their finding that among black homosexuals a "suicide attempt" was five times more frequent than a "serious consideration" but attempt also needs explanation. In addition, more homosexuals than heterosexuals lived alone. Single status, at least among heterosexuals, is a recognized risk factor in suicidal behavior. However, at present there seems to be no way to resolve the methodological problems in comparing the marital status of homosexuals and heterosexuals. Another difference between the two groups was that the homosexuals had lived in the San Francisco Bay area for less time than the heterosexuals. Domestic stability in one's living situation is a factor which protects against suicidal behavior.

With the advent of the AIDS epidemic, there may be a dramatic increase in suicidal behavior among the homosexual and bisexual population. Goedert et al. (1984) reported that half of their male homosexual subjects had contracted the AIDS retrovirus as reflected by their antibody test results, and of those who were sero-positive 6.9% per year developed full-blown AIDS and 13.1% per year developed an AIDS-related condition.

The repercussions of having a sero-positive status or an AIDS-related condition may be particularly difficult for the married bisexual, and for the older homosexual who became aware of his sexual orientation prior to the development of the openly gay subculture. Those who are sero-positive are advised they should inform their prospective sexual partners concerning their antibody status and, in addition, are advised against fathering a child because the risk of transmitting the virus to an offspring is high. The steady partner of a sero-positive subject may be unwilling to continue with a sexual relationship. Setbacks such as these may produce doubts for the subject in accepting his own homosexuality.

The case of L. P. exemplifies some of the risk factors seen in parasuicide. L. P. was 30 years old, single, an unemployed homosexual male. He presented to a Casualty Department in Sydney stating he was depressed and suicidal and that, earlier in the day, he had attempted to drown himself by walking into the surf.

Earlier in the year upon learning that he was sero-positive for the AIDS retrovirus, L. P. had decided to leave his boyfriend with whom he had been living for several years, fearing that his boyfriend might contract with virus from him. He then developed doubts concerning the morality of homosexuality and decided to join a religious sect which endorsed the belief that homosexuality resulted from possession by evil spirits and that by spiritual counseling, it could be exorcised. As a result of joining the sect, he had alienated his friends, who felt that he had "sold out" concerning his homosexuality. For several weeks he had felt fatigued, lost weight, and had bouts of intermittent diarrhea. Because of these symptoms he found it difficult to keep up with the sect's rigorous program and began to have reservations as to whether he had made the correct decision in joining the sect.

One week prior to presentation at the hospital, L. P. had visited a brother who subsequently died of cancer. He had not remained for the funeral because he did not want his family, who were aware of his homosexual orientation, to learn of his AIDS-related symptoms, and he now felt guilty about not having attended the funeral.

There was a history of parasuicide in the family: in separate incidents L. P.'s father and brother sustained serious injuries after attempting to take their lives.

At the interview he was neatly dressed. His speech was logical and there were no delusions or hallucinations. His mood was mildly depressed, but there were no physiological symptoms of depression. He was orientated in time, person, and place. His intelligence was average. Physical examination revealed no abnormalities and previous investigation revealed no evidence of immunosuppression; T4-cells were in the normal range and the T4/T8 ratio was above 1.

L. P. was admitted to the psychiatric ward and given his own room. A few hours after admission he broke his plate and administered superficial lacerations to his left wrist. While the nurse was reporting the episode he took scissors from his bag and further cut himself; however, the cuts did not require suturing. The same evening he was reported by the nursing staff to have made a "provocative and theatrical" attempt to tie his pajama cord around his neck. The following morning he was cheerful. He said he had made a firm decision to return to the sect, no longer felt suicidal, and no longer wanted to remain in the hospital.

Despite the histrionic nature of L. P.'s parasuicidal behavior — walking in the surf, if it actually occurred; superficial wrist lacerations; a "theatrical" hanging attempt — there were enough factors to cause concern. His social network had collapsed: He had alienated his gay friends, disappointed his family by not attending the funeral, and was undecided as to whether to return to the sect. He had doubts about accepting his homosexuality. There was the loss of his lover earlier in the year and of his brother recently. In addition, he was suffering from a stigmatized illness with an uncertain prognosis, and there was a history of serious parasuicide in the family.

Following his brief hospitalization and the firm decision to return to the sect, he improved dramatically. A beneficial cathartic effect is commonly observed following parasuicide, despite there being no change in the circumstances which led to the initial behavior. L. P.'s decision to take a definite course of action — namely to return to the sect — diminished his risk of further parasuicide at least for the immediate future.

PARASUICIDE AND FEMALE HOMOSEXUALITY

Kremer and Rifkin (1969) reported 25 girls, aged 12 to 17 years, who were "thought to be homosexual by teachers" and who were referred by the teachers for psychiatric evaluation. All the girls had "school problems," all were raised in an "unstable" home, and none had grown up in a nuclear-type family unit. The authors found that two had made a suicide attempt and five reported a parasuicide for which treatment was not sought. In another uncontrolled study, Jay and Young (1979) distributed questionnaires concerning female homosexuality to gay periodicals, gay bars, and other homosexual meeting places in Canada and the United States. Approximately 2% of the questionnaires were completed and returned and the authors' report concerned a subsample of 250 female homosexual respondents. Thirty-nine percent responded in the affirmative to the question "Have you ever attempted or seriously contemplated suicide?" One-third felt that the consideration or attempt was related to their homosexuality. The sample was strongly biased toward a high level of education — 60% held at least a college degree. A major weakness with the item in the questionnaire is that it did not differentiate between the attempt and the contemplation of suicide.

Saghir, Robins, Walbran and Gentry (1970b) compared 57 female homosexuals belonging to homosexual organizations in San Francisco and Chicago to 44 female heterosexuals living in a 500-unit apartment complex. The groups were similar in age, race, marital, and socioeconomic status. The authors found that 23% of the homosexuals, compared to 5% of the heterosexuals, reported an "attempted suicide"; only three, all in the homosexual group, required medical attention. The homosexual women were also found to have a high rate of alcoholism and excessive drinking—35%, compared with 5% of the heterosexuals. The high rate of attempted suicide among the homosexual women thus may be related to alcohol use rather than to homosexuality.

A high rate of parasuicide, but not of alcoholism, was found by Climent, Ervin, Rollins, Plutchick and Batinelli (1977) among homosexual female prisoners. The authors compared 26 self-reported homosexuals to 27 non-homosexual prison inmates. They found "suicidal thoughts" and suicidal attempts were more frequent among the homosexuals, whereas alcoholism was more frequent among the non-homosexuals. Factors which may have influenced the results were that the two groups differed significantly in race and type of offense leading to imprisonment.

Bell and Weinberg (1978), using the same recruitment procedure for female subjects as they had for males (as reported above), interviewed 293 female homosexuals concerning their suicidal feelings and behavior. The majority reported themselves to be exclusively or predominantly homosexual. The homosexuals were compared to 140 heterosexuals and categorized by sex and race. Twenty-five percent of the white and 17% of the black homosexuals reported a suicide attempt, as compared to 10% of the white and 16% of the black heterosexuals. These differences were not significant.

MANAGEMENT OF PARASUICIDE

Following parasuicide, patients may require hospitalization because of the immediate effects of the drugs or implements used during the episode. Psychosocial risk factors favoring admission are well-documented and include the risk factors associated with completed suicide. The majority of those who complete suicide communicate their intention to do so during the previous year (Robins, 1981). Statements concerning the hopelessness and the futility of life should be taken even more seriously than reported feelings of depression (Dyer & Kreitman, 1984).

Patients who feel guilty concerning a recent homosexual contact, those who find difficulty in adjusting to or accepting their homosexuality, those whose parents have recently become aware of and been unable to accept the patient's homosexuality, and those who live alone would seem to be at special risk. Homosexual males frequently report negative feelings about their own sexuality (Bell & Weinberg, 1978).

Homosexual patients who present following a parasuicide frequently consume alcohol to excess. It may be warranted to refer such a patient to an alcoholism treatment center, although in many cases they will be unwilling, or initially agree but fail, to attend. Compliance with follow-up arrangements is probably enhanced if the patient is referred to a "gay-sensitive" health care worker.

With regard to the initial assessment, little is gained in attempting to conduct an interview with a patient while he is still toxic from the effects of the alcohol or drugs he has consumed. Not only is the interview painfully slow, but the patient is likely to be labile and disinhibited. In addition, he will remember very little of what has been discussed during the interview.

Statements by the patient concerning his or her motivation for the parasuicide are not necessarily reliable. Older patients may be embarrassed about being brought to hospital and may underemphasize the seriousness of their attempt. On the other hand, especially among younger people if asked directly whether they were attempting to kill themselves, patients may respond in the affirmative even though the events surrounding the parasuicide make it clear that to die was not their intention. Thus, a measure of subtlety in the questions asked by the physician is required in order to collect accurate information. Slipping and falling from heights should be regarded as suicidal behavior until proved otherwise. Many patients on recovery from the parasuicide report a feeling of relief in finding themselves alive, despite the fact that the events that led to the episode remain unaltered.

Information surrounding the events leading to the parasuicide should be collected in detail from those accompanying the patient to the hospital, including acquaintances, police, and ambulance personnel. This information may be critical in assessing the seriousness of the attempt, and should be collected at the time of the incident to ensure its completeness and accuracy. Many patients who present to hospital following a drug-related parasuicide use illicit drugs, which may include heroin. If the patient is unconscious, it is appropriate to search his clothes for evidence of the incriminating drug. (In these circumstances staff must be wary to avoid a needle stick injury, and thereby avoid the albeit unlikely chance of contracting hepatitis B or the AIDS retrovirus.)

Farberow, Schneidman and Leonard (1976) reported a two- to three-fold increase in suicide risk among cancer patients, especially young men with leukemia or Hodgkin's disease. For the patient with AIDS, the stigma of the facial lesions of Karposi's Sarcoma are particularly distressing. The symptoms associated with AIDS are often painful and unaesthetic, and death is slow but inevitable. Lovers and friends may shy away from the patient and he may fear that he will become a liability to those who care for him.

A dilemma for the attending physician may arise when a patient with AIDS announces plans to kill himself, more commonly the patient refuses further medical assistance and medication. If there is no evidence of mental illness nor of cognitive impairment, and the patient is becoming increasingly disabled as a result of the illness, it would seem difficult to interfere with his decision. However, if the decision is made following an upset, for example, the loss of a lover, then he should be requested to delay his decision for at least a few days. In addition, many patients with AIDS develop central nervous system complications, and thus cognitive functions may be impaired. Under these circumstances, it would be very difficult to assume that a rational decision concerning threatened suicide has been made. A second issue concerning threatened suicide in a patient with AIDS is that a depressive illness may develop as a complication of an opportunistic central nervous system pathogen associated with the AIDS retrovirus. Such depressive syndromes may respond to antidepressant medications.

SUMMARY AND DISCUSSION

Anecdotal literature suggests a high parasuicide rate among male and female homosexuals. Most systematic studies do not show a strong association between either male or female homosexuality and parasuicide, although when a difference is reported, it is the homosexuals who show more parasuicide than heterosexuals.

A broken relationship, whether homosexual or heterosexual, is the most frequently implicated immediate precipitant to parasuicide. Homosexual relationships differ in character from those of heterosexuals in that they tend to be unstable, are more often child-less, less monogamous, and have less stereotyping of domestic roles as compared to those of heterosexuals (McWhirter & Matti-son, 1984). Whether these factors influence the rate of parasuicidal behavior remains speculative. In the study by Bell and Weinberg (1978), a broken relationship and parasuicide was considered by the male subjects but not the female subjects to be related to their ho-mosexuality.

Approximately half of the patients presented with parasuicide had ingested alcohol prior to the act and history of alcohol excess is frequent in such patients (Morgan, Burns-Cox, Pocock & Pottie, 1975). Alcohol use is common among homosexuals, and thus a high rate of parasuicide may be related to alcohol use rather than to homosexuality as such. Whether alcohol use follows as a conse-quence of the lifestyle of the gay community, or whether it attracts those who are prone to drink to excess, is not known. The majority of the homosexuals — two-thirds of the males and 90% of the fe-males — in the study by Saghir and Robins (1973) did not regard alcohol use as being related to their homosexuality.

A depressed background is commonly reported by parasuicidal patients (Kessel, 1965), and also by those who have frequent sui-cidal thoughts (Ross, Clayer & Campbell, 1983). A deprived back-ground is also commonly reported by homosexuals (Saghir et al., 1970a, 1970b), especially by male homosexuals with feminine traits (Weinberg & Williams, 1974). The trend for homosexuals to report a high rate of parasuicide may well be related to their de-prived background or to their effeminacy rather than to their homo-sexuality.

Bell & Weinberg (1978) reported that the mean ages of first para-suicide were the same in both heterosexuals and homosexuals, sug-gesting that whatever the risk factors are, they may be the same for both groups. Roesler and Deisher (1972) considered that the high rate of reported parasuicidal behavior among their young homosex-ual subjects could be related to the difficult process of developing a homosexual identity during late adolescence and early adulthood. There is some support for this in the study of Buhrich (1977), in which suicide attempts were reported more frequently in those with the greatest gender dysphoria (namely transsexuals), compared to those with less gender dysphoria (namely homosexuals and trans-vestites). Whether the lower self-esteem and greater guilt over homosexual behavior reported by bisexual males, as compared to predominantly or exclusively homosexual males, predisposes them to parasuicide is not known (Weinberg & Williams, 1974). However, it seems likely that once the individual considers himself to be an integrated member of the gay community, the risk of parasuicidal behavior diminishes.

CONCLUSION

The complexity of suicidal behavior is reflected by the many terms proposed to describe and explain such behavior. Literature tends to categorize such behavior by motivation into accidental overdose, suicide gesture, suicide attempt, and completed suicide. However, it is often not clear, even in the mind of the patient, what the motivation was for the behavior.

Anecdotal reports suggest a high rate of completed suicide among homosexuals, yet systematic studies do not show a greater risk for completed suicide among homosexuals as compared to heterosexuals.

Studies aimed at assessing parasuicide in homosexuals have approached the issue in two ways. First, patients who present with parasuicide have been asked their sexual orientation. Second, homosexuals living in the community have been asked whether they have considered or attempted suicide. A weakness with the former type of study is that the information generally has been collected anecdotally rather than systematically; a weakness of the latter has been that little attempt is made to confirm or characterize the subjects' report of the "attempted suicide."

Review of the literature suggests that, as compared to heterosexuals, both male and female homosexuals are somewhat more prone to parasuicide. Predisposing risk factors in parasuicide related to homosexuality concern the "coming out" process, guilt following first homosexual contact or awareness, and possibly the gender dysphoria or effeminacy seen in some male homosexuals. An increasingly important risk factor among male homosexuals may be associated with the AIDS epidemic.

Risk factors associated with parasuicide among homosexuals, but only tenuously related to it, would seem to be the higher incidence of alcoholism among homosexuals and possibly the greater instability of homosexual relationships.

Homosexuality, as such, would not seem to be an important risk factor in parasuicide when compared to the more commonly recognized factors such as young age, female status, social stress, deprived social background, and current psychosocial instability. Thus, the management of parasuicidal behavior in homosexuals is not dramatically different from that for non-homosexual patients.

REFERENCES

Allen, C. (1962). *A textbook of psychosocial disorders*. London: University Press.

Australian Bureau of Statistics (1983). *Suicides, Australia, 1966-1981, including historical series 1881-1981*. Catalog No. 3309.0. Information Services, P.O. Box 10, Belconnen A.C.T. 2616, Australia.

Barraclough, B., Bunch, J., Nelson, B. & Sainsbury, P. (1974). A hundred cases of suicide: Clinical aspects. *British Journal of Psychiatry*, *125*, 355-373.

Bell, A. P. & Weinberg, M. S. (1978). *Homosexualities: A study of diversity among men and women*. New York: Macmillan.

Buhrich, N. (1977). *Clinical study of heterosexual male transvestism*. Doctoral dissertation, University of New South Wales, Sydney.

Climent, C. E., Ervin, F. R., Rollins, A., Plutchick, R. & Batinelli, C. J. (1977). Epidemiological studies of female prisoners. *Journal of Nervous and Mental Disease*, *164*, 25-29.

Cohen, J. (1961). A study of suicide pacts. *Medico-Legal Journal*, *29*, 144-151.

Douglas, J. D. (1973). *Social meanings of suicide*. Princeton, NJ: Princeton University Press.

Dyer, J. A. T. & Kreitman, N. (1984). Hopelessness, depression and suicidal intent in parasuicide. *British Journal of Psychiatry*, *144*, 127-133.

Farberow, N. L., Schneidman, E. S. & Leonard, C. V. (1976). Suicide among patients with malignant neoplasms. In E. S. Schneidman, N. L. Farberow & R. E. Litman (Eds.), *Psychology of suicide* (pp. 325-344). New York: Jason Aronson.

Goedert, J. J., Biggar, R. J., Winn, D. M., Green, M. H., Mann, D. L., Gallo, R. C., Sarngadharan, M. G., Weiss, S. H., Grossman, R. J., Bodner, A. J., Strong, D. M. & Blattman, W. A. (1984). Determinants of retrovirus (HTLV-III) antibody and immunodeficiency conditions in homosexual men. *Lancet*, *29*, 711-716.

Hetzel, B. S. (1971). The epidemiology of suicidal behavior in Australia. *Australian and New Zealand Journal of Psychiatry*, *5*, 156-166.

Jay, K. & Young, A. (1979). *The gay report: Lesbians and gay men speak out about sexual experiences and lifestyles*. New York: Summit.

Kessel, N. (1965). Self-poisoning—Part 1. *British Medical Journal*, *2*, 1265-1270.

Kremer, M. W. & Rifkin, A. H. (1969). The early development of homosexuality: A study of adolescent lesbians. *American Journal of Psychiatry*, *126*, 91-96.

McClure, G. M. G. (1984). Recent trends in suicide amongst the young. *British Journal of Psychiatry*, *144*, 134-138.

McWhirter, D. P. & Mattison, A. M. (1984). *The male couple: How relationships develop*. Englewood Cliffs, NJ: Prentice-Hall.

Morgan, H. G., Burns-Cox, C. J., Pocock, H. & Pottle, S. (1975). Deliberate self-harm: Clinical and socio-economic characteristics of 368 patients. *British Journal of Psychiatry*, *127*, 564-574.

O'Conner, W. A. (1948). Some notes on suicide. *British Journal of Medical Psychology*, *21*, 222-228.

O'Hara, K. (1963). Characteristics of suicides in Japan especially of parent-child double suicide. *American Journal of Psychiatry*, *120*, 382-385.

Pallis, D. J., Gibbons, J. S. & Pierce, D. W. (1984). Estimating suicide risk among attempted suicides, II. Efficiency of predictive scales after the attempt. *British Journal of Psychiatry*, *144*, 139-148.

Prentice, A. E. (1974). *Suicide - A selective bibliography*. Metuchen, NJ: Scarecrow Press.

Robins, E. (1981). *The final months*. London: Oxford University Press.

Roesler, T. & Deisher, R. W. (1972). Youthful male homosexuality. *Journal of American Medical Association*, *219*, 1018-1023.

Rofe, E. E. (1983). *Lesbians, gay men and suicide*. San Francisco: Grey Fox Press.

Ross, M. W., Clayer, J. R. & Campbell, R. L. (1983). Parental rearing patterns and suicidal thoughts. *Acta Psychiatrica Scandinavica*, *67*, 429-433.

Saghir, M. R., Robins, E., Walbran, B. & Gentry, K. A. (1970a). Homosexuality, III. Psychiatric disorders and disability in the male homosexual. *American Journal of Psychiatry*, *126*, 1079-1086.

Saghir, M. T., Robins, E., Walbran, B. & Gentry, K. A. (1970b). Homosexuality, IV. Psychiatric disorders and disability in the female homosexual. *American Journal of Psychiatry*, *127*, 147-154.

Saghir, M. T, & Robins, E. (1973). *Male and female homosexuality*. Baltimore: Williams & Wilkins.

Spencer, S. J. G. (1959). Homosexuality among Oxford undergraduates. *Journal of Mental Science*, *105*, 393-405.

Stengel, E. (1964). *Suicide and attempted suicide*. Middlesex: Penguin Books.

Swartzburg, M., Schwartz, A. H., Lieb, J. & Slaby, A. B. (1972). Dual suicide in homosexuals. *Journal of Nervous and Mental Disease*, *155*, 125-130.

Weinberg, M. S. & Bell, A. P. (1972). *Homosexuality: An annotated bibliography*. New York: Harper & Row.

Weinberg, M. S. & Williams, C. J. (1974). *Male homosexuals. Their problems and adaptations*. London: Oxford University Press.

Wolfenden, J. et al. (1963). *Report of the Committee on Homosexual Offenses and Prostitution*. London: Her Majesty's Stationery Office.

Homosexuality and Mental Health:
A Cross-Cultural Review

Michael W. Ross, PhD
Flinders University Medical School

James A. Paulsen, MD
Palo Alto, California

Olli W. Stålström, MSocSci
University of Helsinki

It is an additionally provocative thought to consider an APA task force, composed of homosexual psychiatrists, preparing a report addressed to the prevailing theories of the etiology of homosexuality (written, for the most part, by heterosexuals).

(Green, 1972, p.94)

Inclusion of homosexuality in any international classification of disease is problematic, and raises a number of nosologic and value-related issues, as well as cultural ones. It can be argued that the definition of homosexuality as a condition is both culturally and temporally bound in Western society, and thus cannot be used to describe or ascribe characteristics to individuals in other societies. As such, it is inappropriate to even attempt to introduce into inter-

Dr. Ross is Coordinator of the AIDS Program, South Australian Health Commission, P.O. Box 65, Rundle Mall, Adelaide SA 5000, Australia, and Clinical Senior Lecturer in Psychiatry and Community Medicine, Flinders University Medical School, Adelaide.

Dr. Paulsen, now retired, was Lecturer in the Department of Psychiatry and Behavioral Sciences, Stanford University School of Medicine, and was affiliated with the Palo Alto Clinic, Palo Alto, CA.

Dr. Stålström is a member of the Department of Sociology, University of Helsinki, Finland.

Correspondence may be addressed to Dr. Ross at the address above.

131

national classification a behavior which may have been essentialized into an identity in only part of the world, and which may have
multiple meanings in different cultures. Even where homosexuality
is essentialized as a condition or identity rather than as a behavior,
no relationship can be demonstrated between mental health and homosexual identification. Indeed, Cass (1979) suggested that homosexual identification as an exclusive or central definition of one's
identity is only one stage of a developmental process in which the
end point is integration of sexual object preference into other core
identities.

While there may be a causal association between stigmatization
and mental health, this is not linkable to any particular minority or
ethnic status as such but to the stigmatization. This article reviews
the evidence linking homosexual behavior to mental health, cross-
cultural evidence on the status and meaning of homosexual behavior, and evidence for the essentialization of homosexual behavior as
a condition or identity. We then make recommendations on the ex-
clusion of homosexual behavior from the International Classification of Diseases of the World Health Organization.

Any discussion of the terms homosexuality and mental health
must of necessity be based on clear definitions of these two concepts. Previous debate and research has often lead to disagreement
or dubious findings because the meaning and operational definitions
of these two concepts have been assumed to be similar, but have in
fact been dissimilar. Of the two terms, mental health (and its converse, mental disorder) has been the most controversial. Here, mental disorder is defined following the criteria of Freedman, Kaplan
and Sadock (1976).

A mental disorder must meet the following criteria. First, its
manifestations must be primarily psychological — including psycho-
somatic and psychophysiological reactions — and involve alterations
of behavior. Second, the condition in its full-blown state must regularly and intrinsically be associated with subjective distress, generalized impairment in social effectiveness and functioning, or voluntary behavior which the patient wishes to stop because it is regularly
associated with physical illness or disability. Third, it should be
distinct from other conditions in terms of the clinical picture, family
studies, response to treatment, and follow-up. Certain of these
points must be elaborated. First, while the central aspect of Freedman et al.'s definition is the second point, that the condition must
regularly and intrinsically be associated with subjective distress,

care must be taken to distinguish between distress from intrinsic and extrinsic factors. Extrinsic factors impose distress on an individual if a behavior is socially stigmatized. However, social and cultural behaviors may vary widely in terms of presence or absence of stigmatization, and the critical aspect of the definition is the intrinsic nature of the distress. Culturally imposed sanctions which lead to distress are therefore excluded from our definition of mental disorder due to their arbitrary and often contrary nature.

A final point which also bears emphasis is that causation is not a factor on which mental health or illness may be dependent. Mechanism of causation is unrelated to the desirability or otherwise of a behavior, if in fact it is able to be determined. Issues of causation, while important for discussion, are not critical to definition of mental disorder because unless one labels a priori the source of causation pathogenic, one cannot attach the label of pathological to the outcome.

Having set out the conditions on which an objective definition of mental health may be made, it is also necessary to recognize that, as Sedgwick (1973) argued, "mental illness is a social construction," and that "psychiatry is a social institution incorporating the values and demands of its surrounding society." The implication of this is that psychiatric diagnoses may need to be revised with change of public attitudes and attitudes of the psychiatric professions toward certain conditions. Bayer (1981) cited Spitzer as arguing for a narrow and more objectivist view of mental disorder by wanting to include as such only clearly agreed mental disorders, and not psychological developments judged less than optimal. On the other hand, Spitzer also maintained that conditions which are an inherent disadvantage may also be included as mental disorder. Spitzer and Wilson (1975) argued that "Man . . . has developed the concept of illness to identify those conditions for which there exists a consensus that they are bad and ideally should be treated" (p. 826). They thus modified the objectivist stance, but only in terms of general social consensus across cultures. Where a behavior is universally agreed to be bad, then it may be considered to be a disorder. Such a stance admits sociocultural biases while maintaining a fairly objective set of criteria. However, successful application of these criteria depend on taking a fairly narrow view of what constitutes mental disorder. Because the classification of mental disorder depends on having certain objective criteria, this paper follows the three criteria of Freedman et al. and the criterion of Spitzer and Wilson in defining mental health and disorder in relation to homosexuality.

HOMOSEXUALITY: DEFINITION AND PREVALENCE

In Western societies, homosexuality is commonly separated into primary and secondary homosexuality: homosexual acts and homosexual feelings, respectively. Primary homosexuality involves sexual acts between members of the same sex. It may occur transiently in adolescence, in all-male or all-female environments where genital contact may occur with the same sex. It may occur in heterosexual men who desire an outlet less lonely than masturbation. Homosexual orientation, on the other hand, may occur without homosexual acts, in situations where there is an emotional attraction or desire to interact at a physical level between two people of the same sex. It is, basically, a love relationship between members of the same sex.

Thus individuals may indulge in homosexual acts without defining themselves as homosexual, and similarly, individuals may be predominantly attracted to members of their own sex yet never have a physical relationship that is homosexual. Generally, though, in most individuals the feelings and actions are congruent.

From the point of view of classification, it is necessary to point out that there are major differences between homosexual *identity* and homosexual *behavior*. If one is to classify homosexual identity, then one is looking at a process by which individuals come to see gender of preferred partner as a variable which defines other aspects of their lifestyle. If one is to classify homosexual behavior, then, one is looking at behavior which may have multiple meanings between and within societies which are too broad to be classified. Weinberg (1983) noted that many men who have had sex with other males neither suspect themselves of, nor adopt, a homosexual identity. Such people who do identify, at some stage, as homosexuals, are those who are able to conceive a special relationship between *being* and *doing*. It seems nosologically rather arbitrary to classify those who can conceive of this relationship as "homosexuals," and to ignore those who cannot or do not make this link. In looking at mental health and homosexual *identity*, it is also important to realize that this category occurs in only some societies, and may have very different meanings and social sanctions attached to it. We would argue that it is impossible to classify homosexual behavior as having any necessary mental health implications cross-culturally, and exceedingly difficult and culturally bound to classify homosexual identity as having any mental health implications, particularly as a homosexual *identity* usually appears only in societies where it is stigmatized. Any such implications will be primarily relatable to stigmatization, not to the identity; as a consequence, the "condition" of homosexuality as such is probably a *function* of stigmatization and, even where definable, the definition may be cross-culturally variable.

Homosexuality cannot be described as a simple or single behavior any more than heterosexuality can: The homosexual orientation comprises as wide a range of attitudes, practices, and behaviors as the heterosexual one. The very definition of an individual as homosexual *or* heterosexual is misleading because not only may individuals be both to a greater or lesser degree, but homosexual acts may be performed by people with heterosexual orientation, and vice versa. Were it not stigmatized, it is doubtful whether it would need to be emphasized to the point where individuals need to explain homosexual behavior, and thus adopt as part of a self-affirmation a homosexual identity.

Richardson (1983/1984) reviewed the literature on what if anything can be considered essential to the homosexual category, and concluded that not only is the term "homosexual" to designate a particular category of person a recent one, but that in the last century psychiatry has essentialized homosexuality as part of an attempt to explain behavior predefined as immoral or unnatural. In some cases, this was the price to pay for removing such behavior from the realm of the criminal to the medical. She concluded that the definition of homosexuality as an inherent aspect of the structure of society and of individual personality is a history of definitional crises. These crises have arisen in attempting to decide what is essential to the homosexual category: behavior? personal identification? underlying orientation? Maghan and Sagarin (1983) raised additional questions as to whether homosexuality can be seen as a "master status" which colors all other statuses. They noted that in many situations, whether individuals indulge in same-gender sexual activity or define themselves as "homosexual" has no implications for their behavior or the consequences of that behavior. As noted earlier, Cass (1979) suggested that a homosexual identity (in which individuals do see homosexuality as a superordinate defining status) may simply be one stage of accepting one's same-gender sexual behavior. Her stage 6 of homosexual adjustment is defined as the point where having a homosexual sex-object preference is only one facet of, and has few implications for, personality and lifestyle.

We would go further, and argue that the homosexual "condition" is a product of a particular society which stigmatizes homosexual behavior (Western. European) and of a particular period (since the 18th Century; see McIntosh, 1968). Such essentialization, incorporated into Western psychiatric thinking in the past 100 years, bears little relationship to same-sex interactions in other cultures, and must either be seen as a culture-bound classification or rejected as having little meaning in or for mental health in an international context. Prevalence studies dating from the time of some of the most rigid homosexual/heterosexual classifications and punishment of homosexual behavior showed that even in Western society, homosexuality cannot easily be essentialized.

Perhaps the best-known and largest study to look at the prevalence of homosexuality in Western society was that of Kinsey and his colleagues in the United States (Kinsey, Pomeroy & Martin, 1948). They found that male and female homosexuality could best be described as a continuum of degrees of attraction to members of one's own sex, and categorized individuals in terms of this Kinsey Scale. Thus Kinsey and his colleagues found that 37% of the male population had had sex with another male to orgasm between the ages of 16 and 55: over one-third of the population. Of these, only about 4% would be exclusively homosexual all their lives. Nevertheless, their data showed that about 18% of the male population would have as much homosexual as heterosexual experience between the ages of 16 and 55, nearly 1 in 5 of the population. The later Kinsey Report on women (Kinsey, Pomeroy, Martin & Gebhard, 1953) noted somewhat lower figures for female homosexual experiences, 26% of women having been erotically aroused in homosexual situations and half that number reaching orgasm with another woman by the age of 45. As women have become more sexually active since Kinsey collected his data in the 1940s, the female prevalence is probably somewhat higher now.

What is important to note is that homosexuality cannot be described as uncommon or statistically abnormal on this evidence. It is clear that a large proportion of the population has engaged in homosexual activity, and recent studies (McConaghy, Armstrong, Birrell & Buhrich, 1979) have shown that around 40% of men and a higher proportion of women have been erotically attracted to members of their own sex at some time. Thus homosexual attraction, as well, appears to be fairly common. It must be concluded, then, that popular definitions of two classes of people, "homosexual" and "heterosexual," are inaccurate and only serve to draw attention away from the actual proportion of homosexual behavior in the population. What is meant by "homosexual" in the Western scientific literature is usually those individuals who are predominantly homosexual and who acknowledge this fact to themselves or to others. It will be used in the same context here.

However, it must be recognized that dividing individuals up into classes such as homosexual or heterosexual not only ignores evidence suggesting a continuum, but also serves a social function of anxiety reduction. It enables individuals to be typecast with one identity or the other, thus preventing heterosexuals from recognizing their homosocial, homoerotic, and homosexual feelings or behaviors as threatening, and the converse for the persons who have identified themselves as being homosexual. The security derived from such a categorization, while decreasing the individual's examination of their sexual feelings on the basis of gender, does serve to perpetuate the idea of examination of sexual feelings on the basis of gender. It also serves to perpetuate the binary classification of sex object preference and aids in the definition of homosexual interest as a "condition." This is somewhat analogous to the popular concept of mental health in which individuals are branded by society as either "mentally ill" or "normal," essentializing mental illness and ignoring the presence of continua of psychosocial adjustment.

While most data on homosexuals are derived from Western societies, there is considerable agreement that the figures of Kinsey are reasonably accurate. For example, proportions of Kinsey Scale levels 5 and 6 males could be accounted for by number of homosexual acts in a population: In a recent survey in Finland, Talikka (1975) found that in the past two years, 11% of all adult males surveyed had had a homosexual sexual encounter. This survey was based on a random sample of the population.

GENERAL ARGUMENTS OVER MENTAL HEALTH AND HOMOSEXUALITY

The general arguments as to whether homosexuality constituted a mental disorder were extensively canvassed during the debate in 1972 over the classification of homosexuality by the American Psychiatric Association. That debate and its arguments is well-detailed elsewhere (Green, 1972; Bayer, 1981), and as a consequence only the general contentions over classification are reviewed briefly here. Green (1972) was of the opinion that homosexuality was a case of arbitrary definition in which psychiatry used the consensus among society or psychiatrists to impose the status of disorder. He also criticized the assumption that heterosexuality is innate and that the only function of sexuality is reproduction. Further, he questioned the view held in classic psychoanalytic theory that homosexuality is a mark of psychological immaturity, which is based on the theory of the necessity of resolution of oedipal conflict for heterosexuality. Such an approach is based upon a priori assumptions in some psychoanalytic theories about the innate "naturalness" of heterosexuality, and strengthened by reference to psychoanalytic concepts such as oedipal conflict which have not been demonstrated empirically. The whole psychoanalytic construction is thus based upon arbitrary or untestable assumptions. Social learning theory uses the mediators of identification with a sex-inappropriate parent as a model of homosexuality, but this in turn was criticized by Green as making the assumption that sex role deviation (masculinity or femininity) is equivalent to homosexuality. (This assumption is reviewed in detail later in this article.)

The whole concept of whether homosexuality is healthy, and whether a homosexual's psychological functioning is "normal," was questioned by Green (1972), who pointed out that subject to the same criticisms and prejudgments as homosexuality, psychiatrists "might also conclude that *heterosexuality* is a phenomenon of seeking emotional and sexual gratification in a genital relationship between two persons of the opposite sex, associated, to a considerable degree, with symptoms of anxiety, depression, drug abuse, phobias and unfulfilled dependency needs" (p. 87). He went on to question how much of the reported instability of homosexual relationships is inherent, how much the result of societal pressures, and how much is the result of sampling biases and the early emphasis on patients. However, Green also suggested that the essential issue is not whether other psychological systems of homosexuals are in order, but whether homosexuality is an illness apart form being defined one per se: Should quality of sexuality be dependent on direction? Was not the definition of homosexuality as illness simply a moral or value judgment on the part of heterocentric theorists?

Many of the questions raised by Green and others as to whether homosexuality per se is a mental disorder rest on opinion, for the initial assumption of the presence or absence of mental disorder does appear to be a value judgment and is not open to empirical test. Nevertheless, Green's contentions do appear to have greater accuracy and applicability if homosexuality can be shown to have none of the *other* features of mental disorder listed in the introduction to this article. In short, logic requires that if homosexuality is a disorder, then all homosexuals show evidence of psychopathology. If some or most homosexuals can be shown not to have levels of psychopathology outside the normal range, then it cannot be assumed to be a pathological condition. The lack of subjective distress or of problems in social functioning, as specific measures of pathology, are central to rejecting the label of mental disorder.

EXPERIMENTAL STUDIES: HOMOSEXUALITY AND MENTAL HEALTH

The vast number of studies which have looked at the mental health of homosexuals (probably more than 100 since 1960) have almost without exception shown that homosexuals fall within the normal range of psychological adjustment, and that there are few if any significant differences between homosexuals and heterosexuals. Some few studies have actually shown the adjustment of homosexual women to be superior to that of heterosexual controls (e.g., Thompson, McCandless & Strickland, 1971). Such studies have utilized a wide range of psychometric tests, both projective and nonprojective. A few representative examples include studies by Hooker (1957), who found that male homosexuals were indistinguishable on the Rorschach from matched heterosexuals, and Panton (1960), Dean and Richardson (1964), Braaten and Darling (1965), Manosevitz (1970, 1971), Horstman (1972), and Pierce (1973), who all found on the MMPI that male homosexuals did not score outside the normal range of the clinical scales. While some of these studies found significant differences on some scales between homosexuals and heterosexuals, none were outside the normal range. Similar studies using the MMPI with homosexual women reached the same conclusions (Miller, 1963; Ohlson & Wilson, 1974). Using the Adjective Check List, Chang and Block (1960), Evans (1971), and Thompson et al. (1971) achieved similar results. Gonsiorek (1982b) reviewed these findings in detail.

It is important that studies which are clearly unscientific be excluded. Such studies include samples of patient or incarcerated homosexuals, who would be expected to show greater psychological disturbance. As an illustration of this, Turner, Pielmaier, James and Orwin (1974) compared patient and nonpatient homosexual men, and found major differences between them on the EPI and 16PF in the expected direction. Further, there is evidence that homosexual men who volunteer for such studies are less psychologically well-adjusted. Burdick and Stewart (1974) found that those subjects (male homosexuals) who returned for follow-up were significantly higher on extraversion and neuroticism as measured by the EPI than those who did not return. Thus, those homosexuals who volunteer for research are likely to be less well-adjusted than those who do not, and patients even more so.

Some studies which are frequently cited and which suggest that male homosexuals are less well adjusted than heterosexuals are sufficiently unscientific as to be worthless. As an example, Gonsiorek (1982a) cited the research of Bieber et al. (1962). After noting that the sample was composed of patients in therapy, in itself a severe bias, Gonsiorek commented that

> . . . the same group of psychoanalysts developed a theory about homosexuality; developed the questionnaire to test their theory; designed the research study; served as analysts for the patient subjects; served as raters in the research project on their own patients; interpreted the results; and finally concluded that their theory had been verified. (p. 380)

Gonsiorek also made the point that it would be difficult to imagine how to build more potential for research bias into experimental procedures than did Bieber et al.

However, it is important to note that the properly conducted scientific studies, most if not all have found no differences in psychological adjustment in homosexual as compared with matched heterosexual men, and any significant differences have been within the normal range on standardized tests. Nevertheless, it is likely that while there are no apparent differences between homosexuals and heterosexuals as a result of their sexual orientation as such, the position of homosexuality in some societies, where homosexuals are stigmatized minorities, may lead to some homosexuals showing evidence of the effects of prejudice. Accordingly, it is important to review briefly the evidence for extrinsic imposition of psychopathology on homosexuals.

EXOGENOUS FACTORS IN
MENTAL HEALTH IN HOMOSEXUALS

Previous studies of prejudice (e.g., Allport, 1954) have, according to Gonsiorek (1982c), examined the effects of stereotyping and prejudice on minority groups, and found that traits of victimization included feelings of insecurity, self-hate, and neuroticism. As Gonsiorek pointed out, these are precisely the traits that such psychoanalytic writers as Bieber et al. described as inherent and pathological features of all homosexuals. However, the weight of evidence so far suggests that where such traits do occur in homosexuals, they are of extrinsic origin. Theorizing about societal reaction to homosexuality has led to such studies as that of Weinberg and Williams (1974), in which homosexuals in three societies (the United States, the Netherlands, and Denmark) were investigated. Weinberg and Williams argued that because reaction to homosexuality was different in the three societies, then this should be reflected in the mental health of homosexuals in those three societies, with those in the most accepting societies being better adjusted. Yet results showed no significant differences between the societies in this regard, leading Sagarin and Kelly (1975) to claim that "pathology precedes hostile societal reactions and would exist independent of it" (p. 262). The leap from lack of evidence for societally induced psychopathology to the assumption that any pathology is intrinsic, however, is not logically valid unless it can be shown that societal reaction is the critical variable, and that negative consequences do not stem from any variable other than a homosexual orientation. Ross (1978) suggested that the critical variable involved was not the societal reaction itself but the *perception* of societal reaction by the homosexual, and indeed found that expected negative societal reaction predicted more conformity and attempts to deny homosexuality, in line with what would be expected using Allport's model of prejudice. In addition, expectation of negative societal reaction also indicated lower psychological adjustment, measured on the same scales used by Weinberg and Williams (1974). Thus, it would appear that the psychopathology present in some homosexuals may be associated with the stresses of being a homosexual in a society where such a partner preference is stigmatized. Nevertheless, it is clear that homosexuality per se does not have any necessary implications for mental health, although the society in which an individual lives and its reaction to homosexuality may well have implications for the mental health of some homosexual individuals in it.

CROSS-CULTURAL ASPECTS OF HOMOSEXUALITY

The question of whether there is any general consensus on homosexuality as a mental illness was effectively answered by Ford and Beach (1952), who analyzed the human relations area files for 77 societies, and found that in 64% of these societies, homosexual behavior is considered normal or socially acceptable for some or all members of the community. There can be no doubt from these data that homosexuality is present in the vast majority of cultures, and is generally stigmatized in only about one-third of them. Consensus about the deviant status of homosexuality is not present, and would appear in fact to be in the direction of acceptance of same-sex contacts. It is interesting to note that Whitehead (1981), amongst others, reported that the rate of homosexual behavior in the world appears to vary independently of the official cultural "attitude" toward it. The rate may be high where it is condemned (20th Century North America) or low (Trobriands); low where it is permitted (Nambikwara) or high (Desana). She also noted that acceptance of heterosexual expression might appear equally elusive were it not, in some form, universally "institutionalized."

Before looking at the institutionalization of homosexuality and exclusive homosexuality, it is necessary to look at homosexual behavior in various societies in order to ascertain whether it is homosexual behavior per se which has historically led to stigmatization, and whether homosexual behavior can be considered a unitary behavior.

Reviewing sexual variance in history across cultures, Bullough (1976) made the point that homosexuality may be seen as being contrary to a number of perceived purposes. Five major aspects of homosexuality, then, can probably be posited: homosexuality as it is concerned with the procreational aspects of sex, homosexuality as an indicator of social status (dominance-submission), homosexuality as recreation (hedonistic sexuality), homosexuality as an educational activity (mentoring), and homosexuality as an emotional preference (affectional sexuality). There are also some 11 other meanings that sexual interactions (specifically homosexual but also heterosexual) may have to the participants (Ross, 1984); examples may be provided for all of these in various cultures. Clearly, in the course of history, some aspects of homosexuality have been acceptable while others have not. As examples, homosexuality in pre-Christian Jewish society was unacceptable because it did not lead to procreation, which was regarded as the leading imperative for survival of the race. In Egyptian society, homosexuality was regarded as an index of submission if an individual took the so-called passive role in anal intercourse, but as an acceptable behavior for the active partner. After defeat in battle, the soldiers in a defeated army could expect to be sodomized by the Egyptian victors, with stigma attached only to the passive role. This, however, appears only to have been attached to anal intercourse, and not to other forms of homosexual behavior. Hedonistic sexuality in which sexual relations between males was for sexual release, was not and is not stigmatized in many societies, including Roman society and in some middle Eastern cultures, as long as a passive role is not taken. Similarly, in some Polynesian societies such as Samoa (Shore, 1981) and Mexico (Carrier, 1980), it is acceptable for males to engage in homosexual activity as long as there is no deviation in social sex role.

As a subset of hedonistic homosexuality, homosexual behavior as substitution may also be considered in some societies. In such cases, where strict segregation of the sexes between adolescents or adults is practiced, it may be acceptable for homosexual behavior to occur because heterosexual activity is forbidden or impossible. Generally, however, this is referred to as institutionalized homosexuality. It may also become part of educational homosexuality if there is an age or status gap between the partners. Educational homosexuality describes the form of homosexual behavior typical of classical Greece and of several New Guinean societies, in which a youth is adopted by an older man who acts as his mentor. While such homosexual unions serve other purposes as well, including emotional ones, they are recognized as having educational and social importance and accepted as both homosexual and homosocial in nature. Herdt (1981) described the Sambia in New Guinea, in which passive homosexual fellation is universally practiced as a means of developing *masculinity*, as well as having educational and affective functions. Finally, affectional homosexual behavior, which may be subdivided into homosocial and homosexual (although both usually occur together), may be accepted in some societies (for example, contemporary Western society) if there is no overt sexual component or accepted without reservation (as in the Siwans). While these classifications cover the general spectrum of male homosexual relations, they are not exclusive, and one or more categories may coexist. What is demonstrated by these categories is, however, that homosexuality cannot be regarded as a single, coherent behavior, and nor can stigmatization of homosexuality be linked to homosexuality as such, but to homosexuality as it is seen to conflict with various societal values. Thus, it is more correct, as Bell and Weinberg (1978) did, to speak of "homosexualities," than to see it as a unitary behavior. It is equally important to recognize, given that homosexuality is a behavior which reflects a multiplicity of motivations, that the behavioral manifestation of these motivations cannot be considered a distinct condition or to have consistent etiology. Belief in a homosexual identity as it has been essentialized by Western society is culture-bound and socially determined, and thus should not be used to define a behavior and its associated meanings in other cultures.

The wide variation in diagnosis (or labeling) of homosexuality cross-culturally further complicates matters. Behavior that is labeled homosexual, and thus subject in some societies to stigma or to the assumption of mental illness, is not consistent. In Western societies, homosexual behavior is so labeled if it involves genital contact between two members of the same sex, whether manual, oral, anally, or somatic. In contrast, in Mediterranean cultures and their derivatives, the homosexual is regarded as the passive partner in intercourse, and the active partner is neither labeled, stigmatized, nor assumed to be mentally ill (Carrier, 1980). In some cultures, particulary in the New Guinea Highlands and in ancient Greece, there is no stigma attached to either partner, regardless of role (Bullough, 1976; Herdt, 1981). In fact, *failure* to act homosexually would be stigmatized. In yet others, passive homosexuals are considered to be a third sex, functioning as women yet having the soma of a male, and are institutionalized as such (Wikan, 1977). This latter situation can probably be considered an extreme exaggeration of the Mediterranean definition of homosexuality.

Similarly, the cross-cultural literature has abounded with assumptions of what constitutes homosexual behavior, many of which may on examination be shown to be inaccurate. Whitehead (1981), in particular, analyzed the situation of the homosexual in native

North America and found that descriptions of the Berdache phenomenon as institutionalized homosexuality do not fit the data. She argued that the interpretation of homosexuality in other cultures is invariably interpreted in terms of Western notions of homosexuality, and that processes may be quite different in a culture in which they are formally instituted as opposed to those where they are spontaneously expressed. In native North America it was permissible in certain social respects for a man to become a woman (and, more infrequently, vice versa). Homosexual practice was a common accompaniment to this but, as she forcefully pointed out, sexual object choice was outside the realm of what was publicly and officially important about the role of the two sexes: Cross-sex occupational choice and cross-dressing were the two definitive aspects. Sexual object choice variation did not provoke reclassification of the individual, and in fact Berdaches could have sex with either males or females without compromising their status. Conversely, homosexual behavior in males and females was well-known and had specific appellations, but was not considered objectionable.

It is thus clear, as Whitehead (1981) argued, that the Berdache was a case of institutionalized cross-sex status rather than homosexuality, and that analyses of homosexual behavior in other cultures are invariably tainted with Western assumptions about sexual behavior and gender roles. It is also clear that preferential homosexual behavior cannot always be equated with institutionalized homosexual behavior. It could be argued that the homosexual "role" in Western society (McIntosh, 1968) is equally an institutionalization, as a function of the need of medical science and the general population to essentialize sexual preference as an "either/or" phenomenon, and that as a consequence of the conceptualization of sexual preference as either homosexual *or* heterosexual, individuals are forced into socially prescribed categories, and the continual nature of sexual preference as acknowledged by Kinsey et al. (1948) is therefore not recognized.

Implicit in Whitehead's (1981) argument that the definition of homosexuality cross-culturally has been dependent upon imposing Western values and interpretations is the suggestion that homosexuality and deviant gender identity and social sex role are linked. Despite research evidence which illustrates that inappropriate social sex role is not necessarily associated with homosexuality (Heilbrun & Thompson, 1976), the argument that feminine identification is linked with male homosexuality and masculine identification is linked with female homosexuality has continued in psychiatry, probably due to the assumption that in a society where heterosexuality is the accepted relational model, any individual who prefers a same-sex partner must therefore possess attributes of, or consider themselves a member of, the opposite sex (Ross, Rogers & McCulloch, 1978). This is probably a legitimating ploy on the part of a heterosexually based society, but psychiatry has to some degree accepted this societal reasoning in its formulation of homosexuality as psychopathology by arguing that it is psychopathology because of the opposite-sex identification. However, several points must be noted in this regard. First, studies such as those by Siegelman (1972) have shown that femininity in male homosexuals is related not to homosexuality, as such, but to the degree of neurosis in homosexuals. Similarly, Dickey (1961) noted that those male homosexuals who had a traditional masculine role were better psychologically adjusted. The lack of any consistent relationship between homosexuality and social sex role has also been shown by Ross (1983a, 1983b). Ross demonstrated that degree of masculinity or femininity in homosexuals was not dependent on degree of homosexuality, but was in fact dependent on the attitudes toward homosexuality and the rigidity of sex roles in the society in which the homosexual lives. Thus, there is now clear evidence that deviant masculinity and femininity in homosexuals may be dependent on societal factors, and are not necessarily inherent in homosexual behavior. Evidence that in some contexts homosexual behavior may *masculinize* the actor (Herdt, 1981; Carrier, 1980) emphasizes this point.

Psychiatry has, nevertheless, developed the assumption that homosexuality is a function of the disturbance of parental rearing patterns, particularly identification with parental models. While again this has been demonstrated by Siegelman (1974) to be correct only for some homosexuals, by Ross (1980) to be dependent on homosexuals recalling parent-child relations in terms of current theorizing or the etiology purported by psychoanalysts, and by Freund and Blanchard (1983) to be based on increased father-son distance, where it does exist in male homosexuals, that distance being a *result* of the son's sexual orientation rather than a *cause* of it, nevertheless psychiatric theorizing has accepted this as the main basis of psychopathology. The logical fallacy of this has been pointed out by Davison (1982), who stated that:

One cannot attach a pathogenic label to a particular pattern of child-rearing unless one a priori labels the adult behavior pattern as pathological. For example, Bieber et al. found that what they called a "close-binding intimate mother" was present much more often in the life histories of the analytic male homosexual patients than among the heterosexual controls. What is wrong with such a mother unless you happen to find her in the background of people whose current behavior you judge *beforehand* to be pathological? (p. 426)

As Davison so cogently argued, to be consistent one must judge a heterosexual with such a parental constellation to be pathological, as well as all such parents, if homosexuality is to be considered pathological on these grounds. There is of course another argument which illustrates the arbitrary nature of the association between social sex roles and homosexuality, as well as the cultural variation involved. In the New Guinea Highlands, semen which enters the body via homosexual intercourse is regarded as *masculinizing* the individual, whereas in Mediterranean society the same act would be regarded as *feminizing*. Both, it could be argued, involve homosexual behavior: in New Guinea, ritually, and in Mediterranean areas, a socially prescribed institutionalization via the recognized homosexual role for the passive partner only.

Nevertheless, Gadpaille (1980) argued that *preferential* homosexual behavior seems to be universally regarded as deviant. While he noted that much of the anthropological data on cultures accepting some homosexual activity are too vague to permit conclusions about degree of "approval," he failed to distinguish between the bases for homosexual behavior (educational, affectional, and so on) and the different meanings of homosexuality in different cultures and different degrees of institutionalization. It is probably a mistake to assume that preferential homosexuality is not a form of institutionalization in Western society, given the emergence of a clear homosexual "role" (or stereotype) and the tendency of society to classify individuals as either *heterosexual* or *homosexual*. Certainly Saghir and Robins (1973) indicated that some 48% of their homosexual subjects had had heterosexual experience, despite the fact that they were preferentially homosexual at the time they were interviewed.

A second difficulty with Gadpaille's (1980) assertion about pref-

erential homosexuality is the question as to when it becomes preferential. Is it preferential just on the homosexual side of bisexual, or
only when it is totally exclusive? Is the label of preferential homosexuality one which ignores the data of Kinsey et al. (1948), which
indicate that 13% of males will be more homosexual than heterosexual for a 3-year period in their lives, but not throughout their
lives? Given the extreme difficulty of deciding what is preferential
homosexuality, and the point at which it becomes preferential, there
is little point in making the definition of mental health or illness
dependent on this, particularly as preferential homosexuality may
also be seen simply as the Western form of institutionalized, socially imposed homosexuality. For what it is worth, animal studies
involving infra-human primates have also reported preferential homosexuality in some situations, suggesting that it may simply be
one end of the continuum for plasticity with regard to sex of partner
(Erwin & Maple, 1976).

CONCLUSIONS

Any conclusions must be based upon the model of mental illness
or health adopted. In this article, we have adopted one which sees
pathological behavior as being primarily psychological in manifestation and involving alterations in behavior, being regularly and
intrinsically associated with subjective distress and impairment in
social functioning, and being distinct from other conditions in its
clinical picture. Evidence presented here indicates that homosexuality, either within or across cultures, does not meet these criteria.
There is no cross-cultural consensus as to the acceptability of homosexuality, and what data exist suggest that the consensus is toward
acceptance. Cross-culturally, homosexual behavior may have different meanings or be institutionalized to different degrees, and the
reaction of societies to such behavior may range from rejection to
acceptance of an identical behavior. Similarly, different bases for
stigmatization of homosexual behavior may be identified (including
procreation, status, recreation, education and affection), and stigmatization may be directed not so much at the homosexuality, but at
the societal values each of these may transgress.

Given these data, it is impossible to state either that homosexuality is evidence of psychopathology or that there is a common
reaction to it cross-culturally which may lead to stigmatization of
homosexual behavior. In each society, any stigmatization of homo-

sexuality as psychopathological is based upon psychiatry in that society supporting the value judgments made, rather than upon any empirical evidence of psychopathology. The very fact that what is stigmatized in one culture is acceptable in another is evidence of this. While there is no doubt that each society has a right to determine what it regards as acceptable or unacceptable, moral or immoral behavior, psychiatry, as a science, must base its claims on scientific evidence. In the case of homosexuality, it must show that the same consequences stem from the same behavior across discrepant cultures; the evidence clearly shows this not to be the case. Similarly, it is impossible to demonstrate etiology, let alone consistent etiology. In this situation, imposition of a psychopathological label on homosexual behavior would be an act of cultural imperialism without scientific or logical justification.

The evidence does not let us conclude cross-culturally that homosexuality is associated with any necessary consequences. We can only conclude, as did Freud (1920) that "[Homosexuality] is found in peoples who exhibit no other serious deviations from the normal. It is similarly found in people whose efficiency is unimpaired. . . . " Nor can we conclude cross-culturally that homosexual behaviors are essentialized as a condition or identity in societies other than those which create such an identity by stigmatizing homosexual behavior. We should therefore cease to confuse psychiatric diagnosis and moral values, behavior and identity, and remove homosexuality for the International Classification of Diseases.

REFERENCES

Allport, G. A. (1954). *The nature of prejudice*. Reading, MA: Addison-Wesley.

Bayer, R. (1981). *Homosexuality and American psychiatry*. New York: Basic Books.

Bell, A. P. & Weinberg, M. S. (1978). *Homosexualities: A study of diversity among men and women*. New York: Simon & Schuster.

Bieber, I., Dain, J. H., Dince, P. R., Drellich, M. G., Grand, H. G., Gundlach, R. H., Kremer, M. W., Rifkin, A. H., Wilbur, C. B. & Bieber, T. B. (1962). *Homosexuality: A psychoanalytic study*. New York: Basic Books.

Braaten, L. & Darling, C. (1965). Overt and covert homosexual problems among male and college students. *Genetic Psychology Monographs, 71*, 269-270.

Bullough, V. L. (1976). *Sexual variance in society and history*. Chicago: University of Chicago Press.

Burdick, J. & Stewart, D. (1974). Differences between "show" and "no show" volunteers in a homosexual population. *Journal of Social Psychology, 92*, 159-160.

Carrier, J. M. (1980). Homosexual behavior in cross-cultural perspective. In J. Marmor (Ed.), *Homosexual behavior: A modern reappraisal* (pp. 100-122). New York: Basic Books.

Cass, V. C. (1979). Homosexual identity formation: A theoretical model. *Journal of Homosexuality*, *4*, 219-235.

Chang, J. & Block, J. (1960). A study of identification in male homosexuals. *Journal of Consulting Psychology*, *24*, 307-310.

Davison, G. C. (1982). Politics, ethics and treatment in homosexuality. *American Behavioral Scientist*, *24*, 423-434.

Dean, R. & Richardson, H. (1964). Analysis of MMPI profiles of 40 college-educated overt male homosexuals. *Journal of Consulting Psychology*, *28*, 483-486.

Dickey, B. A. (1961). Attitudes toward sex roles and feelings of adequacy in homosexual males. *Journal of Consulting Psychology*, *25*, 116-122.

Erwin, J. & Maple, T. (1976). Ambisexual behavior with male-male anal penetration in male rhesus monkeys. *Archives of Sexual Behavior*, *5*, 9-14.

Evans, R. B. (1971). ACL scores of homosexual men. *Journal of Personality Assessment*, *35*, 344-349.

Ford, C. S. & Beach, F. A. (1952). *Patterns of sexual behavior*. London: Eyre & Spottiswoode.

Freedman, A. M., Kaplan, H. I. & Sadock, B. J. (1976). *Modern synopsis of comprehensive textbook of psychiatry* (2nd ed.). Baltimore: Williams & Wilkins.

Freud, S. (1920). *A general introduction of psychoanalysis*. New York: Boni & Liverright.

Freund, K. & Blanchard, R. (1983). Is the distant relationship of fathers and homosexuals sons related to the son's erotic preference for male partners, or to the son's atypical gender identity, or both? *Journal of Homosexuality*, *9*(1), 7-25.

Gadpaille, W. J. (1980). Cross-species and cross-cultural contributions to understanding homosexual activity. *Archives of General Psychiatry*, *37*, 349-357.

Gonsiorek, J. C. (1982a). Introduction to mental health issues and homosexuality. *American Behavioral Scientist*, *25*, 367-384.

Gonsiorek, J. C. (1982b). Results of psychological testing on homosexual populations. *American Behavioral Scientist*, *25*, 385-396.

Gonsiorek, J. C. (1982c). Social psychological concepts in the understanding of homosexuality. *American Behavioral Scientist*, *25*, 483-492.

Green, R. (1972). Homosexuality as a mental illness. *International Journal of Psychiatry*, *10*, 77-98.

Herdt, G. (1981). *Guardians of the flutes: Idioms of masculinity*. New York: McGraw-Hill.

Hooker, E. A. (1957). The adjustment of the male overt homosexual. *Journal of Projective Techniques*, *21*, 17-31.

Horstman, W. R. (1972). Homosexuality and psychopathology: A study of the MMPI responses of homosexual and heterosexual male college students. *Dissertation Abstracts International*, *33*, 2347B.

Kinsey, A. C., Pomeroy, W. B. & Martin, C. E. (1948). *Sexual behavior in the human male*. Philadelphia: W. B. Saunders.

Kinsey, A. C., Pomeroy, W. B., Martin, C. E. & Gebhard, P. H. (1953). *Sexual behavior in the human female*. Philadelphia: W. B. Saunders.

McConaghy, N., Armstrong, M. S., Birrell, P. C. & Buhrich, N. (1979). The incidence of bisexual feelings and opposite sex behavior in medical students. *Journal of Nervous and Mental Disease, 167*, 685-688.

McIntosh, M. (1968). The homosexual role. *Social Problems, 16*, 182-192.

Maghan, J. & Sagarin, E. (1983). Homosexuals as victimizers and victims. In D. E. J. McNamara & A. Karmen (Eds.), *Deviants: Victims or victimizers?* (pp. 147-162). Beverly Hills, CA: Sage Publications.

Manosevitz, M. (1970). Item analysis of the MMPI *Mf* scale using homosexual and heterosexual males. *Journal of Consulting and Clinical Psychology, 35*, 395-399.

Manosevitz, M. (1971). Education and MMPI *Mf* scores in homosexual and heterosexual males. *Journal of Consulting and Clinical Psychology, 36*, 395-399.

Miller, W. G. (1963). Characteristics of homosexually involved incarcerated females. *Journal of Consulting Psychology, 27*, 277.

Ohlson, E. L. & Wilson, M. (1974). Differentiating female homosexuals from female heterosexuals using the MMPI. *Journal of Sex Research, 10*, 308-315.

Panton, J. R. (1960). A new MMPI scale for the identification of homosexuality. *Journal of Clinical Psychology, 16*, 17-21.

Pierce, D. M. (1973). Test and non-test correlates of active and situational homosexuality. *Psychology, 19*(4), 23-26.

Richardson, D. (1983/1984). The dilemma of essentiality in homosexual theory. *Journal of Homosexuality, 9*(2/3), 79-90.

Ross, M. W. (1978). The relationship between perceived societal hostility, conformity, and psychological adjustment in homosexual males. *Journal of Homosexuality, 4*, 157-168.

Ross, M. W. (1980). Retrospective distortion in homosexual research. *Archives of Sexual Behavior, 9*, 523-531.

Ross, M. W. (1983a). Societal influences on gender role in homosexuals: A cross-cultural comparison. *Journal of Sex Research, 19*, 273-288.

Ross, M. W. (1983b). Gender identity and sexual orientation: Some social and cross-cultural relationships. *Journal of Homosexuality, 9*(1), 27-36.

Ross, M. W. (1984). Beyond the biological model: New directions in bisexual and homosexual research. *Journal of Homosexuality, 10*(3/4), 63-70.

Ross, M. W., Rogers, L. J. & McCulloch, H. (1978). Stigma, sex and society: A new look at gender differentiation and sexual variation. *Journal of Homosexuality, 3*, 315-330.

Sagarin, E. & Kelly, R. J. (1975). Sexual deviance and labeling perspectives. In W. R. Gove (Ed.), *The labeling of deviance: Evaluating a perspective*. New York: Sage Publications.

Saghir, M. J. & Robins, E. (1973). *Male and female homosexuality: A comprehensive investigation*. Baltimore: Williams & Wilkins.

Sedgwick, P. (1973). Illness—Mental or otherwise. *Hastings Center Reports, 1*(3).

Shore, B. (1981). Sexuality and gender in Samoa: Conceptions and missed conceptions. In S. B. Ortner & H. Whitehead (Eds.), *Sexual meanings: The cultural construction of gender and sexuality*. Cambridge: Cambridge University Press.

Siegelman, M. (1972). Adjustment of male homosexuals and heterosexuals. *Archives of Sexual Behavior*, *2*, 9-25.

Siegelman, M. (1974). Parental background of male homosexuals and heterosexuals. *Archives of Sexual Behavior*, *3*, 3-18.

Spitzer, R. & Wilson, P. (1975). Nosology and official psychiatric nomenclature. In A. M. Freedman, H. I. Kaplan, & B. J. Sadock (Eds.), *Comprehensive textbook of psychiatry* (2nd ed.). Baltimore: Williams & Wilkins.

Talikka, A. (1975). Uusia tutkimustuloksia. *Seta*, *3*, 13-15.

Thompson, N. L., McCandless, B. R. & Strickland, B. (1971). Personal adjustment of male and female homosexuals and heterosexuals. *Journal of Abnormal Psychology*, *78*, 237-240.

Turner, R. K., Pielmaier, H., James, S. & Orwin, A. (1974). Personality characteristics of male homosexuals referred for aversion therapy: A comparative study. *British Journal of Psychiatry*, *125*, 447-449.

Weinberg, T. S. (1983). *Gay men, gay selves: The social construction of homosexual identities*. New York: Irvington.

Weinberg, M. S. & Williams, C. J. (1974). *Male homosexuals: Their problems and adaptations*. New York: Oxford University Press.

Whitehead, H. (1981). The bow and the burden strap: A new look at institutionalized homosexuality in native North America. In S. B. Ortner & H. Whitehead (Eds)., *Sexual meanings: The cultural construction of gender and sexuality*. Cambridge: Cambridge University Press.

Wikan, U. (1977). Man becomes woman: Transsexualism in Oman as a key to gender roles. *Man*, *12*, 304-319.

Homosexuals in Eastern Europe: Mental Health and Psychotherapy Issues

Antonin Brzek, MD
Slavomil Hubalek, PhD
Prague, Czechoslovakia

Homosexuals in Eastern Europe face many problems similar to those encountered by their counterparts in the West. In addition, they must deal with problems that arise because of the socialist governments under which they live. This article will discuss both types of problems and will then present how various mental health professionals in at least one Eastern European country, Czechoslovakia, attempt to help homosexuals deal with their problems. First, it is appropriate to consider the general legal and social standing of the homosexual minority in Eastern Europe.

LEGAL AND SOCIAL STATUS

The status of homosexuals from the point of view of criminal law differs in various countries in Eastern Europe (Kosela, n.d.). (In this article, the term Eastern Europe includes the Soviet Union and the European socialist countries; i.e., Bulgaria, Czechoslovakia, Hungary, the German Democratic Republic, Romania, and Poland.) Homosexual behavior was not considered a criminal offense in the U.S.S.R. after the revolution in 1917. However, in 1934 it became a felony. Since then, male homosexuals have been subject to mandatory prosecution. (The criminal code makes no mention of homosexual behavior among women.) Homosexual behavior is also

Dr. Brzek and Dr. Hubalek conduct research and lead psychotherapy groups at the Institute of Sexology in Prague. Correspondence may be addressed to Dr. Brzek, Institute of Sexology, Charles University, Karlovo nam. 32, 121-11 Praha 2, Czechoslovakia.

153

a criminal offense in Romania. In the other socialist countries, homosexual behavior is not a criminal offense generally — only when other circumstances are involved, such as homosexual contact with a minor, abuse of a defenseless or a mentally impaired person, use of violence, performance of homosexual behavior in exchange for payment, or participation in homosexual activity in public (Czechoslovakia).

In Czechoslovakia and the German Democratic Republic, a person under 18 years of age is considered a minor, and adult sexual conduct with such a person is illegal. Hungary's laws vary slightly in that sexual contacts between a person over 20 with someone under 20 are a criminal offense, while sex between persons under 20 and persons between 14 and 20 is not. In Poland, having sex with a person 15 years of age or younger is a criminal offense whether that person is of the same or a different sex.

The marginal social status of Eastern European homosexuals outside the area of criminal justice does not differ substantially from that in Western Europe and the United States. Naturally the situation is worse in those countries where homosexual behavior is a criminal offense. However, some Asian Republics of the U.S.S.R., and above all Armenia, are an exception. There, homosexual behavior is tolerated more by the public (but not by the criminal code) in light of the historical conditions in those areas. In countries where the mandatory prosecution of homosexuality has been abolished, the public is gradually learning to become more tolerant — the highest degree of tolerance being displayed in the German Democratic Republic.

Generally speaking, mental health specialists (and to a lesser extent, medical physicians) in Eastern Europe are very tolerant toward homosexuality. Yet, although a higher degree of tolerance can be found among the more educated, the majority of people in these societies are still intolerant toward it.

With the exception of the German Democratic Republic (discussed below), very few opportunities exist in Eastern Europe for homosexuals to associate with one another. Homosexuals have no opportunities to join associations or clubs where they can make contact with those with similar personal concerns, explore their own identity, identification patterns, and sexual preference, or help each other and publicly advocate their group interests. Citizen associations in Eastern Europe can exist only on a state-organized basis and are expected, above all, to support government policies. Thus, it is next to impossible to obtain approval for an association of homosexual citizens. Nor can restaurants, bars, saunas, or other facilities for homosexuals be established because all means of production as well as provision of services is government-owned.

In countries where it is impossible to own a restaurant privately, as in Czechoslovakia, homosexuals have the opportunity to meet publicly only in those establishments whose service personnel are sympathetic toward them. In Prague, for example, there are two wine cellars with disco programs where the customers are almost exclusively homosexual, as well as certain restaurants where homosexuals tend to meet; but such public places are only found in large cities. (It is interesting to note that they can also be found in countries that prosecute homosexuality.) In countries where restaurants can be privately owned (e.g., the German Democratic Republic), an owner can give priority to homosexual customers, thus providing a meeting place for them. But it is never possible for such a place to be officially set aside for members of the homosexual subculture, or for its name to imply this. Even in the German Democratic Republic, where the largest number of restaurants that bring homosexuals together can be found and where public attitudes are the most tolerant, there are some homosexuals who consider a visit to such a place socially impossible because of public opinion.

There are no journals or magazines in Eastern Europe published by or for homosexuals, or indirectly aimed at the homosexual subculture. Nor are imports of such journals allowed.

Becoming acquainted with a partner through advertisements in state-controlled newspapers (and there are no others) has recently become possible in the German Democratic Republic. In Czechoslovakia it had been possible through hints and allusions; for example, a person was sought for sharing a common interest such as hiking, going to concerts, and so on. But even such advertisements are now forbidden in Czechoslovakia (as of this writing).

Thus, most East European homosexuals are forced to seek out sexual partners anonymously in public toilets, steam baths, saunas, or swimming pools. No such facility can be set aside specifically for such purposes, as in Western Europe, for instance. All such facilities in Eastern Europe serve the general public or some sports club, places where homosexuals will always be invisible.

SEX EDUCATION

Training programs for professionals who deal with homosexuals devote very little attention to this subject in those countries which have mandatory prosecution of homosexuality. For example, textbooks for teachers in the Soviet Union mention homosexuality as a "dangerous perversion and criminal offense."

In countries where homosexuality is not mandatorily prosecuted, medical students receive adequate information about homosexuality and are encouraged to develop tolerant attitudes.

The mass media generally avoid any mention of the subject. In recent years, homosexuality has received tolerant media coverage only in the German Democratic Republic.

JOB DISCRIMINATION

In the socialist countries most workers are employed in state-owned enterprises. All aspects of hiring and terminating an employee are set out in general labor codes and are uniform for the whole country. No official instructions exist which discriminate against homosexuals, other than they cannot work in the police force or as professional soldiers. Discrimination can occur, however, when an employer gives vent to his intolerant attitudes. Employees thus discriminated against can be vindicated if they carry their objections through the proper legal channels. Such difficulties are more frequently encountered by teachers and educators. Employers do not actively investigate whether a job candidate is homosexual or has a criminal record; if he does not use his occupation as a way of making homosexual contacts and does not "scandalize" his colleagues by displaying overt homosexual behavior, he will not be discriminated against. (Homosexuals who have been successful in keeping their sexual lives secret can, in fact, also be found in the army and police.)

PERSPECTIVES

With the exception of the German Democratic Republic, there is no trend in Eastern Europe to change existing criminal codes relating to homosexuality. A slow improvement in public attitudes, hand in hand with increased education about homosexuality, is probably all that can be expected.

Recent developments in this area in the German Democratic Republic have been interesting. The citizens of the German Democratic Republic are much better informed about homosexuality than are the citizens of other Eastern European countries, due in large part to programs shown on television in the Federal Republic of Germany that deal openly with the problems of homosexuals.

In the early 1970s a number of homosexuals in the German Democratic Republic attempted to create an organization within the framework of a government-approved platform. They were not successful. However, their efforts did result in several lectures organized by Urania, a government-controlled institution for education outside the school system.

At the beginning of the 1980s, homosexuals began to organize within the framework of the Lutheran Church, the predominant Christian denomination in the German Democratic Republic. Such a development was possible due only to the relative freedom which the church enjoys in that country. In contrast, in Czechoslovakia the state probably would not tolerate such activities within the framework of any church.

In 1981 an ad hoc group was formed in the German Democratic Republic within the framework of the Student Protestant Association (Arbeitskreis Homosexualitat, Evangelische Studentengemeinde) in Leipzig. Somewhat similar groups are also being organized in other cities. These groups aim to help homosexuals meet one another under socially acceptable conditions, establish their social identity within such a group, identify potential life partners, achieve a greater understanding of themselves, and develop a satisfying lifestyle. Lectures and discussions are organized to inform homosexuals about problems they face, as well as to educate their parents. Cultural activities are also organized — evenings of poetry by homosexual poets, Christmas parties, and so on. These activities are also significant in that they inform the public regarding the homosexual subculture and its problems.

Although it has provided homosexuals with a platform for organizing, the Lutheran Church is still hesitant and somewhat embarrassed by the problem of homosexuality. The church does not educate homosexuals or attempt to introduce specific aspects of Christian morality into their activities. Nor does it strive to counter the homosexual seduction of those individuals who are homosexually oriented but might be capable of adequate heterosexual and matrimonial adaptation.

The fact that in a country with a state Marxist ideology a group of homosexual citizens can organize on a church platform and be publicly active has attracted the exceptional attention of various governmental bodies. However, the situation has not yet provoked state-sponsored repression. Quite the opposite. Numerous articles expressing tolerance toward homosexuality have appeared in the press, written by mental health professionals who think the subject should be dealt with more openly than in the past. One positive indication of change was a scientific symposium held in Leipzig in June of 1985 on the psychosocial aspects of homosexuality.

Because the German Democratic Republic has not yet established its own Institute of Sexology, the Institute of Sexology in Prague was invited to send a member of its staff to present an introductory paper at the Leipzig symposium (Brzek, 1986). After that paper, two Marxist philosophers presented papers explaining that homosexuality does not contradict the morality of a socialist person. (Such an explanation is necessary in Eastern Europe if the phenomenon in question is to be officially acceptable.) Then, a representative of homosexuals, a protestant preacher, reported on the status of homosexual men in the German Democratic Republic, which was followed by an agricultural engineer's report on homosexual women in the same country. Finally, a clinical psychologist and pioneer of marriage and sex counseling in the German Democratic Republic submitted recommendations for the work of these counseling services. He compared homosexuality with heterosexuality as "objectively an entirely full-valued variant of human sexual behavior." After the round table, the chief organizer of the symposium and chairman of the Andrological Society of the Medical Association presented a summary in which he called homosexuality a variant of normal sexual behavior and argued that homosexual behavior should, in itself, not be considered immoral. He asked for tolerance toward homosexuals in restaurants and clubs and that they have the opportunity to seek partners through advertisements. He also urged that information concerning homosexuality be included in teacher training curriculums and in the education of psychologists, physicians, biologists, and other specialists.

In spite of this theoretical, and extremely tolerant, official attitude toward homosexuality, employing homosexuals in the police force or army is not under consideration in the German Democratic Republic. Nor is a change in the criminal code. The only official tolerance is seen in the instructions given to the courts to be lenient in adult/minor sexual contact cases in which the minor involved is almost 18 years old, and to convict the adults involved only in exceptional cases.

PATHOLOGIES

The lack of tolerance of homosexuality by most of Eastern European society leads, as it does in Western Europe, to negative phenomena and medical and social pathologies. The mechanism which gives rise to these phenomena is based on the fact that when a homosexual realizes his deviant orientation, he is not prepared for this revelation, does not find homosexual role models in his environment, and thus tries unsuccessfully to identify with heterosexual patterns and persons. The persons he attempts to identify with have no understanding of his homosexuality and, in turn, the homosexual person has difficulty understanding himself. As a result, maladaptation and malidentification occur in place of identification and social adaptation. Pathological psychiatric phenomena can include neurotic symptoms, depression, suicide, alcoholism, and drug abuse. An inferiority complex may also develop and lead to hyper-compensation in the form of striving to advance occupationally at all costs, or lead to the development of split personalities.

In the area of venerology, widespread promiscuity among male homosexuals (partially caused by their need to remain anonymous) leads to a high incidence of sexually transmitted diseases, above all syphilis and hepatitis B. In Eastern Europe only a few cases of AIDS have been officially recorded. In Czechoslovakia four cases had been reported as of March 31, 1976.

In the area of social pathology, attempts to keep their sexual life secret from members of their own peer group can lead some homosexuals to seek contacts with members of the criminal subculture. Such contacts sometimes influence them to participate in the nonsexual criminality of this subculture (Brzek, 1985). The fact that an adult person can be legally punished if he has a sexual contact with a minor leaves him vulnerable to extortion by a minor (Cerny, 1979). In addition, homosexuals are frequently murdered.

Attempts by homosexuals to hide their sexual orientation through matrimony can lead to dysfunctional, unhappy marriages. Such marriages can generate further psychopathology and have negative effects on the rearing and mental health of children.

THERAPY

In countries which prosecute homosexuals on a mandatory basis, the whole phenomenon of homosexuality is primarily the concern of lawyers and the courts — not therapists.

In the other Eastern European countries (perhaps with the exception of the German Democratic Republic — see above) homosexuality is considered from a medical standpoint to be not quite a disease, but an abnormality — a disorder of sexual health that makes life more difficult and complicated but not one that justifies discrimination. This is also the stance taken by the Institute of Sexology in Prague (Brzek, 1985), as well as psychiatrists and psychologists there who treat homosexuals.

Kurt Freund made a large-scale attempt in Czechoslovakia in the 1950s to change the sexual orientation of homosexuals to a heterosexual orientation through the use of behavioral aversive therapy. He was singularly unsuccessful, openly admitted it, and terminated the whole project. At present, few therapists in Eastern Europe hope to change successfully the homosexual orientation of a person through existing therapies. Only in the U.S.S.R. have there been recent attempts to cure homosexuality, there through the use of autogen training (Vasilitchenko, 1983).

Even if a homosexual orientation is unalterable, its depth is not the same in all homosexuals. Some homosexual men are capable not only of learning to have sexual intercourse with a suitable woman, but also of creating a well-functioning and happy marriage. Having and rearing children within a traditional heterosexual marriage can provide a meaningful alternative existence for some homosexual men. The Institute of Sexology in Prague strives to provide such adaptable men with as much aid and support as possible in this process, aiming to help avoid marriages which would not function properly and lead to further psychopathological phenomena.

If homosexual men are to adapt appropriately to marriage and parenthood, the following conditions should be met. First, the individual's motivation should be strong and authentic, as evidenced by a desire to procreate and rear offspring. False motivation, on the other hand, is evidenced by attempts to take refuge in marriage when faced with an intolerant environment, and by attempts to adapt to what is, for the patient, an unsatisfactory social environment. Second, after spending considerable time with a suitable woman, the homosexual male patient should experience a continued sense of well-being. He should not feel annoyance, discomfort, or otherwise unexplained fatigue. Third, there should be an exceptionally good rapport between the patient and his spouse in the nonsexual sphere. Fourth, the patient should be capable of frequent coital activity with his spouse without dysfunction. And fifth, in the course of living with his spouse, the patient should be capable of giving up even incidental homosexual contacts.

The role of therapists in this adjustment process is limited. They can provide aid to patients who are beginning coital activity by administering drugs and by providing supportive therapy, and possibly also training therapy following the methods of Kaplan (1974) or Kratochvil (1982) just as they do with sexual dysfunctions in heterosexual persons. Otherwise, therapists are basically limited to warning their patients against assessing their situation too optimistically or unrealistically. Most homosexuals who are motivated toward heterosexual adjustment strive for it without the help of a therapist, but what they achieve is often closer to maladaptation than to adaptation. The therapist cannot significantly strengthen the patient's capacity to adapt. His main function is the prevention of maladaptation. For this reason, few homosexuals successfully adapt to heterosexual life as the direct result of therapy. Most such therapeutic attempts end with the patient realizing that he is incapable of such an adjustment, and subsequently returning to the homosexual subculture.

Better therapeutic results are achieved with those homosexual men who, after a period of living in a well-functioning and happy marriage, seek help because that marriage has entered a difficult phase characterized by problems such as the discovery of infidelity with another homosexual, sexual dysfunction, or marital disharmony. Such men are probably examples of those who originally did not require any help in the adaptation process.

Because most male homosexual patients are not capable of authentic heterosexual and matrimonial adaptation, their contacts with sexologists, psychiatrists, or clinical psychologists are limited to supportive therapy which helps them accept their sexual orientation, discover their own homosexual identity, and improve their lives. Our ultimate goal has been to help homosexuals establish permanent love partnerships.

Providing homosexuals with more systematic help in adjusting to their homosexuality is better served by group therapy, which in

Czechoslovakia is provided by two clinics, the Institute of Sexology in Prague, and the Sexological Unit of the Department of Psychiatry of the Medical School in Brno (Bartova, 1979). The group in Brno is similar to a social club for patients, and treats homosexual men, women, and transsexuals together. The Prague group places greater emphasis on a psychodynamic approach. (We have no information about such group therapy existing in other Eastern European countries.) Individual therapy for homosexuals is usually limited to incidental contact for help with secondary psychopathological symptoms.

In the context of therapy for homosexuals, we should also mention requests which arise for sex reassignment. In Western European countries, requests for male-to-female reassignment predominate. In contrast, in Czechoslovakia, where sex reassignment has been carried out for a number of years without resistance from the legal system, female-to-male reassignments predominate (Brzek & Sipova, 1983). This situation appears to be similar in other Eastern European countries where sex reassignment is carried out. It is also interesting to note that some female transsexuals in Eastern Europe are diagnosed as masculine homosexual women in Western Europe. And conversely, homosexual men considered effeminate in Eastern Europe are diagnosed as male transsexuals in Western Europe.

REFERENCES

Bartova, D. (1979). Skupinova psychoterapie pacientus poruchami psychosexualni identifikace (Group therapy of patients suffering from gender identity disorders). Czech., *Moravskoslezsky Referatovy Sbornik, 11*, 92-94.

Brzek, A. (1985). Pohlavni zivot homosexualu (Sexuality of homosexuals). Czech., *Prakt. Lek., 65*(13), 499-501.

Brzek, A. (1986). Psychosoziale aspekte der homosexualitat (Psychosocial aspects of homosexuality). German, Symposium suppl., *Psychosoziale Aspekte der Homosexualitat*, 9-17. Jena: University Press.

Brzek, A. & Sipova, I. (1983). Transsexuelle in Prag. (Transsexuals in Prague). German, *Sexualmedizin, 9*(13), 110-112.

Cerny, V. (1979). Problemy homosexualni prostituce (The problems of homosexual prostitution). Czech., *Kriminalisticky Sbornik, 23*(9), 560-563.

Kaplan, H. S. (1974). *The new sex therapy*. New York: Brunnel/Mazel.

Kosela, J. (n.d.). Homosexualita a jeji trestnost (Homosexuality and penal law). Czech.

Kratochvil, S. (1982). *Terapie funkcnich sexualnich poruch.* (Therapy of sexual dysfunction). Czech., Praha: Avicenum Press.

Vasiltchenko, G. S. (1983). *Tchastnaja sexopatologia II* (Special sexology). Russian, Moscow: Medicina Press.

The Stigmatization of the Gay and Lesbian Adolescent

A. Damien Martin, EdD
Emery S. Hetrick, MD
New York University

As long ago as the 19th Century, Iwan Bloch (1937), the European sexologist whose work so influenced Freud, wrote that:

> . . . [in most homosexuals] manifestations of nervousness and neurasthenia beyond doubt, have developed during life out of an originally healthy state, in consequence of the struggle for life, the painful experience of being "different" from the great mass of people. (p. 490)

Bloch's comment, although referring primarily to adult homosexuals, applies equally well to gay and lesbian adolescents. Although medically based diagnosis and treatment is the traditional approach to the problems of homosexually oriented adolescents, (Socarides, 1978) the cognitive dissonance (Festinger, 1957) that characterizes so much of their emotional and psychological state arises from their membership in a hated and despised minority group—that is, from "the painful experience of being different."

Objections to minority group status for homosexuals have been examined elsewhere (Martin, 1982b). Nevertheless, it may be well

Dr. Martin is Associate Professor in the Department of Communication Arts and Sciences, School of Education, Health, Nursing and Arts Professions (SEHNAP), New York University, and Acting Executive Director and Co-founder of the Institute for the Protection of Lesbian and Gay Youth, Inc.

Dr. Hetrick was a psychiatrist in private practice, and Adjunct Clinical Associate Professor of psychiatry at New York University Medical Center, a co-founder of the Institute for the Protection of Lesbian and Gay Youth, Inc., and the President of its Board.

Correspondence may be addressed to Dr. Martin, 144 East 36th Street, No. 9B, New York, NY 10016.

to define the term as used here. A minority group is any group that suffers from unjustified negative treatment from the dominant group (Allport, 1958). In other words, a minority group is any group that is the victim of prejudice.

An approach based on an understanding of the effects of minority group status provides an alternative to the medically based approaches of the past while in no way implying that gay and lesbian youth are not heir to all the problems faced by humankind, including illnesses like schizophrenia and bi-polar illness. A sociological framework allows for identification of problems and issues shared with other stigmatized groups, as well as specification of those intrapsychic and behavioral problems and issues that are specific to homosexually oriented adolescents. For example, Goffman (1963) pointed out:

> By definition, of course, we believe the person with a stigma is not quite human. On this assumption, we exercise varieties of discrimination, through which we effectively, if often unthinkingly, reduce his life chances. We construct a stigma theory, an ideology to explain his inferiority and account for the danger he represents. (p. 5)

Individual members of a stigmatized group must learn to cope with the intra- and interpersonal implications of the ideology specific to their group. For homosexually oriented adolescents, the psychological, emotional, and social consequences will probably involve ego-dystonic reactions, including but not limited to coping strategies found in all stigmatized groups, such as denial of group membership, withdrawal and passivity, identification with the dominant group with resulting self-hate, aggression against one's own group, and self-fulfilling negativism (Allport, 1958; Hetrick & Martin, 1984; Martin, 1984; Blair, 1982; Baker, 1985).

PRESENTING PROBLEMS

The following discussion will center around the presenting problems of clients at a social service agency serving homosexually oriented adolescents. The authors founded The Institute for the Protection of Lesbian and Gay Youth, Inc. (IPLGY) in 1979. Originally intended as an advocacy group for young people denied services because of their sexual orientation, the group soon moved into a educational mode, providing professional education to youth-serving agencies. In November of 1983, IPLGY opened in New York City as a full social service agency providing services to gay and lesbian youth and their families.

In the first 2 years of operation over 2,000 young people asked for help. Of these requests, 60% involved telephone counseling and crisis intervention; 40% were from young people who came to the agency and underwent an intake interview with a social worker. Clients' ages ranged from 12 to 21, the legal range for defining youth in New York City and State. The median age of clients coming to the agency was 17 years, 1 month; the median age of clients who availed themselves of telephone counseling and crisis intervention was 15 years, 4 months. Of the clients, 40% were black, 35% white, 20% Hispanic, 2% Asian, and 3% "other." This ethnic and racial breakdown matched almost exactly the breakdown in the public school system of New York City. Sixty percent of the clients were male; 40% female. The socio-economic background of the clients ranged from the poverty-stricken through the middle classes to the children of wealthy parents, including children of United Nations diplomats. Similarly, religious backgrounds covered an extensive range, including Roman Catholic, Protestant, Jewish, Moslem, Buddhist, and Native American religions. The presenting problems discussed below are based on both the intake interviews and records of individual and group counseling.

Most problems of gay and lesbian adolescents are strongly interrelated. Yet we have found that each can and should be viewed separately. While this results in redundancy at times, it seems to be a necessary redundancy.

ISOLATION

Isolation is the most prevalent and, for many gay and lesbian adolescents, the most serious problem they face. The isolation is three-fold: cognitive, social, and emotional.

Cognitive isolation reflects the almost total lack of accurate information available to gay and lesbian adolescents. This lack of information, and thus the lack of preparation for management of social identity as homosexuals, is a major differentiator between homosexual adolescents and their heterosexual counterparts in other minority groups. Other minority adolescents, no matter how terrible the social or economic deprivation under which they may exist, have a chance to develop a sense of the "we" versus "they," the very essence of group identity. Dank (1971) highlighted this difference when he wrote:

> . . . the parents of a negro can communicate to their child that he is a negro and what it is like to be a negro, but the parents of a person who is to become homosexual do not prepare their child to be homosexual — they are not homosexual themselves and they do not communicate to him what it is like to be a homosexual. (p. 181)

Lack of appropriate information is not limited to absence of information. Received information is usually limited to the slanders of the "stigma theory." Gay and lesbian adolescents must deal with the most unbelievable antilocutions emanating from all levels of society. For example, in a book sold in many Catholic bookstores in the United States, a Jesuit priest, Father Herbert Smith, and a psychiatrist who teaches creative arts therapy, Dr. Joseph Dilenno (1979) stated:

> Most normal people hate and fear homosexual practices both because they fear their own passions, and because they are afraid for their own children . . . Their fears are not empty. Besides being unnatural and sterile, homosexual acts are a contagious cause of tragedy, and destructive of the natural relationships between the sexes. For heterosexuals reproduce their own kind by the use of sex, but active homosexuals multiply by the abuse of sex — by moral contagion, and by seduction and rape. There are thousands of young boys in large American cities whose services have literally been bought by active homosexuals. It is for these reasons that religious and civil authorities oppose active homosexuality.

Needless to say, Father Smith and Dr. Dilenno did not mention the many more thousands of young girls "whose services have literally been bought by active" heterosexuals.

Homosexual adolescents may accept that homosexuals are predatory (Kardiner, 1954; Gilder, 1979), unsuitable for the "hard professions" (Voth, 1977; Decter, 1980), unable to form mature nonerotic relationships (Pattison & Pattison, 1980), inimical to the survival of the race (Socarides, 1975), criminal seducers (Rupp, 1980), haters of the opposite sex (Stearn, 1962; Kardiner, 1954;

Decter, 1980), immature and the victims of pathological development (Bieber et al., 1962), sexually disordered (Kaplan, 1983), the cause of crime in the streets (Christian anti-communist crusade, 1981) the second World War (Podhoretz, 1977), the Holocaust (Jackman, 1979), lowered SAT Scores (Falwell, 1984), and perhaps most damaging in recent years, the cause of AIDS.

The most immediate effect of such charges on a naive, developing adolescent is a cognitive dissonance that will radically affect the young person's sense of self.

> The standards he has incorporated from the wider society equip him to be intimately alive to what others see as his failing, inevitably causing him, if only for moments, to agree that he does indeed fall short of what he really ought to be. Shame becomes a central possibility, arising from the individual's perception of one of his own attributes as being a defiling thing to possess. (Goffman, 1963, p. 7)

As Festinger (1957) pointed out, accurate information can resolve such crippling cognitive dissonance. Yet, and this is the essence of the cognitive isolation under discussion here, it is this very tool that is denied to the gay or lesbian adolescent. There is little or no opportunity for the homosexually oriented adolescent to discover what it means to be homosexual. Therefore, they cannot plan or sometimes even conceive of a future for themselves (Hetrick & Martin, 1985).

Social Isolation. The negative self-view enforced by the denial of accurate information has both intra-psychic and social effects.

> The awareness of inferiority means that one is unable to keep out of consciousness the formulation of some chronic feeling of the worst sort of insecurity. . . . The fear that others can disrespect a person because of something he shows means that he is always insecure in his contact with other people; and this insecurity arises, not from mysterious and somewhat disguised sources, as a great deal of our anxiety does, but from something which he knows he cannot fix. Now that represents an almost fatal deficiency of the self system, since the self is unable to disguise or exclude a definite formulation that reads, "I am inferior. Therefore, people will dislike me and I cannot be secure with them." (Perry, Gawel, & Gibbon, 1956, p. 145)

Social role by definition involves a set of expectations as to what a person should do (Heiss, 1981). A social identity as a homosexual is so stigmatized, however, that it can lead to a denial of all other social roles for which the adolescent has been socialized (Goffman, 1963). For example, adolescents raised to be Christians are taught that one cannot be a Christian and a homosexual (Baker, 1985; Pattison & Pattison, 1980); adolescents who want to be teachers are told that one cannot be a homosexual and a teacher (Smith & Dilenno, 1979), and adolescents raised to be patriotic citizens are told that one cannot be a loyal American if one is homosexual (U.S. Senate, 1950). In a society in which the leading newspaper, the *New York Times*, can publish an essay that seriously recommends that homosexuals be tattooed on the buttocks as a precautionary identifying measure, without an opposing view published at the same time, and where even a father may indicate that the worst possible thing that could happen to his child is homosexuality (Epstein, 1970), it is not too surprising that the homosexual adolescent develops the self-hatred epitomized in ego-dystonic homosexuality. Sexual desire, a central aspect of the adolescent's developing self, becomes for the homosexual adolescent a threat to everything toward which he or she has been socialized.

Anti-gay activists often argue that homosexuals cannot be considered members of a minority group because, unlike blacks or women, homosexuals can choose to hide (Kelly, 1975; Bryant, 1977). The objection is invalid on several levels. First, not all homosexuals, including homosexual adolescents, can hide their sexual orientation; second, the ability to pass has nothing to do with minority group status. No one would say that a Jew in an antisemitic society is not a member of a minority group because the Jew could escape persecution by pretending to be Christian. Similarly, Catholics in Northern Ireland or light-skinned blacks in the United States are still considered to be minority group members, even though they can pass (Martin, 1982a).

Nevertheless, the ability or non-ability to pass has important implications for gay and lesbian adolescents. Goffman (1963) pointed out that passing divides the stigmatized into two groups: the discredited and the discreditable. Those that are discredited are those whose stigma is known or visible, for example, blacks in a racist society, Jews who must wear a yellow star of David, homosexual males who are "swish" or lesbians who are "butch." Those whose stigma is hidden or not known, but for whom discovery would be disastrous, are discreditable.

Gay and lesbian adolescents can fall into either category with problems that are similar and dissimilar at the same time. The young gay male who is discredited, either because he is "effeminate"[1] or because he has been discovered faces reactions ranging from public humiliation to violence. He can handle this mistreatment in several ways: truancy; withdrawal from activities in school or church, from family or friends; exaggeration of stigmatized behavior through gender deviant mannerisms, cross dressing, and inappropriate sexual acting out. Homosexual adolescents who can pass may also use some of these strategies because of pressures from fear of discovery. Both those who pass and do not pass may engage in dangerous and destructive behaviors. For example, we have had several cases of teenage lesbians who, as a means to hide, have become pregnant. They recognize that the family will accept an unwanted pregnancy more easily than a lesbian daughter. Other adolescent clients have married as a means to "prove" to themselves and others that they are not gay. Celibacy cults like the Christian "ex-gay" movement encourage defense mechanisms like reaction formation, denial, and compensation (Pattison & Pattison, 1980; Baker, 1985; Blair, 1982). For example, in one such cult, homosexuals are encouraged to accept Jesus' heterosexuality as their own and thus to declare themselves heterosexual, even though they still have homosexual desires (Cook, 1985). Denial of the meaning of homosexual desires and actions may be necessary for a time (Hetrick & Martin, 1984). Troiden (1979) found that all his gay male subjects went through a phase that he called "dissociation and signification" during which they recognized certain actions and feelings as homosexual, but denied their significance. Thus, overt homosexual acts became, "a phase," "something I would grow out of," "just because there weren't any girls around," and so forth.

These are not just self-chosen strategies. Adolescents who are discovered are often pushed by parents, counselors, health professionals, and religious zealots into attempts to change or to deny their orientation, despite evidence that such efforts are useless (Martin, 1985; Hetrick & Martin, 1981) or dangerous (Freund, 1977).

These efforts at denial are usually unsuccessful on some level and tend to intensify social isolation. At the least, they lead to a compartmentalizing of one's life. Denied the possibility of non-erotic, non-threatening interactions with their homosexual peers, gay or lesbian adolescents must associate with heterosexual peers who they believe will accept them only if they pose as heterosexual. Even those who hide successfully are socially isolated because the fear of discovery becomes an integral part of their lives. The decision to pass, coupled with the inevitable fear of discovery, is a pivotal differentiator between homosexual adolescents and their heterosexual counterparts in other minority groups (Martin, 1982a, 1982b; Hetrick & Martin, 1984). A Black, Jewish, or Hispanic youngster does not run the risk of being thrown out of the family for being Black, Hispanic, or Jewish; a homosexual adolescent does run that risk. A Black, Jewish, or Hispanic adolescent does not run the risk of losing a religious social identity for being Black, Jewish, or Hispanic; the homosexual adolescent does run that risk. Other minority adolescents do not run the risk of being expelled from their peer groups if they are discovered; the homosexual adolescent does run that risk.

Let us give two examples of the last possibility. One of our clients, a 15-year-old caucasian male from a well-to-do middle class family went to a private school. He suspected that he might be gay and shared this fear with his best friend. His friend, fearful that others might find out and think he was homosexual, immediately told the other boys in the class. The first young man had to leave school because of the subsequent harassment. The dangers of discovery do not come solely from peers, however. A 13-year-old female wrote a poem to her gym teacher. While the young woman did not identify as a lesbian, the gym teacher interpreted the poem in that way and went to the principal. He in turn told the young woman's parents that they could not keep a child "like that" in school. The only placement they could find for her was in a school for the learning disabled. The parents, fearful that their daughter might become publicly known as a lesbian and ashamed of her because they believed she was, refused to fight the principal's decision.

It must be noted that these actions affect not only the adolescents who are discovered, but hidden homosexually oriented adolescents who see what happens to the others. Fear that the same thing might happen to them intensifies their fear of discovery and leads them inexorably to the choice of the "discreditable" position, with all the emotional problems and social difficulties that it represents.

Social isolation, with its consequent emotional and social pressure, seems to be of a paramount importance in adolescent promiscuity, especially among gay males, as discussed in an earlier paper (Martin, 1982a). The teenage gay male, isolated within his family, his neighborhood, religious organization, and school may soon learn that he can make "contact" in certain neighborhoods, bookstores, movies, and parks (Roesler & Deisher, 1972). Unfortunately, this contact is usually sexual in nature. For a few furtive moments the adolescent can achieve some relief from the overpowering tension of hiding. His obsessive concern with his sexual orientation, which results from his fear of disclosure, is transformed into an obsessive concern for sexual behavior. The casual sexual contact also helps to maintain hiding, as it becomes a means to compartmentalize his life and to separate sexual behavior from all other aspects of his life. The setting, the danger, and the type of individuals who exploit young people in this way all tend to reinforce the belief that a homosexual orientation is all that society has said it is—sick, deviant, despicable. The negative self image is intensified. In addition, he grows to view his partners and by extension all homosexual people in the same way, further hindering the development of social networks that will offer support and accurate information.

One product of IPLGY's socialization groups has been a reduction in promiscuous behavior by many of the male clients. The presence of other gay and lesbian teenagers in a supervised setting has led to behaviors, especially dating behaviors, similar to those practiced by their heterosexual counterparts.

Emotional Isolation. Feelings of being alone, of being the only one who feels this way, of having no one to share feelings with, are reported by over 95% of our clients. These complaints do not come only from adolescents living at home. When we were first starting IPLGY, we carried out an informal needs survey of teenage gay males, most of whom were involved in the street scene. We asked them what they would like to have if we were to set up an organization. All of them said they would like to be able to talk to someone gay, especially an adult gay person, without having to worry about "coming across."

In a book that extolled the "Ex-gay" message, a young man tried to explain his feeling of emotional isolation:

Why can't we say where we are really hurting? . . . I was desperate — I wanted to tell you how much I need your help but I couldn't . . . I was convinced that the only way I could be accepted was to remain hidden. I was sure that no one would love me if they knew. . . . I was desperate. I couldn't continue. I withdrew from school and almost killed myself. (Baker, 1985, pp. 76-77)

Bell and Weinberg (1978) reported that 20% of the gay male subjects in their study attempted suicide before the age of 20. Saghir and Robins (1973) reported that 18% of their gay male subjects had attempted suicide before the age of 20. Twenty-one percent of our clients had attempted suicide by the time they came to us; each reported that a factor in their attempt was feeling totally alone with no one to talk to.

Many symptoms of emotional disturbance appear related to isolation. Repeatedly, young people come to IPLGY showing signs of clinical depression — pervasive loss of pleasure, feelings of sadness, change of appetite, sleep disturbance, slowing of thought, lowered self-esteem with increased self-criticism and self-blame, and strongly expressed feelings of guilt and failure. Again, they repeatedly report they feel they are alone in the world, that no one else is like them, and that they have no one with whom they can confide or talk freely.

Yet once they are introduced to their peers, once they are given the opportunity to interact with others who are homosexually oriented in a non-threatening, non-erotic atmosphere, many of these feelings disappear. Emotional isolation, of course, is intricately entwined with both cognitive and social isolation. When the young person has the example of adult as well as peer role models, when the adolescent has someone to talk to openly and has access to accurate information, emotional isolation tends to resolve.

The closet. Social management of stigma through the secrecy affects not only the homosexually oriented; it also affects those who interact with homosexuals, especially professionals who deal with adolescents. In a needs survey of youth serving professionals conducted by IPLGY (Robinson & Martin, 1983), 23% reported no experience dealing with gay or lesbian adolescents, and 69% reported working with less than six during the previous year. Yet most of the professionals responding admitted that, especially in those programs that deal with runaway and homeless youth, homosexually oriented adolescents make up a high percentage of the population.

This finding has two possible interpretations: first, few gay and lesbian youth actually apply for services; second, service providers may work with more lesbian and gay youth than they realize. The first may indeed be a factor. Many of our "street" clients will not go to regularly established agencies because they are afraid. When we referred one homeless client to the largest Catholic youth shelter in New York, he refused, stating "I'd rather take my chances with a kinky John. It's safer." Hunter and Martin (1983) found that among middle-class young people, fear of humiliation often prevented gay and lesbian youth from taking advantage of already available services. This situation has been exacerbated in New York City by the recent law suits by religious social service agencies claiming the right to discriminate against the homosexually oriented.

Nevertheless, there are many unrecognized gay adolescents in client case loads. The number is difficult to determine for several reasons. First, sexual orientation is often ignored, denied, or not considered relevant to the provision of services and thus may not be elicited on intake forms or in client interviews. Second, service providers, often unaware of the numbers of lesbian and gay youth in society, and identifying these youth largely on the basis of cultural stereotypes, may assume that all of their clients are heterosexual. Third, fear of exposure as homosexual often causes many gay and lesbian youth to hide, thus increasing their invisibility within the youth service system. For example, we have had nine clients who were under treatment for suicide attempts but who had not yet told their therapists either that they were homosexual or that that was a factor in the suicide attempt. Fourth, administrative attitudes within the agency may discourage appropriate record keeping or staff training. For example, Roman Catholic social service agencies in New York City will not allow any training on homosexuality that is believed to contradict Church teaching on the subject and some Catholic agencies are not allowed to make referrals to IPLGY. Finally, the very subject of homosexuality and young people creates feelings of fear in homosexual, as well as heterosexual, service providers. At a recent conference of gay-and lesbian-identified health professionals, the first question from a physician was, "How can I risk openly working with gay youth? I would be accused of recruiting and could lose my practice." In the needs survey (Robinson &

Martin, 1983), 61% of the heterosexual respondents feared negative reactions if they or their agencies openly addressed the problems of gay and lesbian youth. Their fears included negative staff assumptions about the respondents' sexual identity with a subsequent endangerment of their jobs, and negative reactions from the community, funding agencies, staff, and supervisors. All respondents reported negative effects on the development and delivery of services to homosexual clients.

If adult professionals, skilled in their work and capable of defending themselves, are afraid to address the issue of homosexuality, is it any wonder that homosexually oriented adolescents stay hidden, and thus isolated, even within those agencies that are supposedly there to help them.

FAMILY

The second most frequent presenting problem is difficulties with the family, which range from feelings of isolation and alienation that result from fear that the family will discover the adolescent's homosexuality, to actual violence and expulsion from the home.

The primary familial problem for the adolescent, even for the homeless adolescent, lies in the cognitive dissonance that arises from a knowledge of the family's expectations and the contradiction that the adolescent's homosexuality poses for those expectations. This sense of contradiction and failure in turn leads to guilt, shame, anger, and a not unfounded fear of rejection. Again, without accurate information, without the opportunity to lessen one's isolation and sense of failure through socialization with peers and adult role models, without the chance to share one's fears and problems with another human being, the adolescent can become progressively more alienated, more depressed, and more isolated.

Parents face similar problems with their realization of a child's homosexuality. Joseph Epstein, a self-described liberal and fighter for civil rights wrote the following for *Harper's* a few years ago:

> They are different from the rest of us. Homosexuals are different, moreover, in a way that cuts deeper than other kinds of human differences—religious, class, racial, in a way that is, somehow more fundamental. Cursed without clear cause, af-

flicted without apparent cure, they are an affront to our rationality . . . there is much that my four sons can do in their lives that might cause me anguish, that might outrage me, that might make me ashamed of them and myself as their father. But nothing they could ever do would make me sadder than if any of them were to become homosexual. (Epstein, 1970, p. 51)

Unfortunately, Mr. Epstein's attitude is not uncommon among parents. Such parental reactions should not be surprising. Like others in our society, they have been taught that gay people are sick, despicable, trivial, and dangerous, that homosexuality is one of the most shameful conditions known to man. They have also been taught, incorrectly, that they are the cause of their child's homosexuality (Bieber et al. 1962; Socarides, 1978; Siegleman, 1974, 1981; Bell, Weinberg & Hammersmith, 1981). Not unexpectedly, parents react with guilt and anger toward their child and each other.

While IPLGY has a family therapy program, several factors inhibit its growth and practice. Confidentiality limits outreach because most clients fear discovery. Family resistance to discussion of the homosexuality one of its members, a resistance strongly supported by social custom and taboo (Goffman, 1963), hinders the implementation of family therapy. Denial ranging from denial of the truth of the discovery to a denial of the child is a third factor. In the former case, families will often insist it is just a phase and there is no need for counseling; in the latter case, the family may expel the adolescent from the home and refuse to have anything to do with attempts at reconciliation. A fourth impediment may be the parents' feeling that a gay-and lesbian-identified agency can not empathize with their feelings as heterosexual parents. Here the resistance lies not so much toward counseling but toward the source of counseling.

Nevertheless, a number of families do seek help in dealing with the shock of discovering a child's homosexuality, and through such counseling are often successful in dealing with it. As with the gay or lesbian adolescent, appropriate and accurate information is often the best therapy. Parents need to learn that evidence indicates that familial background appears to have nothing to do with the development of homosexuality or heterosexuality and that their child is still the child they loved before.

VIOLENCE

The third most frequent presenting problem is violence. By the time they come to IPLGY, over 40% of our clients have suffered from violence because of their sexual orientation. Forty-nine percent of that violence occurs within the family, usually from parents but sometimes from siblings. In a recent conference for New York City high school counselors, participants rated violence as the major problem of homosexually oriented high school students. It must be understood that these counselors usually interact with the discredited effeminate adolescent rather than the student who is successfully hiding. Those at highest risk for violence in all situations are those youngsters who are discredited, usually those who are perceived as effeminate.

When the violence occurs within the family, running away or expulsion from the home are often the immediate result, with prostitution a secondary consequence (Deisher, Robinson & Boyer, 1982; James, 1982). When violence occurs within the school setting, dropping out may be the only solution because most schools refuse even to discuss homosexuality, much less address the problem of violence against the homosexually oriented. Similarly, social service agencies including emergency shelters will admit that they are powerless to protect homosexually identified youngsters in their care. Often as a safety measure, they will put them back on the streets rather than keep them in the shelter.

Rape is a prevalent form of violence against gay and lesbian adolescents, especially in institutional settings. For the gay male in particular, identification as homosexual in a group home or shelter makes rape probable rather than possible. In many instances, the young gay person who is raped is blamed for bringing it on himself. Counselors and childcare workers often see the solution to such violence as the expulsion of the young man who has been attacked. The idea that the victims of homophobic violence are the cause of such violence is not limited to unfeeling or poorly educated childcare workers. Stoller (1975) wrote that homosexual hatred of parents and society, as well as a homosexual's wish to be discovered, is the cause of violence against the homosexual. Stoller's explanation, superficial though it is, may contain a grain of truth. In some few cases, violence against the gay youth may be apparently triggered by the young person's "flaunting."

Flaunting. Some people view simple openness and frankness

about a homosexual orientation, regardless of the accompanying behavior, as "flaunting" and therefore as a hostile act. Others reserve that term for markedly deviant social behavior such as cross-dressing. Although service providers need to clarify for themselves what they mean when using certain terms and to question what those terms reveal about their attitudes and values, it is true that behaviors ranging from simple disclosure of sexual orientation to cross-dressing can evoke major problems within an agency. Heterosexual peers often react with verbal, physical, or sexual abuse of homosexual youth. Service providers may then be torn between the rights and needs of lesbian and gay youth and the need to deal with the disruption caused by their presence or behavior. Lesbian and gay youth themselves may aggravate the situation with hostile acting-out behavior designed to elicit a response. It should be noted that such provocative behavior has been identified as a coping strategy in many minority groups.

The most often cited "flaunting behavior" is cross-dressing. Cross-dressing is not necessarily transvestism. Transvestism is the wearing of the clothing of the opposite sex usually as a means of sexual gratification. While not unknown among the gay and lesbian population, it is primarily a characteristic of the heterosexually oriented (Stoller, 1975). Cross-dressing may indicate transvestism or, for gay and lesbian youth, it may reflect other factors. First, it may be reactive behavior arising from one's minority position. In this case it becomes a means of coping with society's attitudes by exaggerating the behaviors expected by society. When this is the case, it resembles the behavior of a black who shuffles or exaggerates stereotypical "black" behaviors in the presence of whites. Second, cross-dressing may reflect an acceptance of cultural attitudes toward homosexuality. That is, if a male is attracted to a male, then he is not masculine, and therefore he must be feminine. If the young male[2] accepts this reasoning, he often feels that to be gay he must act feminine, and thus cross dresses. This latter factor of cultural expectation also plays a role in the declarations of some young people, especially Black and Hispanic youth, that they are transsexuals. They accept the cultural belief that if one is not "masculine," one is not a male, and therefore one must be a female. Some of our young clients have gone so far as to get hormone injections from unscrupulous physicians or pharmacists without any counseling or preparation for a sex change operation.

Problems with cross-dressing are twofold for the service provider. The most obvious is the disruption and violence that often occur when a young person, the young male in particular, cross-dresses. But there is also the issue of counseling for the cross-dresser himself. He or she must be protected from violence, even violence that occurs because of the individual's own provocative acts, but they must also be counseled as to the meaning of their own behavior. They must be advised as to their responsibility for the consequences when their cross-dressing is primarily an act of provocation, and as to the non-necessity of opposite-sex behavior as an expression of homosexuality. Our experience is that most cross-dressing youngsters, when educated about sexual orientation and exposed to appropriate role models, including peer role models, will often stop cross-dressing.

Youth service agencies are often unprepared to handle in any systematic way issues involving gay and lesbian youth. While space does not allow a detailed discussion of the management of problems elicited by openness of any kind, some suggestions can be offered.

1. Gay and lesbian youth should not have to conform to rules that do not apply to other youth. If there is a rule against affectional behavior, including kissing, holding hands, or necking, it should apply to both heterosexually and homosexually oriented youth. If there are dress codes, they should be applied equally. For example, the wearing of earrings by a heterosexual male will often be accepted as "punk" behavior and an appropriate form of adolescent rebellion; the homosexual male wearing the same earrings will be seen as "cross-dressing."

2. Verbal or physical abuse against gay or lesbian youth is a matter of abuse, not of sexual orientation. The mechanisms used for handling violence in other situations should apply here.

3. Help for the service providers who must deal with the disruption should always be provided. This help can and should include consultation services with gay- and lesbian-identified professional and community groups.

4. Education and training about sexuality, including information about homosexuality, should be directed toward both homosexually and heterosexually oriented youngsters.

5. Referral to an organization experienced in dealing with these problems must always be considered as a possible option.

EDUCATION

Most educational problems faced by gay and lesbian youth relate to issues already discussed. Lack of training, personal attitudes toward homosexuality, and the fear that teachers and other professionals have of addressing the issue, all affect the professional behavior of teachers and others in the educational setting.

The cognitive, social, and emotional isolation discussed above lie at the root of most of the educational problems presented by clients at IPLGY. Students reported they were afraid of discovery, tired of hiding, fearful that if they called attention to themselves by answering in class or attending gym class, they might be attacked or humiliated. Many wanted to drop out (32%), but were dissuaded. Participation in counseling and IPLGY's socialization groups often alleviated the isolation and provided sufficient support for the young people to stay in school. For many who had been discovered, however, especially effeminate males, school became too punishing and dangerous for them to stay. The Harvey Milk High School Program in New York City, run by IPLGY, is one attempt to serve these young people.

SEXUAL ABUSE

Twenty-two percent of our clients report sexual abuse. These reports usually do not occur during the initial intake or the first phone call, however. Before bringing it up with a counselor or in group, clients need a period within which to develop a sense of trust or, and this occurs frequently, the client comes to realize that what had happened was abuse.

Abuse and rape occur in the home, in institutional settings as already discussed, and when the young person, especially the adolescent male, is seeking sexual contact in a dangerous setting like a park, a highway rest area, a movie house, and so forth.

The patterns for sexual abuse and rape of adolescent lesbians follow generally the pattern reported in the literature on sexual abuse of young heterosexual females. Sexual abuse of adolescent lesbians living at home is more likely to be by a member of the family; young lesbians who run away from home are at high risk for rape and prostitution.

Contrary to expectations from the literature, many gay male adolescents have been sexually abused at home. This abuse is usually by an uncle or older brother, but sometimes by the father. Many male clients do not see themselves as abused or raped even when forced to perform acts that they did not wish to perform, or to perform them with people they did not desire. When it occurs within the family, the young male often feels he is to blame because he has sexual desires for men and therefore has brought it on himself. When it occurs outside the home, especially if the young male has been seeking sex, he again feels it was his fault no matter what happens. The phenomenon of self-blame and non-recognition of abuse for gay or lesbian adolescents is related in part to the development of an awareness of the limits of "no." Caught between childhood and adulthood, they often do not have a sense of their right and ability to say no. This difficulty is often exploited by adults who prey on these isolated young people.

Clients who are involved in juvenile prostitution frequently express hatred for themselves and the adult men with whom they have been involved. This hatred becomes especially intense for those adult males who offer them some semblance of emotional or physical security. Because this security is often dependent on the young person's behaving as the adult wants, the juvenile is often returned to the streets, feeling betrayed and abused.

One sees a slightly different pattern with young adolescent males living at home who become involved with "chicken hawks" (older men who prefer having sex with adolescent boys). Initially they report positive feelings because these men have been the only people with whom they could relate. But their feelings change as their options increase. For example, most young people involved in a sexual relationship with an adult will drop that relationship when they have the opportunity to interact with peers.

The major difficulties for young men caught in such relationships revolve around their developing an understanding of the dynamics of interpersonal relationships with men. Because the partners in so-called "intergenerational" relationships are automatically unequal with reference to power, young men involved with pederasts often develop interpersonal skills based on manipulation and sexual bartering. Again, interaction with peers in a non-threatening atmosphere offers the best possibility of developing interpersonal skills that will lead to what Troiden (1979) referred to as a healthy gay identity.

CONCLUSION

Homosexually oriented youth are victims of a society-wide process of stigmatization that has negative social, economic, and emotional effects on its victims. Within this process, young homosexually oriented people become either discredited or discreditable, and each state creates special conditions and problems, not only for the young people themselves but for those who must interact with them. Implicit within this framework is the notion that the youngsters' problems do not stem from their sexual orientation per se, but from the hatred that is directed toward them because of their orientation. Unfortunately, internalization of this hatred intensifies their problems.

NOTES

1. "Effeminate" is an inaccurate term because so-called effeminate behavior has little to do with the way women move, walk, or talk. It is a form of male behavior that differs from the established cultural norm. Similarly, "butch" behavior by the lesbian is not masculine behavior.

2. While lesbians may be penalized for "cross dressing," females have a much wider latitude in dressing than males. Males who deviate from gender expectations in dressing elicit much more severe and frequent reactions. This accounts in part for the far fewer reports of violence against lesbians in institutional settings because of so-called "acting-out behavior."

REFERENCES

Allport, G. (1985). *The nature of prejudice.* Garden City, NY: Doubleday.

Baker, D. (1985). *Beyond rejection: The Church, homosexuality and hope.* Portland, OR: Multnomah Press.

Bell, A. P. & Weinberg, M. S. (1978). *Homosexualities: A study of diversity among men and women.* New York: Simon & Schuster.

Bell, A. P., Weinberg, M. S. & Hammersmith, S. K. (1981). *Sexual preference: Its development in men and women.* Bloomington, IN: Indiana University Press.

Bieber, I., Dain, H., Dince, P., Drellich, M., Grand, H., Gundlach, R., Kremer, M., Rifkin, A., Wilbur, C. & Bieber, T. (1962). *Homosexuality: A psychoanalytic study of male homosexuals.* New York: Basic Books.

Blair, R. (1982). *Ex-gay.* New York: Homosexuality Counseling Center.

Block, I. (1937). *The sexual life of our time* (M. E. Paul, Trans), New York: Rebman, (Original work published 1908.)

Bryant, A. (1977). *The Anita Bryant story.* Old Tappan, NJ: Revell.

Buckley, W. F. (1986, March 18). *Crucial steps in combating the AIDS epidemic.* New York Times, pp. A-27.

Cook, C. (1985). *Homosexuality: An open door?* Boise, ID: Pacific Press Publishing Association.

Dank, B. M. (1971). Coming out in the gay world. *Psychiatry, 34*, 180-197.

Decter, M. (1980). The boys on the beach. *Commentary, 70*(3), 34-48.

Deisher, R., Robinson, G. & Boyer, D. (1982). The adolescent female and male prostitute. *Pediatric Annals, 11*(10), 819-825.

Epstein, J. (1970, September). Homo/hetero: The struggle for sexual identity. *Harper's*, pp. 36-51.

Falwell, J. (1984, April 24). Cited in Flax, E. Falwell packs Irvine for speech on conservatism. *The Daily Pennsylvanian*, pp. 1, 3.

Festinger, L. (1957). *A theory of cognitive dissonance*. Evanston, IL: Row, Peterson.

Freund, K. (1977). Should homosexuality arouse therapeutic concern? *Journal of Homosexuality, 2*, 235-240.

Gilder, G. (1979). Letters from readers. *Commentary, 67*, 4, 8, 12.

Goffman, E. (1963). *Stigma: Notes on the management of spoiled identity*. Englewood Cliffs, NJ: Prentice-Hall.

Heiss, J. (1981). Social roles. In M. Rosenberg and R. H. Turner (Eds.)., *Social psychology* (pp. 94-131). New York: Basic Books.

Hetrick, E. S. & Martin, A. D. (1981). More on "Ex-Gays": A response to Pattison and Pattison. *American Journal of Psychiatry, 138*, 1510-1511.

Hetrick, E. S. & Martin, A. D. (1984). Ego-dystonic homosexuality: A developmental view. In E. S. Hetrick & T. S. Stein (Eds.), *Innovations in psychotherapy with homosexuals* (pp. 2-21). Washington, DC: APA Press.

Hunter, J. & Martin, A. D. (1983). *A comparison of presenting problems in heterosexually and homosexually oriented youth at a student run referral service*. New York: IPLGY, Inc.

Jackman, A. I. (1979). *The paranoid homosexual basis of antisemitism and kindred hatred*. New York: Vantage Books.

James, J. (1982). *Entrance into juvenile male prostitution: Final report*. Washington, DC: The National Institute of Mental Health, Grant #RO1 MH 29968.

Kaplan, H. S. (1983). *The evaluation of sexual disorders*. New York: Brunner/Mazel.

Kardiner, A. (1954). *Sex and morality*. New York: Bobbs-Merrill.

Kelly, G. (1975). *The political struggles of active homosexuals to gain social acceptance*. Chicago: Franciscan Herald Press.

Martin, A. D. (1982a). Learning to hide: The socialization of the gay adolescent. In S. C. Feinstein, J. G. Looney, A. Schwartzberg & J. Sorosky, (Eds.), *Adolescent psychiatry: Developmental and clinical studies* (Vol. X, pp. 52-65). Chicago: University of Chicago.

Martin, A. D. (1982b). The minority question. *etcetera, 39*, 22-42.

Martin, A. D. (1984). The emperor's new clothes: Modern attempts to change sexual orientation. In E. S. Hetrick & T. S. Stein, (Eds.), *Innovations in psychotherapy with homosexuals* (pp. 23-57). Washington, DC: APA Press.

Pattison, E. M. & Pattison, M. L. (1980). "Ex-gays": Religiously mediated change in homosexuals. *American Journal of Psychiatry, 137*, 1553-1562.

Perry, H., Gawel, M. & Gibbon, M. (1956). *Clinical studies in psychiatry*. New York: Norton.

Podhoretz, N. (1977, October). The culture of appeasement. *Harper's*, pp. 25-32.

Robinson, G. & Martin, A. D. (1983). Problems and issues in the delivery of services to gay and lesbian youth: A needs survey, New York: IPLGY, Inc.

Roesler, T. & Deisher, R. (1972). Youthful male homosexuality. *Journal of American Medical Association, 219*, 1018-1023.

Rupp, J. C. (1980). Sex-related deaths. In W. Curren, A. L. McGarry & C. S. Petty (Eds.), *Modern legal medicine: Psychiatry and forensic science*. (pp. 575-588). Philadelphia: F. A. Davis.

Saghir, M. T. & Robins, E. (1973). *Male and female homosexuality*. Baltimore: Williams & Wilkins.

Schwarz, E. (Ed.). (1981). *Christian anticommunism crusade newsletter, 21*, 2-3.

Siegleman, M. (1974). Parental background of male homosexuals and heterosexuals. *Archives of Sexual Behavior, 3*, 3-18.

Siegelman, M. (1981). Parental background of homosexual and heterosexual men: A cross national replication. *Archives of Sexual Behavior, 10*, 505-513.

Smith, H. F. & Dilenno, J. (1979). *Sexual inversion: The questions: The church's answers*. Boston: Daughters of St. Paul.

Socarides, C. (1975). *Beyond sexual freedom*. New York: Quadrangle.

Socarides, C. (1978). *Homosexuality*. New York: Jason Aronson.

Stearn, J. (1962). *The sixth man*. New York: Quadrangle.

Stoller, R. J. (1975). *Perversion: The erotic form of hatred*. New York: Pantheon.

Troiden, R. (1979). Becoming homosexual: A model of gay identity acquisition. *Psychiatry, 42*, 362-373.

U. S. Senate (1950). *Employment of homosexuals and other sex perverts in government*. U. S. Senate, 81st Cong., 2nd sess., Committee on Expenditures in Executive Departments.

Voth, H. (1977). *The castrated family*. Kansas City, MO: Sheed, Andrews, & McMeel.

The Borderline Personality Disorder and Gay People

Charles Silverstein, PhD

New York City

SUMMARY. This paper examines the diagnostic category called Borderline Personality Disorder (BPD) and its relationship to gay people. It discusses the psychoanalytic definition of borderline personalities, and to it adds a cultural definition. In the light of these cultural variables, the diagnosis is defined as a metaphor for the complexities and confusions of modern life. These confusions are important in the lives of gay people, who, it is suggested, are currently more prone to be diagnosed as BPD. Through the life study of a gay man, both the psychoanalytic and cultural variables are identified, then generalized to the problems of gay people in our transitional society.

OBJECT RELATIONS THEORY

The Borderline Personality Disorder (BPD) is a diagnostic construct that originated in the modern psychoanalytic interest in object reactions theory (Kohut, 1971). This theory proposes that pregenital problems, particularly during the phase of separation/individuation of the child (18 to 36 months of age), lead to severe personality disorders in adulthood. It is a theory that primarily implicates the mother as the culprit of the child's later problems by refusing to allow it to develop firm psychological boundaries between itself and others. She does this, it is hypothesized, by withdrawing her love from the child if the child attempts to separate, or by overgratification at the symbiotic stage. This withdrawal produces an *aban-*

Dr. Silverstein is a clinical psychologist in private practice in New York City. He is the founding editor of the *Journal of Homosexuality*, and is the author of three books on gay life. Reprint request may be sent to the author, 233 West 83rd Street, New York, NY 10024.

donment depression in the child, a type of depression that will be experienced throughout the child's life (Masterson, 1981). The theory is an extension of Freud's description of an anaclytic depression (Freud, 1957). Presumably, the child's attempt at separation is experienced by the mother as a parallel abandonment depression.[1] As Rinsley (1982) noted, "The mother is available if the child clings and behaves regressively, but withdraws if he attempts to separate and individuate" (p. 36).

Symptomatology

Perhaps the sina qua non, symptomatically, of the BPD is the concept of *splitting*, whereby all objects, i.e., people, are bifurcated and identified as either all good or all bad.[2] Good objects are safe ones, whereas bad objects are dangerous and bring on the re-experience of the early abandonment depression. This person perception never allows for ambiguity or differentiation because that would lead to confusion, anxiety, and frustration. A bad object may change, and often does, but when it changes, it does so completely and at once, becoming good, so that the person experiences a series of alternations of perception, and hence, alternations of affect. A veridical perception of the assets and liabilities of another person is almost impossible, so that the good becomes bad, and back again. Technically, the person is said to lack *object constancy*. The same process is said to occur in self-perception as well, where a partial self-image inaccurately reflects the person's whole self. Therefore, the person relates to others as parts of a larger and unintegrated ego, rather than as a whole. Kernberg (1975) believes that this good/bad split was originally a simple defect of integration, which then in adulthood is used as a defense of the ego, protecting it from conflicts between libidinal and aggressive identifications.

Kernberg further stated that a person with a BPD fears his own aggression. Good objects protect the person from bad ones, so that he can't be destroyed by self-aggression. It is, therefore, a projection, an externalization of the all-bad aggressive self upon other people. While the borderline person may believe he's protecting himself from the attacks of others, he is really attempting to control them in order to prevent them from, as he sees it, attacking and destroying him. What he does not see is that the aggression he perceives in others is but a mirror of himself.

Kernberg suggested that the syndrome of the BPD is composed

of four symptom groups: diffuse anxiety, multiple phobias, little constancy of sexual behavior, and impulsive and/or addictive states or both. In addition, the BPD person is perceived as compliant and dependent, but often alternates between dependency and self-assertion, depending upon his perception of the benevolence or potential harm of significant people in the environment. He further identified the BPD as a stable, yet pathological, form of personality disorder. To him the "border" was a state between neurosis and psychosis, but he also believed that under stress or the influence of drugs a transitory psychosis can occur.

In practice, people classified as borderline have tended to be quite varied, with some functioning quite well, and others holding on to the barest threads of ego strength. Therefore, Kernberg (1975) suggested a two-fold classification of the BPD into "upper" and "lower" levels. An upper BPD is one in which the principal fear is abandonment and the principal defense is clinging to another person. In the lower level BPD, the principal fear is engulfment and the principal defense is distancing from others. The lower level BPD person is clearly the more disorganized of the two, with feelings of depersonalization and frequent but temporary psychotic episodes which include paranoid ideation. A good review of the dynamics of upper and lower level borderline people can be read in Meissner (1983). Through this dichotomous classification Kernberg noted that the borderline diagnosis includes an unusually large range of individuals, including those, as in the upper level, whose reality testing is fairly good and who learn to function acceptably, to those whose level of functioning is extremely limited, labile in temperament to the extreme, and in whom transitory but frequent psychotic episodes appear throughout life.

At this point even the casual reader may note that the invention of the BPD as a diagnostic category has led to diagnostic boundaries as diffuse as the people it is said to identify, and may soon be said to include an ever expanding segment of the population previously diagnosed as suffering from a variety of neuroses, character disorders, and psychotic reactions. In a book review, Ziesat (1983) noted the potential for using the label as a wastebucket category for cases that were difficult to diagnose. He noted that some psychoanalysts thought the BPD as including essentially neurotic people, with sporadic evidence of psychosis, whereas others thought them to be psychotic with a neurotic veneer. He stated:

If we are going to retain the word "borderline" as a diagnostic term describing this group of patients, we should be clear about which border we are referring to, to wit: Does borderline personality straddle schizophrenia and neurosis, as was originally thought, or affective disorders and character disorders? Or is it a mild form of schizopheniform illness? Or is it simply a type of affective disorder? The reason that such questions are important is that the answers may eventually point to practical treatment strategies. (p. 666)

Even Meissner (1983), who supported the new classification, was cognizant of the hazardous diagnostic foundation of the BPD, and wrote, " . . . the borderline description is so nonspecific that it embraces an as yet unspecified differential diagnosis covering a wide range of disorders" (p. 180).

It is beyond the scope of this paper to argue the validity of the BPD diagnosis, particularly with respect to the etiological beliefs held by object reactions theorists. As we find true of all diagnoses, we can use them as descriptors of behavior without ascribing to the etiological components suggested by theorists. That is precisely what is proposed for the rest of this paper and the case to be presented. Toward that end, we may accept the descriptive statement of the BPD as a diagnostic category listed in the third edition of the Diagnostic and Statistical Manual of Mental Disorders (American Psychiatric Association, 1980):

The essential feature is a personality disorder in which there is instability in a variety of areas, including interpersonal behavior, mood, and self-image. No single feature is invariably present. Interpersonal relations are often tense and unstable, with marked shifts in attitude over time. Frequently there is impulsive and unpredictable behavior that is potentially physically self-damaging. Mood is often unstable, with marked shifts from a normal mood to a dysphoric mood or with inappropriate, intense anger or lack of control of anger. A profound identity disturbance may be manifested by uncertainty about several issues relating to identity, such as self-image, gender identity, or long-term goals or values. There may be problems tolerating being alone, and chronic feelings of emptiness or boredom. (p. 321)

THE CULTURAL BACKGROUND

What seems to this author to have been ignored by object relations psychoanalysts is the question of why the BPD has attained such prominence in the past 30 or 40 years. This question invariably suggests the introduction of cultural factors that have created environmental stressors that increase the likelihood of the kind of personality disorder we now call the BPD. This is not a unique idea. Diagnoses come and go as the times and theories change (Silverstein, 1976/77; 1984). While conversion hysteria was all the rage at one time, hardly any clinicians today meet "glove anesthesia" in a lifetime of practice. Nor is masturbation now listed as a mental disorder. In their places have gone mental disorders that were never listed before, such as anorexia nervosa and bulimia. Also newly listed are those behaviors (e.g., the sexual dysfunctions) that existed in the past but were never labeled mental disorders.

The great increase in the use of the BPD within recent years is unlikely to be the product of inadequate mothering (Chodorow, 1978). Mothers are no less competent today than their mothers or grandmothers were in previous generations. It can even be argued that today's mothers are better educated and more knowledgeable of child-rearing practices. The effects of mothering (and, one would like to think, fathering) are certainly the foundation for adulthood. But other influences come to bear on the child which can ameliorate or aggravate the effects of early childhood. This is particularly true with respect to issues of sexual identity and gender identity.[3] It is in these areas that our society has changed most severely, and this fact, it is maintained, is the reason for the increase in the incidence of the BPD.

Parenting has changed dramatically in this century. In previous generations parents were role models for their children, and this was as true of sexual and gender identities as it was for all other areas of adult behavior. In a sense, it was a vertical system where one generation modeled themselves after the generations that came before them. It was an easy system, and one that produced stability and dependability within the family and the social structure. Moral rules proscribed one's sexual behavior to a relatively small number of acts, with violations of the rules handled harshly. There were rarely conflicts of gender identity, and where they did occur, they were kept secret (Faderman, 1981). In a well-structured society that eschewed ambiguity, few personal choices were made, for few were required. Within the confines of such a system, the BPD was unlikely to appear because one's society created an external structure that ameliorated family inadequacies.[4]

HOMOSEXUALITY AS A CULTURAL VARIATION

Previous to the 19th century, homosexual behavior was not a significant problem for society. Whatever transgressions may have occurred, men and women married, had children, and fulfilled their social roles as parents. In 1869, the ground was broken to change all that. In that year the word *homosexual* was invented (and its counterpart, *heterosexual*) (Lauritsen & Thorstad, 1974; Steakley, 1975). The implications of this fact are seldom discussed. This leads to the suggestion that both sexual identities are artifacts of modern society (MacIntosh, 1968). A social role, in contrast to mere genital behavior, began to emerge for those men and women whose emotional and sexual desires were directed toward the same sex. Confined almost exclusively in the late 19th and early 20th centuries to the realm of medical abnormality (if not curiosity), homosexual couples, what few there were, usually mirrored the social and sexual roles of heterosexual marriage, with one member of the pair playing a rigidly defined male role, and the other a female role, clothes and all (Kiernan, 1884). Many of these relationships lasted for a lifetime, though they would probably have been mystified by a word such as homosexual (Faderman, 1981).

It was only after the Second World War that homosexual love became a possibility for most people, and the rise of the modern gay liberation movement created the environment that encouraged longterm coupling between gay people. Three forces combined to instruct men and women that personal choices were not only possible, but necessary in our modern society.

Alfred Kinsey's Research

The first was Alfred Kinsey (1948), whose monumental sex research profoundly effected our notions of normal and abnormal sexuality. The sexual revolution that he and his colleagues helped to create is often misunderstood. The result is not that people had more or less sex after his work than before. He went after more dangerous game than the mere counting of orgasms. He demonstrated the frequency of various forms of sexual behavior at different ages and at different socioeconomic and educational levels. The very best example of this was his documentation of the normative aspects of masturbation at a time when many medical authorities still diagnosed it as abnormal, and the frequency of homosexual behavior, also condemned as pathological. From a psychological point of view, Kinsey's books were permission-giving for people to experiment sexually.

The Women's Liberation Movement

The women's liberation movement (Flexner, 1975) fought against the traditional social role of women and demanded the same opportunities as our society provides its men. Women were encouraged to join the professions and the business world, and to delay childbearing if they wished. At the same time, a concerted attack upon the traditional hard-nosed image of men was instituted, and a new masculine standard was suggested, the androgynous man who developed his sensitive qualities as well as the customary masculine ones.

The Gay Liberation Movement

The changes initiated by the women's movement led directly to the modern gay liberation movement that began after the Stonewell riot in 1969 (Katz, 1976; Weeks, 1977). This was the third force in our discussion of sexual and social choices. The gay liberation movement was at once an attack upon traditional notions of masculine and feminine, and upon the sexual conservatism of the psychiatric profession. Gay liberation was instrumental in helping millions of gay people to *come out*, and in the organization of a gay service network.

These three forces,[5] the work of Kinsey and his colleagues, the women's liberation movement, and the gay liberation movement have been the foundations of the sexual revolution of the 1970s and 1980s. This revolution, so supportive of individualism, has implicitly instructed the young that a myriad of choices are possible about one's social and sexual roles throughout life. Models from the past have been judged as archaic so that one cannot be instructed, but must learn empirically through experience. But if the individual has been freed from outmoded social and sexual roles, he is nonetheless forced to exact a price for his freedom — to make choices — and this freedom invariably results in personal confusion and conflict.[6]

One needs to remark here that traditional notions of male and female were constructive in society. Everybody knew what was expected of him or her, and knew what to expect from others. There may have been no choice, but there was certainly dependability. The reader should avoid judging this belief as an atavistic call for a return to Victorian standards. It is just the proposition that freedom is not "free," and that some of us are incapable of creating empirical standards for ourselves and first become confused, and finally disoriented.

It is the point of view of this article that the BPD is a direct result of these changing social norms in the 20th century; that it is, in a sense, a social dilemma created by freedom.

The BPD has increased in frequency because the social structures present in previous generations have vanished. Individuals are now forced to make a considerable number of choices over sexual behavior, sexual identity, and gender. It is a task wherein a person is asked to create order out of confusion, and from that ordering of personal and social alternatives evolves a psychological structure that is the modern equivalent of the rules from, say, the Victorian era, but one that is empirically derived. Therefore, the most important responsibility for each person in today's society is to create this personal psychological structure as a replacement for the former social and religious regulations. If one fails to do so, then all subsequent alternatives will be met with even greater confusion. In those who suffer the greatest confusion, disorientation occurs and ego defenses are created to prevent total psychological breakdown. These ego defenses are the symptoms of what is now called the BPD.

This idea is not at all radical. DSM III (APA, 1980) notes that certain personality disorders "have a relationship to corresponding categories in the section Disorders Usually First Evident in Infancy, Childhood, or Adolescence" (p. 305). It goes on to associate the Identity Disorder of Adolescence with the adult diagnostic category of BPD.

DSM III (APA, 1980) states that the Identity Disorder is most common in adolescence, and further that:

> The disorder is apparently more common now than several decades ago, however, perhaps because today there are more options regarding values, behavior, and life-styles open to the

individual and more conflict between adolescent peer values and parental or social values. (p. 66)

What we see today from this perspective and call BPD are a group of people who are incapable of making choices and suffer confusion because of it. Most certainly childhood factors predispose them to confusion. The symptoms of BPD are unlikely to occur in loving and caring families. Disordered nuclear families are a necessary, but not sufficient, reason for the rising incidence of the BPD.

But let us now consider the life of a gay man, Gerard, and follow that with a discussion of his personality dynamics and their implications for all gay people.

THE LIFE-STUDY OF GERARD

"The Train"

(a dream)

"It is dusk. Even in my dream I can feel a cold wind blowing on my naked arms. I can remember feeling goose bumps even with my coat on. The cold seems like it will never end. I am alone on this greyish platform, with no destination. Where am I and why am I so aware of every detail of my position and yet so totally unaware of where I am? I am confused by the terrain around me.

(People enter the train and it leaves.)

"Now the trains are totally unrecognizable to me. They are definitely subway cars, but their destinations are mysterious. One goes to New London, the other to Boston. Somewhere there is a connection to 42nd Street. But I cannot remember where it is or how to get there.

"I retreat to the men's room and take up residence there. The door is locked, so now I can sleep. It is safe, warm, and, when I wake up I can buy a toothbrush and some shampoo and cleanse my body.

"I awaken and try to recollect the dream. I only remember the train station and the john. And being lost. Everything is so easy, if only I could figure it out!"

Patient Information

Gerard is a 32-year-old, white male, employed as an executive by a New York City firm, in psychotherapy for the past year. His entry into psychotherapy was by self-referral, and except for a brief hospitalization at the age of 14 for what appears to have been an adjustment problem of adolescence, this has been his first experience with psychotherapy. He has one brother, 2 years older, and a younger brother and sister. He was born to a working-class family who lived in a rural New England town. His father worked sporadically at a local mill, where employment was seasonal, and at other odd jobs around town. There is no history of mental illness in the family.

Gerard is gay and has lived with a male lover, Alan, for the past 6 years. Previously he lived with his first lover, Tom, for 12 years. Gerard reports no discomfort about his sexual orientation, nor does he remember feelings of guilt, low self-worth, or a desire to become heterosexual, although he did have an affair with a woman during late adolescence. Gerard's sexual behaviors are highly specialized. His typical form of sexual activity is "S & M" sex, where one party plays the role of the sadist, and the other, the masochist. Gerard is a masochist and here, too, he reports his sexual experiences are ego syntonic.

Chief Complaints

Gerard brought to the initial interview one chief complaint from which a number of distressing problems had arisen, leading to his current feelings of discomfort. He felt unloved and deceived about love, and these feelings centered almost exclusively on Alan, his current lover. Gerard did not believe that Alan loved him, though the evidence for this was circumstantial. Gerard said that whenever he tried to express feelings of intimacy, Alan reacted coldly. For instance, Gerard would often prepare breakfast on weekends, but Alan would sleep until noon, or Gerard would plan interesting vacations and Alan would refuse to help in the planning, acting as if the idea of a vacation with Gerard was oppressive. Gerard is very organized about household responsibilities, while Alan is less so, and so cleanliness became another area of conflict. Occasions occurred every day where Gerard interpreted Alan's behavior as rejecting.

Though both hold executive positions and live modestly, they are always having money problems. Gerard is preparing for his retirement by making financial contributions to a fund that are so large that their monthly expenses are not covered by the remainder of their salaries. The excess is put on credit cards and the money conflicts occur as the bills come due. Gerard works hard to budget these bills, while Alan haphazardly throws his into a desk drawer and pays them only when the "dunning" letters arrive. Alan's laissez-faire attitude is hopelessly confusing to Gerard, who is obsessed with accounting for every dollar spent.

Gerard doesn't trust Alan. No one, Gerard believed, could want to hurt him so often, yet be in love with him. He reacted to these slights in two related ways. At first, Gerard would react with rage directed at Alan, accusing him of dishonesty. Alan remained silent during these assaults, refusing or fearing to engage Gerard in discussion, and these sullen responses of Alan's served as further proof to Gerard of his coldness. Then Gerard would ruminate all the more, become convinced that their relationship was a sham, and decide to leave Alan. At this point, some dialogue would occur and Alan would agree to change his behavior to suit Gerard. After awhile, Gerard's anger would mount once again and the cycle of feeling unloved, mistrustful, and hostile would occur once more. Gerard felt out of control, and because his feelings were so strong they were, he felt, destroying him. He could not clear his mind long enough to decide whether Alan did or didn't love him.

Gerard also had problems with his job. He felt that his boss didn't appreciate his work and was overly critical. Gerard typically reacted angrily, and ruminated about quitting. These periods of anger were cyclical, appearing and disappearing suddenly and mysteriously. While Gerard was sure that much of his anger was justified, he wondered at the intensity of it. The parallel affective reactions to lover and employer is obvious.

Two other problems were mentioned at the initial interview. First was his relationship to Tom, his first lover. Gerard still spoke to him every day, saw him occasionally, and considered him a person he still loved. This, too, was a source of conflict because he sometimes felt he should give up his need for Tom, but he wasn't sure. Finally, Gerard had problems with his family, who still live in rural New England. They didn't know that Gerard was gay, though he had been living with men now for the past 16 years. He wanted them to know. Gerard wanted to learn in therapy how to come out to them. When asked why he wanted to come out to them, he replied that he wanted to be able to take his lover home on family holidays, instead of leaving him in New York City. However, when pressed further, he admitted that Alan didn't want to go anyway. Gerard looked confused at this point, knowing that the issue was important to him, but not understanding why introducing Alan to his family was so crucial.

Gerard was asked why he had decided to begin psychotherapy at this time. He responded by first describing some recent transient sexual activities in which Gerard had allowed himself to be abused physically. He feared that he was losing control over his own desires and was inching inevitably toward contacts with "S's" who lacked all impulse control. Gerard described himself as feeling like Sisyphus, the King of Corinth, who was forever doomed in Hades to roll uphill a heavy stone which always rolled down again. This image frightened him.

Developmental History—Early Years

Gerard's memories of early childhood are mostly sad ones. He remembers how often his father hit his mother, and how often he and the other children would console her afterward. He can remember, too, how often, and with such suddenness, his father would physically attack him. One bitter memory is sleeping in bed and suddenly being awakened by his father, who beat him as punishment for running away from home.

He also remembers an unusual relationship with his mother. It was her daily routine from the time Gerard was age 5 to 15 to bring him into bed with her after her husband had left for work. With Gerard in either pajamas or underwear, and she in a slip, she would embrace him and hold him close to her. As Gerard got older he became aware of the potential sexuality of the situation, though he reports not being upset by it. There were times, as he entered adolescence, that he fondled his penis while lying in bed with her, though he states that at no time was there any overt sex between them.

Gerard felt like "Cinderella." He raised his younger brother, was required to sweep the house each day, make the beds, and wash the dishes. Before supper, Gerard ate in the kitchen with his mother, then served the rest of the family in the dining room. He performed these tasks without complaint, although he seethed at its unfairness. He felt trapped by her, forced to spend so much time fulfilling her demands.

The image of the eroticized mother recently appeared in a dream. In it, Gerard and his mother were in bed together. She had an erect penis which Gerard recognized as his own, and he was sucking it. Interestingly, during the therapy session, he noticed that she was wearing long, nylon stockings and this reminded him of his recent fetish for panty hose. The panty hose fetish had begun a few months earlier, had ceased for awhile, and had reappeared recently. He didn't know why, but during the discussion of this dream, Gerard wondered (quite appropriately) whether he was trying to act like his mother, whether he had identified with her sexually.

During this adolescent period, Gerard originated a unique fantasy concerning his parents. He believed that one day his father would come into the bedroom and show Gerard how to have sexual intercourse with his mother, and the sex act between mother and son would be completed with the father watching approvingly.

A number of significant events occurred between the ages of 12 and 14. On two occasions he tried to harm himself. The first one occurred one day as he was walking through the woods. He stopped for a moment, and then picked up a large rock and hammered it against his arm, trying, he remembers, to fracture it. He had no idea why, and ceased only when the pain became unbearable. To this day Gerard does not understand why he did it. Intellectually, he says that he wanted attention from his father (perhaps also to externalize the psychological pain as a sign that he was still alive).

Soon after, Gerard made the first of two suicide attempts. One Sunday morning, Gerard walked to a stone quarry. He tied himself to a rope and jumped into the water expecting to drown, but the water only came up to his chest. He dragged himself back to a boulder, took off all his clothes, and, sitting naked under the warm sun, masturbated.

While still sitting on that rock, Gerard decided to run away to New York City. He did so the next day, but was quickly identified by the police as a runaway and sent home. His father was furious and Gerard was beaten and prohibited from returning to school (where he had been an excellent student) and ordered to get a full-time job in a local mill. He complied, but with yet another resentment to be written on his long list of indignities suffered at home.

Gerard ran away a second time and, arriving at the New York City Authority Bus Terminal, became a male prostitute. By having sex with men for money and spending the night with them, he lived a marginal but satisfying existence. He never felt abused, and claims to be profoundly grateful to these men who helped him. Within a few months he traveled to Washington, D.C., where he lived briefly with a group of gay college students, again "hustled," and then on to Myrtle Beach, South Carolina, where he swallowed a vial of pills in his second and last suicide attempt. He ended up at a psychiatric hospital for a few days and when his parents were called, they told the hospital authorities that Gerard was on his own. He was then 15 years old. He returned to Washington, D.C., where he met his first lover.

Developmental History—Adult Years

At the age of 16 Gerard met Tom, a man of 24. To Gerard, Tom was "a grownup," a man of substance with an education, a responsible job, and a stable home. They became lovers and lived together for the next 12 years. Sex between them wasn't as exciting as Gerard had with other men, but it wasn't as important as his needs for love, security, and a home of his own. In the protection of this environment, Gerard finished high school and eventually got his B.A.

For the first 9 or 10 years, they lived a comfortable life in a New York suburb. Gerard turned over his salary each week to Tom (much as he had earlier to his father). Gerard thought of this relationship as "we," an affair of intimacy and love. But much as Gerard tried, he could not ignore their sexual incompatibility, for Gerard was becoming more passive sexually, and Tom, increasingly distant. Gerard fled to anonymous sexual encounters, most often in "t-rooms," and almost every day. He never told Tom of this. Gerard's sexual feelings also began to change from conventional ones to masochistic ones involving leather and humiliation. He mentioned these fantasies to Tom, who became anxious and refused to discuss them.

Gerard's sexual fantasies continued to change over time. He found himself looking at men dressed in leather walking the streets of New York, wondering about the kind of sex they had, and soon these men appeared in his masturbation fantasies. Again Gerard tried to discuss the fantasies with Tom, who dismissed them as unimportant. Gerard said nothing more, though the fantasies persisted. Within a year their relationship ended.

Upon moving to New York, Gerard experimented with S & M sex. He knew after his first experience that he was a "bottom man." As he says, "It never occurred to me to be a top man." He had all the sex he wanted, yet missed the intimacy of a love relationship.

A year later, Gerard met Alan. Alan was a few years older, and taught at a large urban university. Alan was a "top" and they were sexually compatible. They have lived together for 6 years. Neither asks for sexual fidelity in a lover. While they maintain a good sexual relationship with each other, they also participate in encounters with other men.

In some respects Gerard is tyrannical toward Alan. For instance, Gerard believes that lovers must eat all meals together. Nor does Gerard condone the serving of food that he doesn't like at a meal with Alan (even if Alan likes the food), or if friends are invited to the house for dinner. Not only does he exercise a veritable veto over foods served at home, but he's also offended if Alan orders a tabu food for himself at a restaurant, so that Alan is never allowed to eat any of the foods he enjoys. Gerard does all the planning, including vacations, buying furniture, remodeling the house, and finances. In short, Gerard plans and controls all household and personal functions.

PERSONALITY DYNAMICS—
THE TRADITIONAL BPD SYNDROME

Let us first note that the case of Gerard is that of a reasonably well-functioning person, certainly a high-level BPD as described by Kernberg. There are none of the psychotic episodes or drug addictions as one often finds in borderline people. He also illustrates many of the personality dynamics that are becoming more common in clinical settings, particularly in gay men.

Splitting—The "Good/Bad" Dimension

Gerard's affection dimensions are bifurcated, consisting only of extremes and allowing for no differentiation of meaning; they are categorical judgments of either goodness or badness. Such affective dichotomies can be interpreted as developmentally primitive because they first appear in the earliest years of life, and only with later, more mature learning does differentiation occur, and with it a changed perception of the world and oneself.

Splitting refers to much more than just extremes of evaluative judgment. If we had, for instance, a person who was rigid and un-yielding in perception, and who judged others as either good or bad, we would not have an example of splitting. Such a person would probably fall under the rubric of a character disorder. He would be certain of his judgments, experience problems as externally caused, and, most important, would not experience any conflict. The bad person is bad — period. But in the case of splitting as a personality dynamic, judgments are fluid, and a sense of certainty, impossible. He who is perceived as good during one moment in time may change suddenly to a bad person, someone who inexplicably is transformed from one who loves to one who hates or is dangerous in some way. A sense of psychological stability is therefore impos-sible because the world is ever-changing and always carries the po-tential for threat. It is a psychological plague — and very painful.

Gerard's reactions to present and former lovers, to employers, and to transient sexual partners appear to be all of a kind. One gets the impression that all are invested with the attribute of "father." There is a good/bad affective dimension attached to the concept of father, and Gerard appears to judge potential father figures on the basis of their goodness or badness. In Gerard's history we find an idealized image of a man, say, a lover. To this person, who we may assume has assets and liabilities as any other, Gerard attributes characteristics that represent a fantasy vision of the good and loving father, while ignoring any dissonant information. The perceptual and affectual distortion is two-fold; on the one hand he attributes mythical characteristics to the person, and secondly he represses or ignores those characteristics of the person that are incongruent. Though perhaps not intentional, the process is hostile toward the other insofar as it denies to the other the right to his own individual-ity. The object of this distortion is, in a sense, a metaphorical pris-oner of Gerard's search for the loving father.

The object of Gerard's affection, and most recently this has been his lover, Alan, cannot possibly know or understand that he is re-quired to play the dual roles of the good father from the past and the good lover of today. He is bound to balk at the requirements, which are likely to be experienced as confusion, and to make some gesture of rejection toward Gerard. This conflict, often over symbolic ma-terial, results in the instantaneous metamorphosis of the good father into the bad one, and having done that, Gerard reacts to the disap-pointment in his characteristic ways — anger, attack, and running away to have sexual encounters.

Given this developmental sequence, we have every right to assume that the affective dichotomy of good boy/bad boy occurred earlier than good father/bad father.[7] We may further suggest that "son" and "father" interact in such a way as to show that Gerard's judgment as to his, in contrast to his father's, goodness or badness is in direct proportion to the perceived goodness or badness of the father. This can be easily illustrated diagrammatically. (See Figure 1.)

Box 1 represents the idealized and fantasized relationship between Gerard and his father, and also his perception of romantic and authority figures. Box 4, on the other hand, represents the perceived reality of his relationship to his father, and reasserts itself with each frustration or conflict with a lover or authority figure. Box 4 is also a statement of the genesis of depression because it is a hopeless situation where love, caring, and intimacy cannot exist. Boxes 2 and 3 are, for all intents and purposes, insignificant because not enough individuation between father and son has occurred to allow for judgments to be made of the two independent people.

Father

	Good	Bad
Good	Box 1 Good father Good son	Box 2 Bad father Good son
Bad	Box 3 Good father Bad son	Box 4 Bad father Bad son

Gerard

Figure 1

The Abandonment Depression

This repetitive pattern of disappointment in love in adulthood leads to deep feelings of depression in Gerard, much as the disappointments in childhood led to depression during those early years. A chronic depression is, in fact, one of the most prominent aspects of Gerard's personality. The feeling of having been rejected by his father (who also failed to protect him from his mother) in his early years is not yet history because the feelings of rejection are continually re-experienced in adulthood. Though the relationship between any son and his father is important, it is possible that the relationship between a gay-to-be son and his father is even more important (Silverstein, 1981). Additionally there are the morning bed experiences with his mother, a seductive scene to which Gerard acquiesced and entwined in the fantasy that his father would teach Gerard how to have sex with his mother. It would be hard to imagine those experiences and fantasies without the production of guilt. Though he rarely expresses guilty feelings, one might reasonably hypothesize that beneath the smoke screen of verbal attack lies low self-esteem and feelings of guilt. One therefore needs to explain how Gerard defends himself against the feelings of depression, guilt, low self-esteem, and the fear of abandonment.

The dynamics of depression suggest that it can be dealt with in at least two ways: It can be expressed, leading to reduced motoric activity and the feeling of helplessness, or it can be defended against through a form of reaction-formation, leading to increased motoric behavior and the pretense of domination over the environment. In the former, a passive orientation to the environment is suggested, while the latter suggests an active orientation. Of these two orientations to depression, Gerard has chosen the latter ego syntonic approach, whereby he defends himself against depression through acting-out behavior, convinced not that there is something wrong with him, but that he must protect himself from the malevolence of others.

Two events in Gerard's history show how early his defenses against depression began, and how they relate to current adult behaviors; the arm wounding and the suicide attempt. Self-harm was the result of depression and the feeling of extreme isolation. In the arm-wounding incident, Gerard remembers hoping that his father would take care of him, and so this suggests a manipulation tied to depression. In the second, the suicide attempt, we have for the first time an association between depression and sexual excitement. One might hypothesize that by the age of 14 Gerard had learned to adapt to depression by transforming it into excitement, and then to release the excitement through orgasm. Because the masturbation, a motoric act, substituted for the affect of depression, we are entitled to call it an acting-out behavior and to hypothesize that adult sexuality may share the same characteristics as these early adolescent experiences; namely, manipulation of others by self-harm, and sexuality as an acting-out behavior to camouflage depression. Of course, we would also expect the origins of these dynamics to be placed much earlier chronologically, but those memories are still subject to repression.

This acting-out as a defense against the depression created by feelings of abandonment takes two forms; toward his lover, Gerard attacks, punishing Alan for reminding him of his feelings of early abandonment, and at the same time, Gerard acts out sexually, seeking a new transient love object. The alleviation of depression by sexual release had begun the day when Gerard tried to commit suicide in the quarry, and that dynamic continues. Confusion results because he is at once attacking one man (Alan) while showing love toward another (during anonymous sex). The totality of this behavior would have to be mystifying.

Identity Diffusion

Lack of individuation from both parents is one of the most significant variables in Gerard's depression and acting-out behavior. While he is clearly aware of his judgments toward his father, Gerard is less aware that they are also a projection of his feelings about himself, and that these feelings are the most significant, therapeutically speaking.

The identity diffusion involves the mother as well, and this is indicated by the incestuous fantasies, his dreams, and his current, though sporadic, interest in panty hose. One gets the impression from Gerard that ego diffusion toward the father concerns goodness and badness, while toward the mother it concerns sensuality, sexuality, and sensitivity. One would also think that over time these ego diffusions toward both parents would lead to resentment on Gerard's part because of his perceived loss of psychological freedom, illustrated so poignantly by him in this recital of the myth of Sisyphus. Gerard reacts toward these identity diffusions differentially; toward those with power, as with lovers and employers, he acts aggressively, as if he were the bad son, and they, the bad fathers. Anonymous sexual partners, however, more likely represent the maternal diffusion and hence are more sensual, more pleasing sexually, and interpreted as more intimate. It is now clear why Gerard ran away from home at ages 14 and 15. It was an attempt to find his own identity and to define his own ego boundaries, though he would hardly have understood this at the time. His running away behavior in recent years is merely a repetition of his search for his individuality.

The identity diffusion has markedly effected Gerard's experience of sexuality. While his sense of being a gay man has always been secure, his specific sexual behaviors have shifted over time. He began with "vanilla" sex, then turned to hustling, and, during a brief period in adolescence, to an affair with a woman. During his 12-year relationship with his first lover, he began the period of anonymous sex in t-rooms. After their break-up, Gerard came out once again, this time into S & M sex as a bottom man, and currently continues his outside sex while in his current love relationship. Most recently, he has experimented having sex while wearing pantyhose, a sexual variation that causes him a great deal of anxiety, perhaps because of the fear that a greater propensity toward "drag" lurks not too far from the surface of consciousness. For our purposes, it is not relevant whether Gerard is in "the closet" with respect to women's apparel (he isn't). His anxiety is caused by the feeling of helplessness over his own sexual fantasies.

One needs to be careful here because it's easy to fall into Victorian standards of sexuality. In the modern gay male community, versatility is valued. A gay man can voluntarily choose between a variety of sexual acts to please himself or a partner, or alter his sexual needs to complement a transient mood. This versatility is an asset when under voluntary control, but in the history reported here, it is not so much versatility as it is a dramatic change in sexuality, wherein a past mode is given up and replaced by a new one.

S & M Sex

Gerard's current sexual behavior appears to be another important dynamic in his search for a good father to take care of him. S & M sexuality is ideally suited to Gerard's adoptive behavior because it creates a clear structure around sexuality. In the first place, the "slave" is taken care of by his "master," a responsibility that is taken very seriously by mature advocates of S & M. To Gerard, who certainly plays a child-like, obedient role, the master, not unlike his father, instructs him as to proper behavior, punishes violations, and rewards obedience. All of this is done according to mutually agreed upon rules. Gerard is also punished physically by the "top," as he was by his father many years ago. It therefore avoids any ambiguity as to status and responsibility. At the same time it allows Gerard to please his mentor for the night, which, in a sense, makes the top man less threatening. The punishment may also alleviate the feelings of guilt, and help Gerard to feel alive and worthwhile.

More recently, Gerard's need to be punished has gotten out of control, perhaps because depressed feelings have been rising to consciousness. His fear that he may allow himself to be seriously abused is well-founded. What has happened from a dynamic point of view is that Gerard has sought out impulse-laden sadists who lack control, whereas in the past he was quite adept at choosing sadists who were highly sensitive to Gerard's physical and psychological limits. The harmful S & M experiences, then, are a result of the return of depressed feelings to which are attached feelings of guilt, and for which extreme physical punishment for fantasized crimes are arranged. These fantasized crimes are likely to be incestuous mother/son feelings.

Problems in the area of independence/dependence affect all aspects of Gerard's current life, and this conflict is often acted-out in the drama of S & M encounters. The forceful demand for independence from Alan is more likely a defense by Gerard against his own desire for, and fear of, passivity—the desire to be taken care of, and a passivity that is expressed sexually when he plays a dependent role, but not in his love relationship, where-in trust many lead to feelings of abandonment. As independent as he may pretend to be, and as far away as he may be from his family, for Gerard individuation is not yet an accomplished fact, which probably explains why he continues to hold onto former lovers. Another example of Gerard's conflict in the independence/dependence continuum is his compulsive need to return to his parent's home periodically, trying to create a loving relationship to his parents, only to become disillusioned once again and leave in anger.

Finally, we might note the particular effect of anxiety on Gerard, which is, once again, common in the borderline personality. Such people are not more anxious than others, nor do they typically decompensate if they experience a high level of anxiety. Kernberg

(1975) illustrated this well. Whether the person typically experiences high or low anxiety in day-to-day living, he becomes accustomed to it and copes well with it. It is only when the anxiety reaches a point much higher than the person's norm that anxiety leads to acting-out behavior. For one person, it may be a relatively low level of anxiety, whereas for another person, a very high level of anxiety is needed to lead to acting-out. In low-level borderline people, the overproduction of anxiety may lead to transient psychotic episodes or drug addiction. In high-level people, it leads to depression and, as in this case, to sexual acting-out. Seeking transient sexual experiences is Gerard's characteristic way of coping with higher than normal anxiety levels. These sexual experiences are a good palliative to anxiety, and after them the anxiety level returns to normal. Without them, a slow but steady decompensation results. It should also be noted that sexual versatility is an asset in Gerard, so that his transient encounters are almost always pleasing for him and his partner.

GERARD FROM A CULTURAL PERSPECTIVE

A shifting world is very unpleasant. Even when change is explicable, many people have a hard time feeling competent, but when the change comes from within the psyche, and is experienced as involuntary, confusion results.

Gerard is an excellent example of a person most vulnerable to external change. Early experiences make it difficult for him to perceive the world accurately. What are Gerard's alternatives when finding his experiential world constantly shifting, and when loved ones like family and lovers can take on the lineaments of Dr. Jeckel? How often such a person must wonder, "Can no one be trusted?" The experiential world is, for Gerard and for many gay people today, a dangerous place that must be controlled for the sake of personal safety.

No doubt Gerard has been difficult at home. He demands behavior from his lover that is unreasonable. This is not compulsivity. It results from two things: the first is his fantasy of creating a more stable home then he came from, and the other is a reaction against Alan's laissez-faire behavior. The tidiness that Gerard demands of Alan is a mechanism to control internal confusion by creating external order—having everything, out there, in its proper place relieves the feeling of disorder within.

A metaphorical concept would be helpful now, the idea of an

expanding ego. Those of us trained in traditional analytic theories are used to thinking of the ego—the reality testing part of one's personality—as a boundary between the person and the outside world. In textbooks, it is most commonly illustrated by a circle— "me" in the center, and everything else outside. We've been taught that the rigidity of this boundary, or its fluidity, typified either the neurotic or the normal person. But for each individual the size of the circle remained essentially the same.

Might we suggest that there are people, like Gerard, whose ego boundaries expand and contract depending upon the individual's perception of safety or threat?

No one can live in a psychological world composed of chaos. Such deterioration could only end in psychosis, suicide, or drug addiction. A person's self-esteem must be restored in some way. If a person's ego lacks the power to control its own impulses and feelings (some colleagues would insist on calling this an id/ego conflict), it can expand into the outside world to control it, thereby restoring for awhile the internal confusion.[8]

It is not unusual for a person with a deficient concept of self to symbolize the internal disorder through projection of the self onto the environment. The boundaries of the self expand, in a sense, marching over the usual demarcation between self and the outside world, and end up treating the immediate external environment as if it were the ego itself. In Gerard's case, the untidiness of home is menacing because it becomes a vivid representation of his own internal untidiness. The laissez-faire behavior of his lover must be controlled because it might magically transport him back to his original home, the one he hated and feared so much. When Gerard no longer feels attacked, and internal order is restored, the ego contracts and he can experience feelings of love toward Alan and others.

Please do not be confused about the expanding ego. It is not an indication of psychological strength. For instance, it does not show the ability to experience intimacy. Intimacy results when an outsider is allowed through a person's ego boundaries and into the person's concept of self—a potentially threatening thing—creating an acceptable feeling of vulnerability. This is very different than an expanding ego, whereby the person throws a net around others to capture them, control them, and make them safe. Intimacy allows the other to be free, while an expanding ego encapsulates them like flies in amber.

What an exhausting process this is, remaining vigilant against

any sign of external disorders. Someone less capable than Gerard
would live a different lifestyle, fearing the danger of intimate relationships and therefore seeking only serial relationships with others.
Gerard's solution is to have serial, time-limited, transient relationships in his outside affairs, in which his partners are experienced as
all good, and a stable home life with his lover, who is perceived
sometimes as good, and at other times bad.

From this cultural perspective, we can see Gerard's behavior as
an attempt to create order in the world. To a large extent he has
been successful. As a matter of fact, one might marvel at how well
he has coped, given his early experiences. He has remained and
been successful in his profession for many years, and is now an
executive. Nor had Gerard given up in his demand for a loving gay
relationship. His first lasted for 12 years, and his second is now as
of this writing in its 6th year. He may often want to walk out, but
he's never so foolish as to actually do it.

BORDERLINE PERSONALITY AND GAY PEOPLE

There is no question that the concept of the Borderline Personality has important consequences for gay people. It makes no difference whether the etiological theory suggested by object relations
analysts is accurate. From a metaphorical point of view, the diagnostic category viewed from a cultural perspective highlights the
problems of social change for many gay people.

We do not all come from loving families. Those who do not, and
even those who do, are faced with a world that presents a confusion
of alternatives. This is true of all of our citizens, homosexual as
well as heterosexual. But the heterosexual world, as it is changing,
at least is changing from a recognized standard, and the changes
from the past can be charted and evaluated. The heterosexual man,
for instance, need only ask of himself, "What kind of man do I
want to be?" It is unlikely that he would even think of asking,
"What kind of heterosexual man do I want to be?"

But the gay individual must solve questions of both gender identity and sexual identity. The levels of potential confusion for gays
are, therefore, twice that of heterosexuals. This obviously leads to
considerably more alternatives, and hence, more potential confusion. We might hypothesize, therefore, — and this is my second
point — that the more the innovations in society favor the acceptance
of variations in lifestyle, the greater the confusion in those groups

that vary the most form the norm—such as gay people. Again, *as discrimination is reduced, we should expect some gay people to experience more confusion*. The Bell and Weinberg (1978) study, albeit with data collected before the "Stonewall," confirms this. Gays attempted suicide 5 times more often than heterosexuals, and experience more depression and loneliness. One also tends to see this disorganization more clearly in the gay male world than in the lesbian one because men are more visible and open. One also finds it in the difficulty of some gay men to participate in an intimate relationship , and in some lesbians who cannot help from merging with a lover.

This itself may sound confusing. It may sound like the traditional argument that gay people are psychologically disturbed. But that is not the intention. The psychological problems of gays will be *different* after gay liberation than they were before it. Let's make the contrast in time periods more clear.

Before gay liberation, self-loathing and guilt were common enough in the gay community. Depression was probably the single most important psychological dynamic for a number of reasons, with suicide commonly enough the result. Society's oppression took an awesome toll in gay lives.

Now there is less guilt in the gay world. More gay people are open with family, employers, and friends—and reap the rewards of a person who removes the chains of fear from his or her body. Consequently, depression has become *less* of a problem than it was earlier. But if gays have few, if any, stable standards of behavior from the past and now have more internal problems to solve in order to create a sense of psychological stability, then it follows that more of them will experience confusion, and even sexual fluidity.

Does this argument suggest that gays are "sicker" than heterosexuals? No, it does not. The question "are homosexuals sick?" was specious 20 years ago, and is irrelevant today. A sexual orientation is not "healthy" or "sick" (Begelman, 1977). To perceive it in these terms requires acceptance of the medical model as the only arbiter of social behavior.

What we might expect to find in the gay population is a bimodal curve of social and personal adaptibility. On the lower end of the curve are those gay people—like Gerard—whose early experiences limited their capacity to deal with conflict and ambiguity. There are probably many gay people, men and women, in this category.

But we are likely to find another group of gay people who learned to cope with the newly allowed freedoms, people who probably come from more nurturant families or who for reasons we ill-understand turn society's approbrium into psychological strength. These gay people may even turn out to be more adaptable to social and psychological vicissitudes than the average heterosexual person.

From this vantage point, we might predict that over time, as standards of conduct become more predictable in the gay community, the curve of adaptibility between these two groups should change to a normal one. It further suggests that a homogenization will occur in the area of sexual identity.

A FINAL NOTE

What should we make of this new diagnostic category, the "Borderline Personality Disorder?" Does it exist, and if so, what diagnostic areas lay on either side of the boundary? The question assumes that one diagnostic system is more accurate than another, when in fact diagnostic systems are themselves a reflection of the culture, the times, and, though many professionals dislike admitting it, political negotiation and compromise. The battle over the status of homosexuality in the psychiatric nomenclature is a good example of politics and negotiation in diagnosis (Bayer, 1981).

What is of importance to those of us who work with gay people is the idea that they are faced with a disproportionate number of problems. The new cultural belief in individualism has its price: taking responsibility and making choices within a confusing array of possibilities. Those gay people who come from disoriented families will face this freedom ambivalently, unconsciously missing the former social structures that ameliorated family deficiencies. It is toward those people, like Gerard, who live and love in a hostile world that we need to direct our professional competence so that the cultural freedom becomes a personal one as well.

NOTES

1. There is a tendency on the part of some psychoanalysts to lean heavily upon the mother as the "cause" of all future dire consequences that befall the child. One cannot help wondering whether hidden amid all this theory is a rage toward mothers on the part of the theorists.

2. This is Kernberg's definition of splitting. Splitting to Kohut and Masterson is more complicated and tied to etiological theory.

3. These two are often confused. Sexual identity refers to one's sexual orienta-

tion, homosexual, heterosexual, or bisexual. One's gender identity, on the other hand, is one's concept of male, female, or androgeny (Bem, 1974). Either can be confused in a person.

4. One should also note that the extended family was the norm in previous generations, whereas today the nuclear family keeps other relatives at a distance. Previously, extended family members could make up for the deficiencies of a child's parents.

5. One could reasonably argue that "the pill" was another force, but it is not relevant to a discussion of homosexuality.

6. One might hypothesize that the failure of the churches to control the mind and actions of its members, particularly in large urban areas, has contributed to the insecurity and confusion of us all.

7. One would expect a similar dichotomy to exist with regard to the mother, but this has not yet emerged.

8. The idea of an expanding ego is a metaphor; it is not a real thing. It is not like a balloon expanding with the introduction of puffs of air. Nor is the ego a real thing; it too is a metaphor. The diagnostic system, our present one or previous system, are also metaphors, albeit complicated ones, for the worries and concerns of a particular society at a particular time in its history. This is as true of early societies that explained human behavior in terms of dybbuks and demons intruding into the consciousness of the victim, as it is for our modern society that explains human behavior in intrapsychic terms. Descriptions of diagnoses, ego defenses, indeed, all psychological jargon, are not characteristics of the person being described. They are merely convenient, and one hopes useful, ways of organizing the observations of the perceiver.

REFERENCES

American Psychiatric Association. (1980). *Diagnostic and statistical manual of mental disorders* (3rd ed.). Washington, DC: Author.

Bayer, R. (1981). *Homosexuality and American psychiatry*. New York: Basic Books.

Begelman, D. A. (1977). Homosexuality: The ethical challenge: Paper 3. *Journal of Homosexuality, 2,* 213-219.

Bell, A. P., & Weinberg, M. S. (1978). *Homosexualities: A study of diversity among men and women*. New York: Simon & Shuster.

Bem, S. (1974). The measurement of psychological androgyny. *Journal of Consulting and Clinical Psychology, 42,* 155-162.

Chodorow, N. (1978). *The reproduction of mothering: Psychoanalysis and the sociology of gender*. Berkeley: University of California Press.

Faderman, L. (1981). *Surpassing the love of men: Romantic friendship and love between women from the renaissance to the present*. New York: Morrow.

Flexner, E. (1975). *Century of struggle: The women's rights movement in the United States*. Cambridge: Belknap Press of Harvard Universities Press.

Freud, S. (1957). On narcissism: An introduction. In J. Rickman (Ed.). *A general selection from the works of Sigmund Freud*. New York: Liveright. (Original work published 1914.)

Katz, J. (1976). *Gay American history: Lesbians and gay men in the U.S.A. — A documentary*. New York: Crowell.

Kernberg, O. (1975). *Borderline conditions and pathological narcissism*. New York: Aronson.

Kiernan, J. G. (1884). Insanity: Lecture XXVI. — Sexual perversion. *Detroit Lancet, 7*(11), 481-484.

Kinsey, A. C., Pomeroy, W. B. & Martin, C. E. (1948). *Sexual behavior in the human male*. Philadelphia: Saunders.

Kohut, H. (1971). *The analysis of the self*. New York: International Universities Press.

Lauritsen, J. & Thorstad, D. (1974). *The early homosexual rights movement*. New York: Times Change Press.

Masterson, J. M. (1981). *Narcissistic and borderline disorders*. New York: Brunner-Mazel.

McIntosh, M. (1968). The homosexual role. *Social Problems, 16*(2), 182-192.

Meissner, W. V. (1983). Notes on the levels of differentiation within borderline conditions. *The Psychoanalytic Review, 70*, 170-209.

Rinsley, D. B. (1982). *Borderline and other self disorders: A developmental and object-relations perspective*. New York: Aronson.

Silverstein, C. (1976/77). "Even psychiatry can profit from its past mistakes." *Journal of Homosexuality, 2*, 153-158.

Silverstein, C. (1981). *Man to man: Gay couples in America*. New York: Morrow.

Silverstein, C. (1984). The ethical and moral implications of sexual classification: A commentary. *Journal of Homosexuality, 9*(4), 29-38.

Steakley, J. (1975). *The homosexual emancipation movement in Germany*. New York: Arno Press.

Weeks, J. (1977). *Coming out: Homosexual politics in Britain, from the nineteenth century to the present*. London: Quartet.

Ziesat, H. A., Jr. (1983). Borderline personality: On which border is the line located? [Review of *Borderline and other self disorders: A developmental and Object-Relations perspective.*] *Contemporary Psychology*, [28], 665-667.

Index